CONSTRUCTING
ADOLESCENCE IN
FANTASTIC
REALISM

Children's Literature and Culture
Jack Zipes, *Series Editor*

Children's Literature Comes of Age
Toward a New Aesthetic
by Maria Nikolajeva

Sparing the Child
Grief and the Unspeakable in Youth Literature About Nazism and the Holocaust
by Hamida Bosmajian

Rediscoveries in Children's Literature
by Suzanne Rahn

Inventing the Child
Culture, Ideology, and the Story of Childhood
by Joseph L. Zornado

Regendering the School Story
Sassy Sissies and Tattling Tomboys
by Beverly Lyon Clark

A Necessary Fantasy?
The Heroic Figure in Children's Popular Culture
edited by Dudley Jones and Tony Watkins

White Supremacy in Children's Literature
Characterizations of African Americans, 1830–1900
by Donnarae MacCann

Ways of Being Male
Representing Masculinities in Children's Literature and Film
by John Stephens

Retelling Stories, Framing Culture
Traditional Story and Metanarratives in Children's Literature
by John Stephens and Robyn McCallum

Pinocchio Goes Postmodern
Perils of a Puppet in the United States
by Richard Wunderlich and Thomas J. Morrissey

Little Women and the Feminist Imagination
Criticism, Controversy, Personal Essays
edited by Janice M. Alberghene and Beverly Lyon Clark

The Presence of the Past
Memory, Heritage, and Childhood in Postwar Britain
by Valerie Krips

The Case of Peter Rabbit
Changing Conditions of Literature for Children
by Margaret Mackey

The Feminine Subject in Children's Literature
by Christine Wilkie-Stibbs

Ideologies of Identity in Adolescent Fiction
by Robyn McCallum

Recycling Red Riding Hood
by Sandra Beckett

The Poetics of Childhood
by Roni Natov

Voices of the Other
Children's Literature and the Postcolonial Context
edited by Roderick McGillis

Narrating Africa
George Henty and the Fiction of Empire
by Mawuena Kossi Logan

Reimagining Shakespeare for Children and Young Adults
edited by Naomi J. Miller

Representing the Holocaust in Youth Literature
by Lydia Kokkola

Translating for Children
by Riitta Oittinen

Beatrix Potter
Writing in Code
by M. Daphne Kutzer

Children's Films
History, Ideology, Pedagogy, Theory
by Ian Wojcik-Andrews

Utopian and Dystopian Writing for Children and Young Adults
edited by Carrie Hintz and Elaine Ostry

Transcending Boundaries
Writing for a Dual Audience of Children and Adults
edited by Sandra L. Beckett

The Making of the Modern Child
Children's Literature and Childhood in the Late Eighteenth Century
by Andrew O'Malley

How Picturebooks Work
by Maria Nikolajeva and Carole Scott

Brown Gold
Milestones of African American Children's Picture Books, 1845–2002
by Michelle H. Martin

Russell Hoban/Forty Years
Essays on His Writing for Children
by Alida Allison

Apartheid and Racism in South African Children's Literature
by Donnarae MacCann and Amadu Maddy

Empire's Children
Empire and Imperialism in Classic British Children's Books
by M. Daphne Kutzer

Constructing the Canon of Children's Literature
Beyond Library Walls and Ivory Towers
by Anne Lundin

Youth of Darkest England
Working Class Children at the Heart of Victorian Empire
by Troy Boone

Ursula K. Le Guin Beyond Genre
Literature for Children and Adults
by Mike Cadden

Twice-Told Children's Tales
edited by Betty Greenway

Diana Wynne Jones
The Fantastic Tradition and Children's Literature
by Farah Mendlesohn

Childhood and Children's Books in Early Modern Europe, 1550–1800
edited by Andrea Immel and Michael Witmore

Voracious Children
Who Eats Whom in Children's Literature
by Carolyn Daniel

National Character in South African Children's Literature
by Elwyn Jenkins

Myth, Symbol, and Meaning in *Mary Poppins*
The Governess as Provocateur
by Georgia Grilli

A Critical History of French Children's Literature
by Penny Brown

Once Upon a Time in a Different World
Issues and Ideas in African American Children's Literature
by Neal A. Lester

The Gothic in Children's Literature
Haunting the Borders
edited by Anna Jackson, Karen Coats, and Roderick McGillis

Reading Victorian Schoolrooms
Childhood and Education in Nineteenth-Century Fiction
by Elizabeth Gargano

Soon Come Home to This Island
West Indians in British Children's Literature
by Karen Sands-O'Connor

Boys in Children's Literature and Popular Culture
Masculinity, Abjection, and the Fictional Child
by Annette Wannamaker

Into the Closet
Cross-dressing and the Gendered Body in Children's Literature
by Victoria Flanagan

Russian Children's Literature and Culture
edited by Marina Balina and Larissa Rudova

The Outside Child In and Out of the Book
by Christine Wilkie-Stibbs

Representing Africa in Children's Literature
Old and New Ways of Seeing
by Vivian Yenika-Agbaw

The Fantasy of Family
Nineteenth-Century Children's Literature and the Myth of the Domestic Ideal
by Liz Thiel

From Nursery Rhymes to Nationhood
Children's Literature and the Construction of Canadian Identity
by Elizabeth A. Galway

The Family in English Children's
Literature
by Ann Alston

Enterprising Youth
*Social Values and Acculturation in
Nineteenth-Century American Children's
Literature*
edited by Monika Elbert

Constructing Adolescence in Fantastic
Realism
by Alison Waller

CONSTRUCTING ADOLESCENCE IN FANTASTIC REALISM

ALISON WALLER

Taylor & Francis Group
NEW YORK AND LONDON

First published 2009
by Routledge
711 Third Avenue, New York, NY 10017

Simultaneously published in the UK
by Routledge
2 Park Square, Milton Park, Abingdon, Oxfordshire OX14 4RN

Routledge is an imprint of the Taylor & Francis Group, an informa business

First issued in paperback 2010

© 2009 Taylor & Francis

Typeset in Minion by
Swales & Willis Ltd, Exeter, Devon

All rights reserved. No part of this book may be reprinted or reproduced or utilised in any form or by any electronic, mechanical, or other means, now known or hereafter invented, including photocopying and recording, or in any information storage or retrieval system, without permission in writing from the publishers.

Trademark Notice: Product or corporate names may be trademarks or registered trademarks, and are used only for identification and explanation without intent to infringe.

Library of Congress Cataloging-in-Publication Data
Waller, Alison.
Constructing adolescence in fantastic realism / by Alison Waller.
p. cm.—(Children's literature and culture ; 55)
Includes bibliographical references and index.
1. Adolescence in literature. 2. Young adult fiction, English—History and criticism. 3. Fantasy fiction, English—History and criticism. 4. Young adult fiction, American—History and criticism. 5. Fantasy fiction, American—History and criticism. 6. Teenagers in literature. 7. Group identity in literature. 8. Realism in literature. I. Title.
PR830.Y68W36 2008
823'.0876609282—dc22
2008002336

ISBN13: 978-0-415-95832-5 (hbk)
ISBN13: 978-0-415-89774-7 (pbk)
ISBN13: 978-0-203-89413-2 (ebk)

For Anna and Lucy

Contents

Series Editor's Foreword		xi
Preface		xiii
Acknowledgments		xv
Introduction		1
Chapter 1	Developing through Fantasy: From Stasis to Transformation	29
Chapter 2	Fantasies of Identity: The Self and Individualism	55
Chapter 3	Fantasies of Empowerment and Agency: Gender and the Burden of Responsibility	91
Chapter 4	Writing Fantastic Spaces: Real, Virtual and Textual Teens	145
Conclusion	New Evolutions: Fears and Pleasures of Young Adult Fantastic Realism	187
Notes		199
Bibliography		207
Index		217

Series Editor's Foreword

Dedicated to furthering original research in children's literature and culture, the Children's Literature and Culture series includes monographs on individual authors and illustrators, historical examinations of different periods, literary analyses of genres, and comparative studies on literature and the mass media. The series is international in scope and is intended to encourage innovative research in children's literature with a focus on interdisciplinary methodology.

Children's literature and culture are understood in the broadest sense of the term 'children' to encompass the period of childhood up through adolescence. Owing to the fact that the notion of childhood has changed so much since the origination of children's literature, this Routledge series is particularly concerned with transformations in children's culture and how they have affected the representation and socialization of children. While the emphasis of the series is on children's literature, all types of studies that deal with children's radio, film, television, and art are included in an endeavor to grasp the aesthetics and values of children's culture. Not only have there been momentous changes in children's culture in the last fifty years, but there have been radical shifts in the scholarship that deals with these changes. In this regard, the goal of the Children's Literature and Culture series is to enhance research in this field and, at the same time, point to new directions that bring together the best scholarly work throughout the world.

Jack Zipes

Preface

Ask most British adults what they read when they were teenagers and the answer is likely to be 'nothing' or 'the classics', 'Ian Fleming' or 'Agatha Christie'. Adults of a certain age might mention Robert Cormier's *The Chocolate War* (1974) or Judy Blume's *Forever* (1975), key landmarks in early young adult realism. Now and then someone will recognise the names of Alan Garner or Robert Westall, Margaret Mahy or Louise Lawrence, and will vaguely recall that strange worlds of magic and metamorphosis invaded their reading for a year or two. In fact, a plethora of extraordinary and exciting novels that merge fantasy and realism have been successfully published over the last forty years, and I have gathered them together under the label 'fantastic realism'. Such texts have been read by teenagers and held in school or public libraries throughout Britain. That the majority of adult readers outside of specialist spheres (such as education, librarianship or publishing) have forgotten these books suggests a strange cultural amnesia and one that has generally been exacerbated by critical silence. This book is an attempt to reassess texts that have previously been ignored or under-theorised by examining them through their shared generic features. In particular, I want to ask whether a potentially subversive genre such as fantastic realism offers its readers new and interesting ways of becoming and being adolescents, because this project has also grown out of a fascination with what adolescence means in the late twentieth century. Beginning to plan the doctoral work on which this book is based at a moment when I was technically just beyond adolescence, I was struck by how distant I felt from being 'grown up'. Indeed, I was curious about the emotional and practical markers confidently used to define young people, and how far they relate just as effectively to modern adulthood. This book is concerned with how traditional views of adolescence are constructed and how they permeate fictional representations, as well as what these views say about adult reactions to changing images of youth.

There were certain novels that set my adolescent self whirling with their weird mixture of fantasy and reality and their glimpses of transformation and growth: Robert Westall's *The Devil on the Road* (1978), Margaret Mahy's *The* xiv • Preface

Changeover (1984) and Robert Cormier's *Fade* (1988) are a few of the texts that appear in *Constructing Adolescence* and which have a role in my own production as adolescent reader. The main part of this study provides close readings of these texts and other fantastic realist novels for teenagers from the late 1960s to the current day.

* * *

> If Laura had been asked how she knew this reflection was not hers she could not have pointed out any alien feature. The hair was hers, and the eyes were hers, hedged around with the sooty lashes of which she was particularly proud. However, for all that, the face was not her face for it knew something that she did not. It looked back at her from some mysterious place alive with fears and pleasures she could not entirely recognize. There was no doubt about it. The future was not only warning her, but enticing her as it did so. (*The Changeover* 3–4)

> I looked down and saw nothing. Only space. Although my body retained its weight, I felt a sensation of lightness, as if my body could soar through the air [. . .] Standing [. . .] in that strange new state, present but absent, transparent, my head spinning [. . .] I wanted to cry out: Get me out of this, take away the fade, let me wake up from this dream, this nightmare [. . .] I was suddenly whole again, restored, intact, visible, *here* and *now* [. . .] Everything the same as before.
> But not really the same again.
> Never to be the same again. (*Fade* 71–72)

These two extracts offer a starting point and could easily describe the status of adolescence in any one of the fantastic realist texts discussed in the following chapters. Each protagonist is projected into a mysterious place of magic or time-travel, metamorphosis and the supernatural, that exists alongside their ordinary world. Mahy's heroine perceives such a new space as 'alive with fears and pleasures' and this book suggests that her ambivalent feelings precisely echo the uncertainty evident in adult representations of adolescence. Although the teenager is often a figure to celebrate through fantastic growth and possibilities, teenagers also threaten to disrupt liberal humanist certainties about an idealised state of adulthood and, as such, they are bound by the very conventions of an ultimately conservative realism.

I begin with an introductory chapter, which provides a theoretical and methodological discussion of the discourse of adolescence, and of the fields of young adult fiction and fantastic realism. Throughout the book, a range of theoretical and critical apparatus informs the arguments, and textual readings engage with theories of genre and representation, identity, power and fantasy.

Acknowledgments

I am grateful to the AHRC and the British Academy for awarding funds enabling me to research and write this book. I would also like to acknowledge the institutional support I have received from Oxford Brookes University, Nottingham Trent University, and the National Centre for Research in Children's Literature at Roehampton University.

Many people have offered advice and assistance in different forms. Thanks therefore go to Joelle Adams, David Belbin, Vicki Bertram, Sandra Byatt, Kerry Davies, Ian Gadd, Ruth Griffin, Faye Hammill, Susan Hancock, Mary Hine, Peter Hunt, Murray Knowles, Gillian Lathey, Jenni Lewis, Sean Maher, Fiona Maine, Sharon Ouditt, Rob Pope, Lisa Sainsbury, Liz Thiel, Estella Tinknell and Lynette Turner. I am also particularly grateful to Russell Jackson, David Waller and Jennifer Waller for their personal support and encouragement.

Finally, I would like to thank Jack Zipes and all the staff at Routledge.

Parts of Chapter Three first appeared in '"Solid All the Way Through": Margaret Mahy's Ordinary Witches.' *The Fiction of Margaret Mahy*. Eds. Sarah Winters and Elizabeth Hale. Wellington, NZ: Victoria University Press, 2005. 21-43.

Introduction

In a society that worries about its own infantilism there is a general atmosphere of uncertainty surrounding the concept of adolescence. These anxieties are crucial to understanding modern subjectivity and they result in extreme—often nostalgic—attempts to fix adolescence as a separate state. Adolescence is always 'other' to the more mature stage of adulthood, often perceived as liminal, in transition, and in constant growth towards the ultimate goal of maturity. Yet our own experiences tell us that human beings never truly become unified, active or powerful selves. Indeed, some contemporary theory would suggest that identity is fluid, plural or fragmented at all stages of life. My first intention in writing this book, therefore, is to examine and try to understand our own *adult* attitudes towards adolescent identity. I want to ask whether adult sensibilities construct fictional teenagers in order to maintain their own sense of coherent selfhood, and to manage ambivalent feelings towards the potentially dynamic state of adolescence. To answer this question, *Constructing Adolescence in Fantastic Realism* examines those fundamental themes which inform our understanding of 'the teenager'; themes which emerge in both literary and cultural contexts. Its general argument is that models of adolescence do not arise solely from professional discourses such as psychology, sociology, cultural studies and education, or from commonsense voices in the media, but are also produced in and through fictional representations.

This leads me to the book's second purpose: to provide a critical overview of some of the extraordinary and exciting novels successfully published for teenagers over the last forty years that merge fantasy and realism, and which I have gathered together under the label 'fantastic realism'. It seems to me that the models or frameworks we use to understand adolescence—including developmentalism, identity formation, social agency and subjectivity within cultural space—can also be found symbolically represented in the common tropes of teenage fantastic realism and its sister genres. In these books, incredible, supernatural and magical elements invade the adolescent's everyday and diurnal world: elements such as metamorphosis, hauntings, doppelgangers, invisibility, magic gifts, witchcraft, time-slip, cyberspace and virtual reality. The readings offered in this book explore how adolescence is represented in young adult fantastic realism, not only through an examination of the main features of teenage characterisation, but also by analysing the thematic and structural elements of these novels as the fantastic and the real collide.

In the subsequent chapters I will analyse fantastic realist novels for teenagers from the second half of the twentieth century and the beginnings of the twenty-first. This is partly an attempt to reassess texts that have previously been ignored or under-theorised by examining them through their shared generic features. This enables older, overlooked novels to be considered alongside more recent texts, particularly those that have benefited from current critical and popular interest in both teenage fiction and forms of fantasy. My readings are informed by the concept that fiction and theory emerge from shared attitudes towards adolescence, and that themes and ideological perspectives are embedded in literature aimed at young people. I will question these attitudes, asking whether parallel realities and fantastic identities produce forms of adolescence that are dynamic and subversive or whether they act to keep the teenager in check through essentially humanist and pedagogic urges.

The rest of this introduction outlines ways of conceptualising and understanding adolescence before turning to defining the genre of young adult fantastic realism.

Theorising Adolescence

Theories of the Child

> [Word children] are cast within the domain of texts and of images. In that sense, they are of exactly the same order as the children and childhoods that inhabit, say, the pages of developmental psychology journals, which are also re-presentations: word children and iconic-children. What we call the study of children is, on this reading, always the study of re-presentations of children. (Stainton-Rogers and Stainton-Rogers 193)

There is an ongoing project among theorists of all kinds to problematise aspects of childhood and age. The Stainton-Rogers' 'word children' offer a vivid illustration of this project; they are textual or iconic representations of children that are inscribed through discourses and reproduced in fiction. 'Word children' and 'word teenagers' are inevitably controlled by adult systems of communication. Since this is the case, it is possible to uncover some of the prevailing ideological attitudes towards young people in the shared themes that exist across fictional, theoretical and popular discourses. Such a concern with issues of age and representation reflects a more general late twentieth-century interest in theorising and deconstructing identity within cultural and literary studies. The theoretical drive to question ideas of the self and the politics of representation is found in a number of key works from historical, philosophical and literary fields. Therefore, a publication like Allison James and Alan Prout's important collection of sociological essays on the construction of childhood, *Constructing and Reconstructing Childhood*, which appeared in 1990, can be located alongside studies of racial, sexual and gendered identities by Edward Saïd, Michel Foucault and Chris Weedon.

Underlying these approaches is the post-structuralist notion that identity is not an organic whole but is divided into *identities* that allow an awareness of differences in age, ethnicity, sexuality, gender and class. Stuart Hall argues that identities are endlessly fascinating because they are 'never unified and, in late modern times, increasingly fragmented and fractured; never singular but multiply constructed across different, often intersecting and antagonistic, discourses, practices and positions' ('Who Needs Identity?' 4). Problems arise when the concept of identity becomes so fragmented that it is impossible to use without employing a confusing series of caveats. Critics are in danger of being immobilised by nuances and contradictions. How can 'the adolescent' be discussed when *adolescence* is a phenomenon that not only varies across different cultures, historical periods and individual experiences, but is also cross-cut by identifiers such as gender, race and class. Hall has a solution, which draws on Derridean deconstruction and suggests putting key concepts 'under erasure': 'This indicates that they are no longer serviceable—"good to think with"—in their ordinary and unreconstructed form. But since they have not been superseded dialectically [. . .] there is nothing to do but to continue to think with them' (1). Thus, despite its complexities and problems, identity can remain a useful umbrella term under which the variants of modern subjectivity can be explored. By ensuring that original paradigms are not reproduced—so that we no longer think of women solely within Patriarchy, or indigenous people merely in the context of Colonialism—we free up the terminology of identity for further use and scrutiny.

Age is a relatively late addition to this post-structuralist enterprise and Chris Jenks complains that at the point where gender and class were shifted into 'the post-structuralist space of multiple and self-presentational identity sets' (*Childhood* 3) childhood remained locked in a simple child–adult binary. Jenks and other theorists in the field of childhood studies have sought to deal with the dilemma of speaking of a universal, essential or unproblematic childhood and have found Hall's solution useful.[1] James and Prout, for instance, argue that childhood presents 'an interpretive frame for understanding the early years of human life', but point out it is not a unified concept because 'it is biological immaturity rather than childhood which is a universal and natural feature of human groups' (*Constructing and Reconstructing Childhood* 3). Before I turn to the implications of such an approach for ideas of *adolescence*, I want to trace a particular strand of theoretical thought about the child to show how literary study is inextricably connected to notions of deconstructed identities.

'Constructionist theory' takes as read the premise of *social* constructionism: that identity is significantly formed by social and cultural contexts rather than being fixed through age, race or sex, for example (this position is also known as the Standard Social Science Model or SSSM, and I shall return to this version of constructionism in my Conclusion). Constructionist critics go further and suggest that descriptive discourses—from history to art—act to *construct* identity, and that identity is not dictated by external forces but is mutable. Jacqueline Rose is perhaps the best known proponent of this approach. Her *The Case of Peter Pan: or the impossibility of children's fiction* (1984) reads J.M. Barrie's character as a paradigm of how the child is created and consumed.[2] Rose takes an explicitly psychoanalytic angle, discussing literature through the economies of desire and repression, and her main thesis is that the 'real child' can never exist within a literature that is produced by adults, other than as a figure of fantasy or desire:

> There is no child behind the category 'children's fiction', other than the one which the category itself sets in place, the one which it needs to believe is there for its own purposes. These purposes are often perverse and mostly dishonest, not wilfully, but of necessity, given that addressing the child must touch on all of these difficulties, none of which it dares speak. (10)

Rose suggests that children's literature is an institution that presents images of childhood for consumption by children and by adults reading to/for children. But she points out that the process of representation is not transparent; that portrayals of childhood only refer back to essential notions of the child, constructed through adult discourse, and that the 'real' child reading the book is no less constructed by the institution of literature. Crucially, Rose suggests that the impossibility of children's literature resides in adult perceptions of childhood itself, as a universal, innocent and primitive state which transcends the complexities of language and meaning. By representing the child, she argues, literature is seen as reverting to pure meaning, untrammelled by adult confusion or complication, and it is imagined that the essential truth of a text can be uncovered through the innocence of children's books. In other words, children's literature and its criticism deal with a fantasy of origins:

> in the analysis of children's fiction, the child seems to become implicated in the process [of uncovering primary meaning]. It is as if the child serves to sanction that concept of a pure origin because the child is seen as just such an origin in itself. The child is there, and the original meaning is there—they *reinforce* each other. (Rose 19)

Of course, in some respects children's literature is actually very much distanced from the idea of original meaning: indeed from any meaning at all. Rose is surely right when she claims an impossible layer of adult perspective and desire in the creation of literature for and about childhood. But she fails to note that a text that can be imagined as transparent innocence of language and meaning might also be envisaged as a void and a site for meaninglessness and nonsense. The child, it seems to me, can still signify obfuscation and darkness.

Rose's general premise continues to be influential, however. Karín Lesnik-Oberstein has extended her argument by examining ways that critical treatments of the child (in history, art history, psychology and children's literature criticism) ignore the textuality of childhood. She argues that this occurs because of a prevailing unconscious desire for meaning and truth ultimately to be located in a moral, caring and emotional society based around 'family'. Thus, for Lesnik-Oberstein, dominant critical approaches judge representations of childhood through reference to the 'real' child (discoverable through biological, psychological or psychoanalytical data), expressing a desire to retain a particular image of childhood that allows a positive view of humankind more generally. She argues that 'the creation and protection of an essentialist "childhood" and the "child"' asserts 'the existence of an emotional tie to children which is "normal", which endures [. . .] the loving family, with the child at its vital heart, redeems humanity morally and existentially' ('Childhood and Textuality' 18).

This romantic assertion can certainly be found in recent critical approaches to children in literature, such as Roni Natov's poetics of childhood, which 'addresses the persistent longing for childhood in adulthood' and represents the child as a 'source of hope' (6, 7). Both Rose and Lesnik-Oberstein suggest that childhood is not a comforting or coherent reality that can simply be 'discovered' in literary representations, but is rather 'a mediator and repository of ideas in Western culture' ('Childhood and Textuality' 6) which reveals as much about adult desires (for the pure child who morally redeems them) and fears (of the instability of history, art and ideas in representing themselves) as it does about the nature of children. Rose points to the fact that these qualities romantically attributed to children are in direct opposition to concepts of adulthood (which signifies corruption, decay and complexity) but that such oppositions cannot reflect essential truths about the child: 'instead they produce a certain conception of childhood which simply carries the weight of one half of the contradictions which we experience in relation to ourselves' (50). In other words, adults use the concept of childhood as a way of containing confusing 'non-adult' aspects of our own identity. The child here does not speak for themselves, but represents aspects of humanity supposedly lost to adults.

Rose and Lesnik-Oberstein provide a useful starting point for an exploration of what adult concerns are at stake in the representation of *adolescence*, but their work also has limitations for this line of enquiry. Whilst childhood is seen as a kind of alter-ego for the adult, there is no theoretical place for the adolescent. Lesnik-Oberstein collapses ideas of adolescence and childhood, using criticism of young adult novels simply as further evidence for her theories about constructions of the child. She will sometimes include adolescence in her discussions, but only bracketed as an afterthought, as in the phrase 'the child (or adolescent)'. Yet the 'set of meanings' contained in adolescence is quite distinct from childhood and cannot be described in straightforwardly oppositional terms. For instance, adolescence does not clearly refer to ideas of innocence, origin or moral security, and it is located, not merely as 'other' to adulthood, but also as 'other' to childhood. It is a liminal space onto which a distinct dichotomy of desires or fears cannot easily be projected. I would argue, moreover, that the literature and critical work surrounding adolescence is less blinkered with regard to the textual nature of its subject. The category of 'teenager' is a recent one, and has had less time than childhood to build up those concrete layers of meaning in social history, art, religion or, indeed, fiction. Adolescence is, after all, a less stable and more fluid concept, defined by its 'in-between-ness', its transitory position between childhood and adulthood, and its dependence on fleeting popular culture. Although the teenager is not always thoroughly theorised in critical analyses, there *is* a more general acceptance of the teenager's inherently constructed nature. For example, adolescent identity formation is a central theme in sociology and sociologically influenced literary criticism, and often relates to techniques of borrowing from, or distorting, mainstream styles. Teenagers are described as constructing their own identities through absorption, rejection or 'bricolage' of the dominant ideologies and social patterns of their parents or educators. For this reason, Stephen Thomson considers the defining quality of adolescence to be performative, each alternative identity or youth subculture merely being 'one possible décor draped over an abiding and essentially unchanging scene of youth' (24).

Young adult fiction requires the same kind of rigorous critical treatment that children's literature has been subject to. An exploration of the adult concerns and preoccupations behind teenage fiction is essential in addition to endeavours in children's literature criticism, as the discourses and themes of adolescence are considerably different. The following sections set out how I intend to use and adapt constructionist theory to explore the idea of 'adolescence' and offer some parameters to what I, as adult critic, understand by this concept.

The Discursive Field of Adolescence

In the following chapters, the features and concerns of young adult fantastic realism are read against the discursive field of adolescence. Drawing on Foucauldian thinking, Christine Griffin defines discourse as a 'system of statements which constructs an object. This fictive object can then be reproduced in the various texts written or spoken within the domain of discourse' (7). A 'discursive field', then, is a theoretical matrix where different types of knowledge, fictive representations and dominant themes intersect to produce meaning. The field of adolescence indicates all those moments when imaginative, theoretical or professional discourses are specifically concerned with the teenager or when adolescence is conceptualised through 'discursive frameworks'. Overlaying this complex matrix onto primary texts helps us to understanding how adolescence is represented in young adult fantastic realism and what adult concerns and ideologies underpin the genre.

A discourse can be a disciplinary area such as psychology or biology, or a professional subject such as law or education, or imaginative systems like literature and art. Furthermore, discourse can be tied to a strong sense of subject so that adolescence might be seen to be formed through discourses of family, and teenagers through the discourse of culture. Clearly none of these systems are neutral and all are capable of revealing ideological intentions towards the concepts they construct and describe. The adolescent inscribed through biological discourse serves a different purpose to the one who figures in discourses of war or in pedagogical discourse. The first might well portray an enduring and immutable pattern of human change, the second might represent innocence in the face of tragedy, and the last might explain the educational problems of teenagers.

Discourses that are related to powerful or privileged voices are most likely to appear 'truthful'. Scientific, academic, legal or other official discourses, for example, seem to give an incontestable picture of adolescence, while it may appear easier to question the creative versions produced in fictions. These apparent hierarchies of discourse are not fixed, however, but contingent on shifting public perceptions. It is possible to argue thus that fictional portrayals—particularly in the media of television, film and music—are more powerful than official voices in representing ideas of what adolescence constitutes because of their pervasiveness in modern society and their special relevance to teenage culture. Moreover, post-structuralist understandings suggest that, as well as constructing meaning through representations, discourse also wields power. Foucault shows that power does not exist simply as an external force but is brought into being through discourse—just as discourse is generated through power (*Power/Knowledge*). Ultimately this means that dominant and persuasive discourses can coerce subjects into conforming to conventions of behaviour. In other words, by producing adolescence in a variety of ways that appear to be natural and innate, discourse helps to replicate those norms in the expectations and actions of future individuals.

This book examines interlinking 'discursive frameworks' that formulate common ways of representing adolescence: development, identity, social agency and subjectivity in space. These frameworks thread through the discursive field providing unifying themes that relate to a central concept. They are not tied to one particular discourse but are employed across disciplines. It is these frameworks that produce the links and interstices between theory and fiction, allowing young adult fantastic realism and models of adolescence from psychology, psychoanalysis, biology, sociology and cultural theory to communally construct teenagers as 'word children'.[3] In examining a number of key theories that have shaped late twentieth-century ideas of adolescence, I am not attempting to offer any expert judgement of their validity, but I am using influential works to show what general themes permeate the discursive field.[4]

Defining Adolescence

Throughout this book I use the terms 'adolescence', 'teenager', 'youth' and 'young adult'. They are clearly related to one another, but have subtle distinctions relating to history, culture and the body. To be youthful is to be almost any age, any class and any gender (although the singular 'youth' most often refers to a boy, and the terms 'decadent youth' and 'disaffected youth' have quite different social connotations). For any greater sense of meaning, the concept of youth is dependent upon historical and social contexts. In his history of Western youth, Michael Mitterauer takes what might be deemed a constructionist approach and argues that:

> in conditions not complicated by civilization, neither emotional puberty nor the so-called [rebellious years . . .] would be recognized or recognizable [. . .] they appear to represent symptoms and expressions of the particular historical-cultural setting of a young person. (7)

Adolescence describes a stage of life featuring emotional and social qualities that are caused by, or are dependent upon, a specific historical-cultural setting. Although the *Oxford English Dictionary* records the earliest use of 'adolescence' as 1430, the modern use of the term owes much to professional and academic acceptance of emergent social and psychological sciences in the late nineteenth and early twentieth centuries. Since Granville Stanley Hall's 1904 study on adolescent psychology is often cited as the point of 'invention' of modern adolescence, the term seems to be firmly grounded in the social sciences. For instance, cultural historian Lucy Rollin dismisses the 'the sociological tone of adolescence' for her own purposes in preference for terminology of the 'teenager' (ix). Mitterauer states that adolescence primarily refers to psychological and social aspects that correspond to 'puberty', a time of biological change where children develop mature sexual characteristics. However, in the same way that James and Prout are careful to distinguish between childhood and 'biological immatury', Christine Griffin questions the assumption that the biological domain is 'inherently "natural", inevitable and irrevocable' and offers a more dynamic way of understanding adolescence as informed by biological changes and social factors that work upon each other (10–11).[5] In other words, the biological process of puberty in isolation does not automatically engender the state of adolescence, which also has psychological, social and cultural imperatives. Indeed, it is these imperatives that will be crucial in the textual readings in later chapters.

Whereas adolescence is codified through various professional, academic and physical or social discourses, the concept of 'the teenager' is predominantly a cultural one. Despite its ostensibly pragmatic definition as an individual aged between thir*teen* and nine*teen*, the term refers more accurately to a member of a cultural group or sub-section of society that developed out of post-war affluence and social readjustment in the United States. Increased spending ability, the influence of mass marketing, and media representations of young people, particularly in film and music, helped to shape a social group that had previously lacked coherence. Natalie Babbitt light-heartedly describes this process from the vantage point of 1978: 'The category *teenager* itself is a new one, of course. It made its first appearance during the Second World War and was created partly by parents, partly by manufacturers, and partly by Frank Sinatra' (33). Despite Babbitt's specific allusion to *American* popular culture, sociologist Mark Abrams claims that by the 1950s British youth culture had adopted a similar cohesive form, defining itself as different or other to mainstream society, and finding pleasure in its disposable income and lack of responsibility.

If the teenager was to some extent created by commercial interest as Babbitt suggests, it is no surprise that teenage fiction emerged in the 1960s, partly as a response to consumer needs and partly as a means for shaping them. British publishers recognised a distinct young adult market: Penguin initiated the first teenage imprint, Peacock Books, and Macmillan and Bodley Head followed with 'Topliners' and 'New Adult' series. Commentators have identified a variety of 'first' young adult novels to be published in Britain, including *The Catcher in the Rye* by J.D. Salinger (first published in book form in America in 1951 and in Britain in 1954), Beverly Cleary's *Fifteen* (1956/1962), S.E. Hinton's *The Outsiders* (1967/1970) and Paul Zindel's *The Pigman* (1968/1969), as well as a much earlier Australian contender, Louise Mack's *Teens* (1897). In the very early stages of this process a new term was introduced to the field. In 1957 the Young Adult Services Division of the American Library Association was established (YASD, known since 1992 as the Young Adult Library Services Association or YALSA). Since then, 'young adult' or 'YA' has been used as a classification for fiction and other commodities aimed to appeal to a teenage market, although what it actually means in terms of age is not always clear. YALSA's guidelines specify twelve- to eighteen-year-olds but in Britain 'young adult' often means no older than fourteen or sixteen. On the other hand, author David Belbin argues that true young adult novels are seriously aimed at the fourteen-plus group and that there is a set of novels aimed at and read by ten- to fourteen-year-olds that require a different terminology ('The David Belbin Interview'). The term 'young adult' is often used to try and bracket together young people in a non-patronising manner, but in practice the label is not often recognised and usually refers less to the age, experience or social group, and more to the products and lifestyle aimed at that sector. It is to these literary products we can now turn.

Young Adult Fantastic Realism: Defining a Genre

Young adult fiction, and literature in general, plays an ambiguous part in the academic and cultural life of contemporary teenagers. According to one study carried out in October 1994 just over half of the fourteen-year-olds questioned had read a book in the previous month that was not part of a lesson or homework. Boys' reading in particular drops dramatically at this age and the range of reading material diversifies for both sexes, expanding from children's story books to include adult novels, newspapers, magazines and non-fiction.[6] The principal site for reading amongst teenagers is within schools where a wide range of literature is recommended, and fiction is privileged as a form of instruction in a humanist tradition, either in terms of learning formal reading and comprehension skills or, more obliquely, in terms of a moral and social education. In the introduction to his 1978 collection of American short stories to be used in schools, Thomas West Gregory argues that '[a]dolescents have been fascinating personalities in American literature ever since Mark Twain set Huck Finn on his odyssey down the Mississippi' and encourages adolescent readers to engage with literary works, not only to help understand their own identities, but also to improve themselves by consuming 'good' literature (xv). Today, English guidelines for the National Curriculum at Key Stage Four (years ten and eleven, or ages fourteen to sixteen) emphasise reading as a function for learning about language and form ('to extract meaning beyond the literal, explaining how the choice of language and style affects implied and explicit meanings'). The curriculum also lays emphasis on a kind of moral education that uses novels as a way of thinking about interpersonal issues ('to identify the perspectives offered on individuals, community and society' and 'to understand the values and assumptions in the texts').[7]

Fiction aimed at teenagers is not always deemed the stuff of good literature or high culture. Indeed, the teenager exists primarily within the sphere of popular culture and subculture, and the prevailing interest is in commodities *for* teenagers, rather than art *about* them.[8] Teenage fiction resides in a rather uneasy position between high and low culture. Although it alludes and relates to the popular cultures of adolescence through music, magazines, fashion, drugs or alcohol, sport, and ideas of leisure and disposable lifestyle, it remains a part of high culture through its affiliation to the institution of literature. Teenage fiction is not about teenagers actively creating their own culture but rather about allowing them to absorb it from an adult point of view.[9] In this uneasy position, there is a continued suspicion of the merits of teenage fiction, of its very form and meaning, and of the wisdom of giving it its own space for analysis. Before I go on to outline the debates surrounding young adult literature and define the specific focus for this book's attention, it is worth exploring why it might be important to consider the nature of genres such as young adult fantastic realism.

Genre Theory

My argument has always been, and remains, that carving up fantasy and the fantastic and jamming its literature into a series of discrete, neatly labelled boxes kills literature dead. (Armitt, *Contemporary Women's Fiction and the Fantastic* 13)

Why should we be interested in identifying and examining a specific genre within young adult literature? Armitt points to serious failings in genre criticism: pigeonholing, prescriptive labelling, and a closing down rather than an opening up of critical approaches. She argues that ground has been lost while 'critics of fantasy have been futilely squabbling over whether a text is marvellous or fabulous' (13). Still, she notes the shared concerns and characteristics of uncanny, gothic, grotesque and utopian literature, and discusses their significance. Distinguishing genres is an essential process in the growth and development of literature and its criticism, and this is exactly what the field of young adult literature studies needs. Analysing a particular genre does not simply result in the deadening meticulousness of definition. Genre is, as Alastair Fowler argues in his introduction to genre theory, 'an instrument not of classification or prescription, but of meaning' (22). In other words, the process of distinguishing young adult *fantastic* realism from young adult realism is not only necessary for constructing a more finely shaded taxonomy of texts available to teenagers, but is also a useful tool for noting significant trends in the field. If authors of young adult literature have branched out from the original and central form of realism into other genres then these differences are relevant to how the texts can be understood and how they are placed in a wider context. Ute Heidmann and Jean-Michel Adam refer to this movement as 'genericity', stressing the dynamic processes at play when a text conforms to, or subverts, an existing genre. They also point to the significance of classifying by genre amongst different actors in the textual field: author, editor and reader (to which we might add teacher and librarian).

A good case study for this process can be found in Peter Hollindale's categorisation of 'the novel of ideas'. In his critical survey of excellence and 'rubbish' in young adult fiction, Hollindale argues that to some professionals in the field the 'adolescent novel' has come to be identified with 'a simple children's book with added sex, violence, and family collapse' ('The Adolescent Novel of Ideas' 85) when instead it should be recognised as part of a complex body of work that 'addresses a multitude of themes from the everyday-realistic to the abstract, theoretical, and conjectural, or uses a range of modes from parochial urban naturalism to cosmic fantasy' (84). From his particular focus on the 'adolescent novel of ideas' or literature aimed at teenagers which attempts to 'grow the mind a size larger', it is clear that his aim is to study types of 'quality' fiction for young people. This kind of text is often highly political or philosophical and therefore appeals to adult sensibilities as well as to teenage readers looking for a challenge. It is attractive to the critic because of its complexity, literary intertextuality, and its tendency to be canonised in curriculum reading lists. As a minor literary movement, Hollindale's adolescent novel of ideas proves to be less a generic form and more a value judgement, revealing adult perspectives about what teenagers should be reading. In this book I also recognise value in tracing popular or generic patterns or forms, and argue that attention to generic breadth is important to map out any new literature, helping to establish young adult fiction as more than merely a set of 'problem novels'.

The development of genres in young adult literature reveals ways in which authors, publishers and readers choose to represent and recognise adolescence in fictional terms. The last decade has seen some excellent critical considerations of young adult genres and their wider implications, although these remain relatively isolated. As well as Hollindale's identification of the adolescent novel of ideas, other critics have explored the intricacies and significance of genre fiction in horror, high fantasy and science fiction, subversive fiction, and dystopic novels (Reynolds, *Radical Children's Literature*; Sambell; Sarland 'Attack of the Teenage Horrors'; Sullivan, *Young Adult Science Fiction*). Cart's cultural history of teenage fiction indicates the progression of different generic forms that seem to have captured the teenage market across fifty years. His study covers realism, naturalism, romance and horror but does not note any specific niche for fantastic literature of any kind (possibly due to its failure to win American prizes or feature in high-selling series). His final chapter indicates a desire for a more intellectual and experimental teenage fiction, one that has relevance but still remains an art.

Modern genre theory recognises that genres—as well as individual works or authors—play a part in exposing and producing social meanings and ideologies. Genre is inherently social and historical as well as aesthetic, and the process of any particular genre being recognised, organised and allowed to flourish owes much to ideological climates and dominant discourses. Genres also form an intrinsic part of the matrix of literary, social and cultural elements that make up those discursive practices and positions over a period of time. David Duff describes such a 'sociology of genre' as a critical methodology which 'examines the social and economic factors affecting the production and reception of literary (or other) genres' (xv). This methodology accepts that conscious historicising is not simply a way of contextualising tangible cultural items such as authors or texts, but that genres—indeed whole aesthetic forms—can themselves illuminate social realities. Duff's approach is especially valuable in a field such as young adult literature, where issues of market, pedagogy and ideology are so close to the surface, and where generic matters of form can easily be ignored in preference to content.

For instance, the conventions of teen realism foreground social problems and a concern with the teenage protagonist's solutions through interpersonal growth. A fantastic realist text might cover similar ground but pay more attention to the relationship between what is real and unreal, shifting interpretive activity from social reality to metaphysical questions. This distinction will become clearer as I go on to describe the differences between realism, fantasy and fantastic realism in young adult literature in the subsequent sections, but for now two novels about discovering long-lost family members illustrate the point. Sarah Ellis's *Out of the Blue* (1995) and Peter Dickinson's *The Lion Tamer's Daughter* (1997) both tell the story of a teenage character finding out that they have a previously unknown sister. Where Ellis's realist novel focuses on Megan's relationship with her parents and on her own maturing idea of family, Dickinson's story is dominated by the fact that Melly and her newly found twin were originally conjured out of one baby and are, in effect, fantastic mirror selves that cannot exist in the same world. The supernatural trope foregrounds concepts of identity and selfhood, whereas a realist novel is more likely to deal with interpersonal development.

Both texts, however, share concerns and characteristics that emerge from the shape of their parent literature: teenage fiction, or young adult literature. Before I can produce successful readings of novels such as Dickinson's, it is necessary to define young adult literature and fantastic realism.

Defining Young Adult Literature

> Although teen-age fiction cannot boast of such masterpieces as *Alice's Adventures in Wonderland* or *The Wind in the Willows*, it is possible to point to a marked improvement in the quality and stature of recent books. (Matthews, 'Writing About Adolescent Literature' 36)

Thomas West Gregory's primer for adolescent readers referred to above does not include fiction aimed specifically at young people (its authors include Philip Roth, Joyce Carol Oates and John Updike). This fact, alongside Dorothy Matthews' assessment quoted above, perhaps indicates a continuing suspicion of teenage fiction in the late 1970s. Robert Bator once complained that children's literature is too often considered to be 'a peninsula dependent on and emanating from the main body of literature': it now seems possible to argue in much the same tone that teenage fiction continues to be regarded as an outcrop on that peninsula (xiii). Journalists seek to promote texts by comparing them sympathetically with children's or adult classics. Much is made, for example, of Robert Cormier's adult literary influences, which range from Ernest Hemingway to Graham Greene, while on a different note, Cecily von Ziegesar's 'Gossip Girl' series has been described in reviews as '*Sex and the City* as told by Carrie Bradshaw's kid sister' (Cooke 1).

Voices from academia and education are wary of dedicating special space to young adult literature. From Matthews' gentle lament that 'teen-age fiction' does not have the quality found in the work of such masters as Lewis Carroll and Kenneth Grahame, to the practice of relegating teen novels to the final chapter of a scholarly study of children's literature, there remains a lack of confidence in the intrinsic value of young adult literature and an anxiety about how critics should approach it. Critics feel the need to defend their interest in this literature by showing that their knowledge of 'quality' children's literature is close at hand to frame and validate the more recent books in the branch of young adult literature. The implication is that teenage fiction cannot be left to stand on its own. The established field of children's literature, on the other hand—even if it still sometimes lacks a place in academic studies—can always fall back on its relative longevity and canonised 'classics' such as *The Wind in the Willows* to confer a sense of old-fashioned quality and the 'test of time'. Introducing a special issue of *Children's Literature Association Quarterly* ten years ago, Caroline Hunt identified a continued tendency for critics to subsume the newer literature of teenage fiction within a broader spectrum of a more established children's literature: 'Obviously, a literary subgenre that has existed for twenty-five to fifty years will accrue less commentary than an older one; typically, too, critics begin by considering a subgenre within its class and only gradually detach it for separate examination' (5).

However, it may not be useful to continue to consider teenage fiction as a sub-genre of either children's literature or adult literature. The differences become cumbersome and preclude more detailed criticism. For instance, comparing a picture book for five-year-olds (such as John Burningham's *Granpa*, 1984) to a teenage novel (such as Tim Bowler's *River Boy*, 1997) might produce interesting longitudinal readings of a particular theme like the death of a grandfather, but would generate few scholarly insights about the state of teenage fiction itself. Considering a teenage novel as part of a wider field of adult fiction, on the other hand, might also help develop ideas of how different texts deal with specific subjects or identify narrative patterns. But it would not address the ideological implications of the fact that most teenage fiction is created by adults for young readers. A separate critical methodology is necessary in order to theorise young adult literature's very in-between-ness or liminality. There have been moves to begin this work: Robyn McCallum's excellent Bahktinian reading of teenage novels, for example, examines the novels on their own terms and makes no attempt to fit them into a continuum of fiction from children's books to adult literature. Roberta Seelinger Trites further contributes to a theoretical underpinning in criticism of teenage fiction in her discussion of power and literature for young people, while Marc Aronson considers teenage fiction important enough to have its own critical history. There is, however, still much work to be done in defining boundaries, building a specific criticism, and theorising the field.

Identifying what we mean by 'young adult literature' or 'teenage fiction' continues to generate difficulties. It is easy to sympathise with Michael Cart when he refuses to play the game:

> Whatever happens, the field is in flux; but then, it always has been, and why not? For what is adolescence but a state of continuous change—of becoming, not being. For that reason alone, I believe the best definition of 'young adult literature' will be the least specific one. And frankly, since it is such a function of our ever-changing ideas of and attitudes towards adolescence, I'm not sure we need a formal definition. (11)

We might also throw in the towel with author Isabelle Holland, who asks 'What is Adolescent Literature?' and comes to the expansive conclusion that 'adolescent literature is whatever any adolescent happens to be reading at any given time' (61). Both Cart and Holland rely on a stable concept of adolescence (even if Cart considers the main and enduring quality of adolescence to be changeability) but they differ in their basic approach to the literature. Where Cart considers young adult literature to be the *result* of adult attitudes towards adolescence, for Holland, teenage fiction becomes a 'reading event' rather than a text,[10] privileging reading contexts over the formal distinctiveness of young adult literature. However, the very inclusiveness of this approach renders it almost too broad to be useful to the literary critic. As novelist Nicola Morgan notes, one teenager's reading may be completely different from another's, and both may be as diverse as any other individual's choices, regardless of age. According to Morgan, if one were to pursue this line of thinking it would make as much sense to have a separate category for 'Dog-owning Middle-aged Mother in Nuclear Family Fiction' (124). Certainly, studies of adolescent reading suggest that individual teenagers read widely amongst children's and adult literature, as well as non-fiction, or that they simply do not read at all.[11]

If defining teenage fiction by extra-textual means and readership is problematic, classification through textual features is also plagued by difficulties. As with any field of literature, it is impossible to construct an infallible list of features common to all individual instances; the impulses behind any field are also practical, political, ideological and dictated by fashion. A feasible solution is to state what kind of characteristics are expected—by authors, publishers, teachers and readers—in a book aimed at teenagers and to use this as a guideline for defining teenage fiction. For instance, it might be agreed that a young adult novel is generally shorter than an adult novel, has fewer or no subplots, and uses language that is accessible and appropriate to young readers. It might also be widely accepted that a young adult novel should be *about* adolescence in some way; that is, it should have a teenage protagonist and a plot that incorporates elements of adolescent experience or interest. There are always exceptions in any formal taxonomy. Philip Pullman's *His Dark Materials* series (1995–2000), for example, defies the model on several counts despite often being classed as *for* young adults; each part of the trilogy is as long as an adult novel, with several subplots and a number of complex political and philosophical themes that are sometimes described in highly scientific or theoretical language. Other novels appear to have few of the first-person, taboo-breaking credentials that are used to define teen fiction, yet they are habitually published, shelved or taught as young adult fiction because of a teenage character or a storyline that is relevant to adolescent readers. Gillian Cross's *Pictures in the Dark* (1996), for example, has many features of a children's novel, and yet is regularly found on teenage shelves due to its themes of identity and development, and the fact it features a GCSE class.

These norms are propagated through conceptions on the part of authors, publishers, teachers and readers of what a teenage novel might be, but also through commercial and institutional pressures. Books that are organised, marketed, sold, lent (in libraries) and taught as young adult literature *become* young adult texts and in this way cultural, economic and educational forces dictate the definition. After struggling heroically with a number of attempts to organise his thoughts on children's literature, John Rowe Townsend finally concludes that definition must ultimately be left to the publishing industry (10), and relying on the concrete decisions of publishers and cataloguers is indeed tempting in its simplicity. It is also a useful method for tracing wider indications of how teenagers and their cultural artefacts are shaped and understood by the adult institutions that surround them. The manipulation is a two-way process, however. Scholars need to be aware that the 'canon' of young adult literature shifts more quickly than most, as teenage readers appropriate adult texts and publishers pick up on the trend and re-issue a subversive adult text as a 'teen pick'. Nicholas Tucker and Julia Eccleshare's recent *Rough Guide to Books for Teenagers* illustrates this process, listing amongst its recommendations novels by Iain Banks, Isabelle Allende and Jane Austen, as well as Robert Westall, Gillian Cross and Jacqueline Wilson. Teenage novels themselves can be re-marketed as 'crossover' fiction, originally published for one readership and subsequently recognised or reissued as appealing to a wider audience.[12]

Some novels originally aimed at children or at adults can be appropriated by teenage readers and retrospectively added to the teenage canon (J.D. Salinger's *Catcher in the Rye*, 1951, has followed this trajectory). In addition, there are some novels—most often 'problem novels'—that have a clear ideological purpose in educating or informing specifically teenage readers. Judy Blume's *Forever* (1975) is a notorious example, in which the reader learns about contraception, first-time sex and the potentially transitory nature of young love alongside heroine Katherine. In this novel, content and style are also indicators of teenage fiction status, and certain themes or features can likewise be used as 'checks'. A number of crucial events often occur around adolescence or signal a stage of development or a coming of age: first experience of death; first sexual encounter; first relationship; movement between schools or into work; cultural signifiers such as alcohol, drugs, music, film or computer games; and general markers of identity achievement or maturation and empowerment (these will be explored further in later chapters). Young adult fiction might be identified where two or more of these practical checks apply to a text.

Peter Hunt suggests that children's literature can be defined as 'a particular text [...] written expressly for children who are recognizably children' ('Defining Children's Literature' 16). It is a position that draws on mainstream reception theory, arguing that an ideal reader is one who has the appropriate abilities and knowledge to allow them to read and interpret texts in acceptable ways (Fish; Culler). Young adult fiction, in this view, is written expressly for an implied adolescent reader; it is clearly aimed at teenagers as they are recognised as such through various (usually adult) discourses. We might depart from Peter Hunt's criteria in one respect, however: he demands that children's literature be written expressly for children who represent a childhood that is 'recognizable *today*' (my italics) ('Defining Children's Literature' 16). This demand for currency certainly helps to indicate fluidity in the teenage literature market but, for a study that is concerned with how adolescence has been represented in fiction over a period of time, it is as important to understand what was considered to be suitable for the implied adolescent thirty years ago as it is to define what is now described as teenage fiction. It is also valuable for scholars of teenage fiction to notice that their own critical work begins to reshape the boundaries of the literature itself.

Alan Garner's *The Owl Service* was published in 1967 and, for the purposes of this study, Garner's work is a reasonable starting point. It not only coincides with the advent of publishing for teenagers in Britain and with the publication of classic American young adult texts by Hinton and Zindel, it is also the first significant fantastic realist novel for teenagers. For, as well as tracking the shape of teenage fiction over time, it is also important to consider the different genres within young adult literature, as fashions in taste change, and the cultural mood shapes how teenagers read and how they are represented. In this book, I am specifically concerned with the genre of 'fantastic realism'.

Defining Fantastic Realism

I have written elsewhere about my first encounter with teenage fantastic realism (Waller, '*Fade* and the Lone Teenager'). Robert Cormier's *Fade* was published in 1988 and it tells the story of a young adolescent called Paul Moreaux who discovers the incredible ability to 'fade' or become invisible seemingly at will. A number of things about this novel are notable. To begin with, although Cormier plays with narration and story expectations in ways that he has already experimented with in *I am the Cheese* (1977) and *The Bumblebee Flies Anyway* (1983), this is the first of his novels which explicitly includes a fantastic element.[13] And the fantasy of invisibility is not accepted by Paul as a child might accept it in a book for younger readers (as natural); nor does the special power open up parallel worlds where everyone can fade. *Fade* details Paul's isolated struggle with his discovery and its intervention in the everyday and realistic occurrences in this ordinary boy's life. Young adult fantastic realism combines the characters and events of contemporary or recognisable adolescence found within teenage realism with some aspect of the consensually impossible, supernatural or unreal. This genre merges teen realism (and its sub-genre the problem novel) with elements of fantastic literature, including fantasy, horror, supernatural tales, fairy tales and—to a certain degree—science fiction or speculative fantasy. The dominant tone and style is realism: events are generally described 'as they really are' without recourse to overtly metaphorical, allegorical or archaic language. Third-person narration offers an unobtrusive 'mirror' or window onto reality, and focalised or first-person texts present an immediate adolescent voice. The fantastic occurs at the level of story as an impossible event or situation that invades the realist narrative. This provokes an initial hesitation on the part of character and/or reader. The fantasy is not absorbed into reality; it remains strange and impossible either to the reader, or to the character it affects, or to both.

The term 'fantastic realism' has an existing critical history in the field of nineteenth-century literature. Rosemary Jackson uses it to describe work by authors such as Charles Dickens, Charlotte Brontë, Elizabeth Gaskell and Fyodor Dostoevsky, drawing attention to their use of the gothic alongside social realism (123–140). Mikhail Bakhtin also describes Dostoevsky's mode of writing as 'fantastic realism' and yet his use of the term 'fantastic' is in many ways misleading. Rather than referring to strange and impossible events or elements that occur within a narrative, Bakhtin refers to Dostoevsky's method of heightened realism, which produces the most realistic and truthful representation of man through completely unfeasible access to his inner workings (54–55). Alison Lee asserts that such '[r]ealism has little to do with reality' and is instead a critical construct indicating that artists have a privileged insight into reality and truth (3).

In many respects it could be argued that the young adult fiction under inspection in this book has no such lofty ideals to reveal truth and beauty, and for this reason it is necessary to distinguish my use of the term 'fantastic realism' from Bakhtin's. The two forms of fantastic realism do, however, share some ground in their forms of realist representation. Dostoevsky's work aims to construct reality through artificial acquaintance with the interior life of characters. Similarly, young adult fantastic realism does not attempt a completely naturalistic portrayal of mundane everyday existence, although neither does it consciously aim to offer broad truths about society or humanity (in contrast to classic, socialist or psychological realism). Instead it employs the conventions of young adult realism to represent contemporary teenage life, narrating events that could conceivably occur in reality and evoking characters who are recognisable and consistent. In this respect its representational aspirations are very close indeed to the tenets of classic realism according to Catherine Belsey, who suggests that its basis is 'the assumption that character, unified and coherent, is the source of action' (73).

Realism, or the attempt 'to show things as they really are' as Raymond Williams puts it (218), is the most recognisable form of young adult fiction. Hollindale describes young adult realism as 'taboo-breaking realism in the depiction of teenage social experience and conflict [. . .] which purports to offer teenage readers a mirror image of their lives' ('The Adolescent Novel of Ideas' 84).[14] Examples range from S.E. Hinton's *The Outsiders* (1967), which tracks the exploits and crises of rival teenage gangs through the voice of young Pony Boy to Jenny Downham's recent *Before I Die* (2007), a harrowing narrative tracing the last few months of sixteen-year-old Tessa's life after she has been diagnosed with leukaemia. Hollindale's definition is limited in one respect though, because breaking taboos—while important in early work by authors such as Paul Zindel and Judy Blume—does not take into account more recent realism. There are still taboos to be broken, often by Melvin Burgess who writes about drugs, sex and gender roles in *Junk* (1996), *Lady: my life as a bitch* (2001), and *Doing It* (2003), yet taboos shift over time so that the topics that were unmentionable in the 1970s are often expected subject matter for contemporary young adult fiction. A great deal of realist fiction for young adults also covers less controversial subject matter, which implies an understanding that taboo-breaking does not mirror every teenager's experience. Hollindale is guilty of conflating all teenage realism into the 'problem novel', which can be described as being primarily driven by a social condition or concern rather than character or story, and which often has recognisable stylistic characteristics such as a first-person, confessional voice and colloquial language.[15]

As a narrative form, realism is crucial to the history of teenage fiction; but the fantastic impulse is also important. The fantastic is a flexible and wide-ranging mode of narration, not one merely represented by the bounded worlds of fantasy, where the reader enters a self-contained secondary world, or where stories are self-coherent but 'impossible in the world as we perceive it' (Clute and Grant 338). The fantastic signals a structural rather than a thematic form, and one that has been eloquently formulated by Tsvetan Todorov in his *The Fantastic: a structural approach to a literary genre* (1973). Todorov's three genres—the 'marvellous', 'uncanny' and 'fantastic'—subtly delineate the potential for different interpretations of fantastic actions dependent on their *logic*. Where impossible fantasy events are contained within a discrete and other world (such as Tolkien's 'Middle Earth', for instance) they have their own logic and can be termed marvellous; the uncanny represents narratives where strange happenings can be rationalised through psychological explanations (many ghost stories turn out to be examples of the uncanny because the supernatural suggestion is disproved). The fantastic proper is located between these two points.[16] In other words, logic fails in fantastic literature and impossible events can be explained *either* through supernatural terms *or* by psychological reasoning. This ambiguity forces the protagonist and/or reader to hesitate between versions, creating tension and allowing the prospect of completely readjusting beliefs and ways of perceiving reality. Todorov's approach is crucial in challenging conventional approaches to fantastic fiction for young people. Most critics of teenage fantasy prioritise a rational reading of the fantastic focusing on socio-physiological development of adolescents. Magic is explained away as a purely imaginative product of awakening sexuality, and ghosts are read as fabricated alter-egos. To return to Cormier's *Fade*, for example, Patricia Head, amongst others, argues that whether or not the 'fade' actually exists is not the main concern of the novel. What is significant for her is what the *pretence* of invisibility says about the protagonist's personality.[17] I would argue that the protagonist's ability to become invisible provides the primary interest for the reader. Straightforward psychological readings of fantasy do not always provide the fullest interpretations. I will show below that it is also important to consider issues of empowerment, alternative perceptions of the world, and the potency of metaphor as a way of representing adolescence.

Rosemary Jackson's seminal work, *Fantasy: the literature of subversion* (1984) defines the narrative qualities of literary fantastic, using concepts from psychoanalysis and applying them to cultural activity. For Jackson, the literary fantastic:

> has to do with inverting elements of this world, re-combining its constitutive features in new relations to produce something strange, unfamiliar and *apparently* 'new', absolutely 'other' and different, and it includes works by Mary Shelley, Edgar Allan Poe and Franz Kafka to name a few. (8)

Jackson's classification relies on structural influences from Todorov and Fredric Jameson, suggesting that fantasy/the fantastic is important as a mode from which more discrete genres emerge. For her, the fantastic reveals widely held 'phantasies', that is, the unconscious imaginative activities that occur in response to some internal frustration in the individual. She is thus predominantly concerned with how the fantastic works as an impulse to subvert social and psychological norms: 'Literary fantasies, expressing unconscious drives, are particularly open to psychoanalytic readings, and frequently show in graphic forms a tension between the "laws of human society" and the resistance of the unconscious mind to those laws' (6–7). In other words, Jackson interrogates the very reasons behind the production and function of fantasy. Her explanation relies on structural rather than thematic arguments, as she maintains that the content of fantasy is not in itself subversive. Instead, it is the way that fantasy undermines realist techniques and unities that provides a parallel to social and psychological resistance to dominant ideologies. It is possible to follow Jackson in tracing culturally embedded attitudes towards adolescence in the very fantastic structures that feature in young adult fantastic realism. While I would question the assertion that all fantasy must reveal subversive reactions to the laws of human society, it is certainly true that tensions exist in the form of fantastic tropes found in young adult fiction and that, to a certain degree, these tensions reflect 'unconscious' ambivalence about the fantastic teenager.

Jackson's is just one way to regard the fantastic and its literary and cultural importance. Other critics are sceptical of fantasy's place in the literary canon, arguing, as Colin Manlove does, that the distance between real worlds and fantastic realms creates an aesthetic and moral problem for the reader from a secularised world that lacks belief in supernatural forces (258–261). Others claim that the distance is not so very great, since all literary creation is a form of fantasy, and the fantastic mode—with its impulse to create something new—

pervades all literature. These debates are usefully summarised by Millicent Lenz and Peter Hunt, who provide an account of fantasy's colourful critical legacy:

> [Fantasy] is the root of all literature, an area of advanced literary experimentation, and essential to our mental health; *or* it is regressive, and associated with self-indulgent catharsis on the part of the writers; *or* it is linked to a ritualistic, epic, dehumanised world of predetermination and out of tune with post-romantic sensitivity; *or* it symbolizes the random world of the postmodern. (2)

Sister Genres

What seems certain is that where realism purports to show things 'as they really are', the fantastic shows things that *are not*, creating worlds unlike our own, creatures that do not exist, and events and actions that would prove impossible in our common diurnal world. Fantastic realism has several 'sister' genres, which are perhaps more familiar but which are subtly different in tone or intention. Magic realism, for example, creates a world that appears like ours but which is supernaturally or magically unlike it at a structural level. The generic difference between magic realism and fantastic realism resides in the idea of strangeness or unnaturalness, since in fantastic realism the protagonist does not expect the impossible to happen and when it does it is beyond their ordinary lived experience. In magic realism those impossible happenings are incorporated into a worldview that the characters—if not the reader—find natural or acceptable. Both magic realism and fantastic realism can employ realistic and reliable reportage, but magic realism describes impossible elements as if they were of the same ontological quality as possible events, whereas fantastic realism indicates the discrepancy between the expected and unexpected. For this reason, magic realism is often more playful and has a tradition of being overtly political.[18] Fantastic realism also bears similarities to domestic fantasy, but again the two are not quite the same. The domestic elements of domestic fantasy tend towards themes of children's, rather than young adult, literature, with the fantasy often related to toys, games or animals and the setting based around the safety of family. Certainly, Peter Hunt uses the term to refer to comforting and contained narratives based in an enchanted space. As such, it is quite distinct from fantasy or fantastic realism, which is generally more disquieting (Hunt, 'Winnie-the-Pooh and Domestic Fantasy'; Louisa Smith). Finally, fantastic realism also has features of content in common with high fantasy, which locates action within a wholly imaginative and 'other' world and has its own internal logic where witches, magic powers and time-travel are inherently possible. But here I think the differences are clear: unlike fantasy, fantastic realism's main concerns and focus remain at least equally located within a contemporary realist narrative. In other words, the centre of these fantastic realist texts is not what C.S. Lewis would call the 'secondary world',[19] but rather the way in which aspects of such a secondary world interact with and affect the 'real' teen world.

Genre boundaries are not unassailable, of course, and a number of fantastic realist texts in this study display features and characteristics of these other sister genres, as further discussion below will explain. For now, an example will suffice: Margaret Mahy's *The Changeover* (1984) is included in this book as a fantastic realist text, but other critics describe it as magical realism (Kimberley Reynolds 21). There are certainly some elements of the carnivalesque in Mahy's style, but my readings stress the protagonist's isolated experience of the fantastic as it is embedded into a recognisable world. I am also aware that a text can move between genres depending on its reader and their understanding of what is real and what is impossible, as well as that text's impact when set against others.

Texts that can be classified as examples of fantastic realism prioritise a reading of the impossible element as authentic rather than a psychological or metaphorical phenomenon. For instance, a story about a teenage girl moving to a new rural home and falling in love for the first time is intercut with the appearance of ghosts and their attempts to affect the girl's decisions (*Unquiet Spirits* by K.M. Peyton, 1997). The ghosts are fantastic instances of the impossible—that is they do not fit into the rational and ordinary world portrayed in the rest of the novel—yet they are represented as utterly real rather than as aspects of the girl's imagination or tricks of the light or mechanical devices. Another example is the story of a boy who belongs to a contemporary acting troupe and who suddenly swaps places with a sixteenth-century counterpart (Susan Cooper's *King of Shadows*, 1999). The boy's modern concerns about bullying, bereavement and belonging are transposed to the Elizabethan period and are played out there, before the boy is returned to the twentieth century. There is, however, no suggestion that the trip has been a dream or a phantasy evoked by his own subconscious to help him resolve his problems. The time-travel is tangible and explicitly pertains to the contemporary narrative.

Types of Fantastic Realism

These examples point to two of the different manifestations of teenage fantastic realism: the haunting novel and time-travel/time-slip. It is worth briefly setting out here some of the key types of fiction this book examines, although, as I have already indicated, the boundaries are sometimes blurred and at times texts fall into more than one category. These types figure as thematic links which may have some structural similarities and which all exist in the wider genre of fantastic realism.

The haunting novel as it appears within fantastic realism is distinct from both children's ghost tales and pre- or early twentieth-century ghost stories. Rather than aiming to frighten the reader or to examine the metaphysical meanings of visitations from beyond the grave, young adult haunting novels are more concerned with the protagonists, how they cope with being haunted, and their place in time and reality. In most haunting novels the spirit is benign and in need rather than malevolent, and the story often revolves around righting a wrong that the ghost suffered when alive (although if there is a distinct horror element to the narrative a malicious ghost is possible). Concepts of the ghostly can also function symbolically to highlight trans-historical assumptions about adolescence such as transience, 'otherness' and being in between worlds. Examples from this sub-genre include: Gillian Cross, *The Dark Behind the Curtain* (1982); Penelope Farmer, *Thicker than Water* (1989); Pete Johnson, *We, the Haunted* (1989); K.M. Peyton, *Unquiet Spirits* (1997); Julian F. Thompson, *Ghost Story* (1997); Celia Rees, *Ghost Chamber* (1997); David Almond, *Kit's Wilderness* (1999).

Closely related to haunting novels are stories dealing with time-travel or time-slip. According to Tess Cosslett, time-*slip* occurs where 'the protagonist slips back in time, characters from the past reappear in the present, or both' ('History from Below' 243).[20] Cosslett's definition can be supplemented by more nebulous types of slippage, such as a fantastic connection or merging with a place, object or character from a different time. Time-*travel* is more likely to appear in science fiction than in fantastic realism, as pseudo-scientific time-machines allow movement backwards and forwards in history. In some instances, however, time-travel is instigated through magical means, often by the power of a talisman or a magical person. In fantastic realist time-slip and time-travel, the contemporary world always plays a significant part in the narrative and does not merely form a framing device for a series of historical adventures, as often happens in children's literature. Examples include: K.M. Peyton, *A Pattern of Roses* (1972); Ann Pilling, *Black Harvest* (1983); Robert Westall, *The Wind Eye* (1976); Tim Bowler, *River Boy* (1997); David Almond, *Kit's Wilderness* (1999). Time-travel novels include: Robert Westall, *The Devil on the Road* (1978); Ruth Park, *Playing Beatie Bow* (1980); Geraldine Kaye, *Forests of the Night* (1995); Susan Cooper, *King of Shadows* (1999); Marianne Curley, *Old Magic* (2000). Alan Garner's *Red Shift* (1973) is also unquestionably concerned with time but is more difficult to classify. Although the main characters do not explicitly travel through history or slip between different times, they do experience flashes of colour and sensation from the past or the future, and this element of fantasy persuades me to include the text within the category.

Witchcraft forms a recurring theme in teenage fantastic realism and a number of texts relate episodes where apparently 'ordinary' teenage protagonists emerge as a witch of some kind. Like haunting novels, witchcraft narratives tend to focus on the affirmative qualities of the fantasy rather than any fearful properties of black magic (unless they are part-horror). Most protagonists in witchcraft novels are female and it seems that authors are eager to explore issues of matrilineal power and contemporary female identity through mythological and historical frames. Historical tales that chronicle the consequences of being a witch at a time of persecution, such as Katherine Lasky's *Beyond the Burning Time* (1994) are not truly fantastic realist because they aim to present accurate versions of social history, but they can provide an interesting comparison. Witchcraft novels include: Louise Lawrence, *The Earth Witch* (1982); Margaret Mahy, *The Haunting* (1982), *The Changeover* (1984) and *The Tricksters* (1986); Robert Westall, *Yaxley's Cat* (1991); Jean Thesman, *The Other Ones* (1999); Marianne Curley, *Old Magic* (2000); Susan Price, *The Bearwood Witch* (2001); Marcus Sedgewick, *Witch Hill* (2001); Cate Tiernan, *Wicca: book of shadows* (2001). Melvin Burgess's *Burning Issy* (1992) and Celia Rees's *Witch Child* (2000) employ fantastic elements in their historical accounts.

In a further sub-genre of fantastic realism protagonists develop magical powers without any suggestion that they have taken on the role of witch. In these narratives there is usually a specific magic gift (such as invisibility or superhuman powers) that affects the individual teenager and their otherwise ordinary day-to-day experiences. Robert Cormier's *Fade* (1988) and Peter Dickinson's *The Gift* (1973) are examples of the magic gift narrative, and Lois Lowry's *The Giver* (1993), although essentially futuristic, shares some of these fantastic realist traits.

The literary fantastic in the adult canon is full of tales of metamorphosis; this is also a popular form within teenage fantastic realism. The teenage protagonist transmutes into animal form, either permanently or in a series of episodes that are interspersed with the contemporary realist narrative. The metamorphosis can be played out in a number of ways, from being a fantastic flight from reality, to constituting an inherent part of the individual's identity, to a test of character. The relationship between the adolescent as a normal human character and their alter-ego as metamorphosed creature is central in these texts. Examples of metamorphosis narrative include: Alan Garner, *The Owl Service* (1967); Peter Dickinson, *Eva* (1988); Patrice Kindl, *Owl in Love* (1993); Sue Welford, *The Night After Tomorrow* (1995); Melvin Burgess, *Tiger Tiger* (1996); Gillian Cross, *Pictures in the Dark* (1996); David Almond, *Secret Heart* (2001); Melvin Burgess, *Lady: my life as a bitch* (2001).[21]

A number of teenage novels fall under the wide category of fantastic realism, which deals with general supernatural or uncanny themes. Freud's concept of the '*unheimlich*' helps to explain this sub-genre as one which mixes the familiar with the bizarre to a disturbing or extraordinary effect. In these narratives a realistic representation of contemporary experience is invaded by an element that cannot be explained through rational methods. Such novels are usually unsettling in their synthesis of recognisable experience set beside alien, unnatural or supernatural events. Examples of uncanny/supernatural novels include: Alan Garner, *The Owl Service* (1967); Louise Lawrence, *The Power of Stars* (1972); Peter Dickinson, *Healer* (1983); Phillip Gross, *The Wind Gate* (1995); Margaret Mahy, *The Tricksters* (1986); Tim Bowler, *River Boy* (1997); David Almond, *Skellig* (1998); Charles Butler, *Calypso Dreaming* (2002). In addition, Lois Duncan's *Stranger with my Face* (1981) and Peter Dickinson's *The Lion Tamer's Daughter* (1997) provide two interesting instances of the uncanny by using 'doppelgangers' or 'doubles', motifs that are more prevalent in adult literary fantastic. These novels are both nominally about twins but in each case the relatively commonplace relationship is complicated by a fantastic element as the characters and their doubles are linked by magical rather than natural means.

Finally, I have included a number of texts in Chapter Four which are not strictly fantastic realist but which might more accurately be termed 'speculative fantasy'. These novels maintain a distinction between a realistic situation and an element of fantasy invasion, but the goalposts indicating reality are shifted slightly so that the situation is no longer identical to that of a contemporary reader. In other words, these texts are most often set in the future. This makes little difference to the fundamental tone of the narratives, however. I am particularly interested in the developing role of technology, and it is clear that where computers or electronic devices make the transition from ubiquitous futuristic tool to supernatural force, the teenage protagonists are still amazed by its strangeness: these books do not deal with a future world where fantasy is normalised. In a way, individuals in cyber speculative fantasy have much in common with characters in time-travel or magic gift narratives: the only difference is that their reality is rather more technologically advanced than the reader's and their fantastic experience or powers occur in cyberspace. Clearly, there are times when speculative fantasy might just as legitimately be categorised as science fiction, but I am keen to draw attention to the role of fantasy in these texts, and the qualities they share with fantastic realism more generally. Speculative fantasy under consideration in Chapter Four includes Gillian Cross's *New World* (1994); Michael Scott's *Gemini Game* (1993); Alan Gibbons' *The Legendeer* trilogy (2000–2001); Vivian Vande Velde's *Heir Apparent* (2002); Leslie Howarth's *Ultraviolet*; and a collection of short novels under the collective title of *The Web 2027* (ed. Simon Spanton, 1997).

A final word should be added regarding the scope of this book, terminology used, and methods used for identifying texts. The terms 'young adult literature', 'teenage fiction', 'literature of adolescence' or 'writing for older readers' often overlap or are used interchangeably when in fact there are subtle but specific connotations to each expression. Most crucially, the term 'literature' may be understood to refer exclusively to a set of texts with high cultural value and yet it can also be used without an evaluative function, in order to describe a whole body of imaginative writing. In some respects this ambiguity makes 'literature' awkward to apply to teenage fiction, which is often considered to be a narrow collection of texts, untested by time. Because we are concerned with the novel form, rather than poetry, drama and other creative texts that might be incorporated in the idea of 'literature', I generally use the term young adult fiction, by which I mean novels aimed at readers who are between twelve and sixteen years old (this inclusive range reflects the increased blurring of age boundaries at adolescence and means that representations of *early* adolescence can be examined). The texts analysed are selected from those novels available to a British reader during the last forty years. My readings encompass mainly British and American authors due to their predominance in the field. A small number of fantastic realist texts from Australia, New Zealand and Canada are also included where they have been available to British readers. Although there are clearly cultural and geographical distinctions to be made, this study focuses on common themes across the field, especially since most fantastic realism published in Britain has tended to collapse cultural difference in favour of a naturalised Anglo-American teenager. There is additionally some evidence that those models of children's and young adult fantastic fiction of all kinds that originate in Great Britain have also developed in Commonwealth countries (Smith, *The Fabulous Realm*). Similarly, differences of race, class, sexuality and ability are generally underdeveloped in fantastic realism. Although an exploration of these gaps would be useful and interesting, here the focus will be primarily on issues of age and, to a lesser degree, gender.

Ideological assumptions about adolescence, its form, its status, and its wider meaning permeate a number of different discourses, from psychological models to media portrayals, and these are clearly bound to fiction that aims both to describe something of that state of being and to somehow affect (through reading, and however subtly) the thoughts or behaviour of adolescents themselves. Moreover, fantastic realism, compared with other genres, offers a potentially more complex matrix of representational and ideological meaning. Whereas teenage realism purports to portray teenagers and their lives *as they really are*, fantastic realism has the potential to disrupt these representations, subvert the dominant discourses of adolescence and offer an alternative set of ideological positions, as Jackson argues all fantastic literature has the ability to do. Part of the purpose of this book is to question whether this subversion happens in young adult fantastic realism or whether, in fact, the form still presents conventional and conservative representations of adolescence.

Chapter One focuses on developmental theories of 'normal' adolescence and shows how ideas of social and physical transformation are metaphorically formed through fantastic tropes of witchcraft, metamorphosis and time-travel. Time shifts, in particular, offer symbolic patterns of desirable forward-movement. Building on these readings Chapter Two deals with the developmental necessity of forming an individual, unique and personal identity at the stage of adolescence. Fantastic narratives question the unity of the self (for example, through doppelgangers and ghosts) and express anxiety where identity appears to be lost (dissolved or made invisible). Chapter Three problematises the assumption that fantastic power provides true agency for the teenage protagonist. Using social theory of teenage subcultures as a framework and drawing on findings from the previous chapters, this chapter tests the overall thesis through a consideration of gender expectations in young adult fantastic realism. In particular, the witch and superhero are considered in terms of both adolescent and gendered fantasies. Chapter Four turns to cyber versions of adolescence in speculative fictions of computer games and virtual reality. These online identities are assessed in terms of the new forms of space they allow their young protagonists, and *textual* selves are offered as an alternative spatial subjectivity for adolescence.

Chapter One
Developing through Fantasy: From Stasis to Transformation

Maria Nikolajeva identifies a series of narrative patterns in children's fantasy fiction. She argues that '[c]ircular journeys are more common in fantasy for children than linear ones, which is natural; the child characters return to their own safe home' (*The Magic Code* 42). Other critics concur, Jacqueline Rose suggesting that children's literature seeks the safety of the nursery at the beginning and ending of each narrative (37), and Sarah Gilead wondering whether the closure of a realistic return home means that fantasy itself is a dangerous space to be escaped *from* (80–109). In contrast to Nikolajeva's child, the adolescent no longer has the option to return home to the safety of comforting familiarity. Discourses of development state that they must move on: to their own home, to the next stage, away from childhood and towards adulthood. This chapter examines ways that fantastic tropes and structures depart from childhood patterns of circularity and instead share common ground with developmental theories and frameworks of progression. The narrative pattern of these discursive frameworks will be familiar to anyone interested in childhood and adolescence in the twentieth and twenty-first century: indeed, it is the dominant model for understanding the concept of youth, and has influenced practical and analytical approaches to education and the social sciences. Nevertheless, despite this familiarity—or perhaps because of it—developmental theory is worth outlining and examining in some detail.

Developmental Theory

Transition and Developmentalism

John Coleman and Leo Hendry agree that transition has been the 'customary' way to describe adolescence within psycho-social discourses. They argue, 'we believe it makes sense to consider adolescence as a transition, while at the same time acknowledging that within this stage there are many turning points which have key significance for later adaptation' (11). Coleman and Hendry's model figures adolescence both as a distinct state of change and as a series of stages that aid development into adulthood. In doing this it effectively fuses two vital frameworks for adolescence. On one hand, *transition* locates adolescence as a set of meanings between, and in conflict with, childhood and adulthood. The child and the adult adopt opposing positions: innocent and experienced, immature and mature, pure and sexual, free and responsible. However contestable these positions are they function successfully as binaries, but those gaps between the two states are more problematic. The teenager resides in the indefinable space between innocence and experience, or asexuality and sexuality, forcing a definition that relies on transitory and unstable signifiers. Coleman and Hendry do question the validity of a framework of sudden and dramatic transition, since their own temporal conception of adolescence spans seven or eight years (as puberty begins to occur at earlier ages and social maturity extends beyond the teen years) (7–19).[1] Their series of 'many turning points', therefore, suggests a more gradual and measured alteration. This approach is much less closely related to the 'storm and stress' of sudden change and is more concerned with the adaptive nature adolescents require in order to cope with constantly shifting social and psychological terrains.

Coleman and Hendry's method is a sophisticated manifestation of the developmental theory that has dominated work in the field of adolescence since the 1920s. These theories concentrate on explaining how humans change over the span of their lives, implicitly supporting broader humanist impulses of education and personal or social improvement that are crucial to modern attitudes towards young people. Indeed, the speedy and conspicuous changes that occur in the early stages of life have provided the focus for most developmental studies, which are generally less concerned with changes later in adulthood and old age. Although Plato and Aristotle originally conceptualised age periods as stages of infancy, boyhood and young adulthood, it was the rise of psychology and sociology as new sciences in the early twentieth century that instilled developmentalism as the governing framework for adolescence. Rather than being fixed as a single point between childhood and adulthood the teenager is seen to progress through a series of stages or tasks that lead towards maturity. As adulthood is often (though not always) posited as the completion of development, adolescence is crucial as a preparatory, intermediary stage and is considered to be key in the sequence of stages as the moment or phase where identity begins to be crystallised, cognitive skills sharpen, social roles are adopted or anticipated, and solipsism gives way to a more inclusive moral outlook.

A cluster of influential theorists with training in clinical psychology are key, not only in the way they have shaped professional fields, but also due to their influence over practical issues and other discourses, including critical approaches to literature for young adults. Jean Piaget collated clinical evidence and wrote on child psychology from the 1920s to his death in 1980.[2] He argues that cognitive processes, along with factors of environment, have a direct and profound effect on personality and that children progress through a set of stages, each one of which involves an improved cognitive ability and each one of which presents problems. The 'formal operational' stage of adolescence, for instance, refers to the point when an individual can make hypotheses and consider outcomes without having concrete terms to rely upon. It is also the moment when there is a progression to 'thinking about thinking': becoming reflective as well as empathic. Educational and social contexts affect how soon or how well children reach this stage of reasoning (Piaget suggests around fourteen- to fifteen-years-old for Western cultures) but because an innate structure of human development exists that follows a strict pattern, formal operational thinking will only be achieved if it can be built on previous stages (Piaget, *Growth of Logical Thinking*; Muuss 140–175).

Erik Erikson draws on Piagetian and Freudian ideas in his psycho-social theory of identity development. Instead of these phases being wholly psychological or sexual, as Freud would have it, or cognitive, like Piaget's schema, Erikson's stages represent tasks of social integration and integrity of identity. His argument is that at each stage the individual must resolve a conflict in order to progress successfully to the subsequent level of development. For Erikson, the main focus at adolescence is on the gradual establishment of a mature identity. Rapid changes in physical and social arenas force the adolescent to question previous assumptions and develop a clearer sense of who they are, what they believe and what they will become (Erikson, *Identity and the Life Cycle*, 'Youth: fidelity and diversity').[3]

James Marcia's work on psycho-social 'fidelity' at the stage of adolescent identity achievement (the schema outlined by Erik Erikson) identifies four potential attitudes to this task amongst teenagers. According to his theory, two of these are described as successful and healthy: 'identity achievement' (when an individual commits to an appropriate social role) and 'moratorium' (the process of searching for this role). In contrast, foreclosure (unquestioningly adopting the roles of others) and diffusion (not searching for any kind of psycho-social role) are considered to be psychologically damaging for the individual's future (Marcia 551–558). This is one way that the binary of ordinary/deviant functions in theoretical models. It will prove to be demonstrated fictionally in both time-travel and metamorphosis narratives in this chapter, and also in later chapters where discussion turns to teenagers achieving a *fantastic* identity, such as the role of witch or wizard. The dominant ordinary/deviant binary can also relate adolescence to the biological determinism that helps to tie teenagers to their bodies, gender roles and sexualities in conventional ways. Biological changes are linked to other forms of development at adolescence, and menstruation or sexual maturity are symbolic of wider personal and social transformations in many of the primary texts, although it is often also made clear that sexual awakening is not necessarily indicative of a complete transition into adulthood.

Piagetian theory is innately rigid in the order and timing of these stages, and many of his critics suggest that Piaget and his followers depend too much on the implication that the process of development is from a low state in childhood to a 'higher' state of maturity. James, Jenks and Prout claim that Piaget's theory is the 'most absolute, if materially reductive, image of childhood structured by biological stages' (17). Certainly, Piaget sees childhood and adolescence as intrinsically different from adulthood, and in some ways he presents children and adolescents as lesser beings. Although this may sound reductive, it is a philosophy that pervades Western socialising and educational culture.

Liminality

Liminality is conceptually linked to theories of development, and particularly to transition, but offers a less prescriptive framework for adolescence. Liminality is an anthropological term that refers to the ritual stage or space existing between two states. French anthropologist Arnold van Gennep first characterised liminality as one of the three phases of any 'rite of passage' across cultures. These rites are rituals that accompany every change of place, state, social position or age, and are therefore crucial wherever there is a sense of children becoming adults. Rites include a phase of *separation* (detachment from previous social or cultural status), *liminality* and *reincorporation* (where the individual returns to a new and stable state). Victor Turner employs van Gennep's universal concepts to examine the notion of liminality in specific African tribal rituals and it is here that explicit ritual processes are most obvious; adolescent liminality in an African tribe incorporates a literal separation from the usual space and status of village life and is imposed by elders as a form of initiation into adulthood. It also often involves the reversing or inverting of current status roles, in a form of humiliation or trial (Turner 94–95).

In modern Western culture there is no clear identifiable space or time for the withdrawal from normal modes of social action at the time of adolescence, nor is there an explicit ritual process imposed by elders (unless one considers formal schooling and examination to be comparable). However, adolescence *is* formulated as a period when individuals are neither institutionalised as children nor accepted into adult roles and society fully, and it is also conceptualised as a series of rites of passage, such as a first sexual experience, first encounter with death, or first paid work. While individuals are going through these various events they are in a liminal state to some degree: performing ritual versions of adult life in preparation for their actual change of status.

Teenage fiction itself is also affected by the liminal status of adolescence. It is located in an uneasy position as neither children's storybook nor adult literary novel, and is not necessarily read exclusively within its intended readership of adolescents who move between the literary worlds of children's literature and adult texts.[4] The differences between Western and non-Western forms of liminality are partly conflated in young adult fantastic realism. Teenage characters exist in a contemporary world where the markers of adolescence remain linked to a material and contemporary world. That is, young adult texts value successful negotiation of romantic relationships or economic achievement. Fantastic realism, however, often locates these markers within a role or space that can more accurately be defined as liminal, even ritual in essence. Turner lists a number of symbols that express the ambiguous and indeterminate attributes of liminal entities: 'liminality is frequently likened to death, to being in the womb, to invisibility, to darkness, to bisexuality, to the wilderness, and to an eclipse' (95). These are metaphors that regularly occur in teenage fantastic realism. David Almond's *Kit's Wilderness* (1999), for example, employs games of death and darkness in its narrative and Robert Cormier's *Fade* (1988) tends towards Freud's sense of 'entropy' (as the opposite of energy, and the longing for death or Nirvana) in its treatment of invisibility. Other textual examples describe fantastic space or time where the adolescent protagonist prepares for future adulthood: in particular, the 'changeover' ritual in Margaret Mahy's *The Changeover* (1984), animal space in *Pictures in the Dark* by Gillian Cross (1996), and past time in time-slip novels such as *King of Shadows* by Susan Cooper (1999). *Fade* will be discussed in the context of identity loss in the next chapter, and I will examine the feminised realm of teenage witchcraft in Mahy's work in Chapter Three, but we shall come across the last two texts later in this chapter.

Narrative Implications

Both developmentalism and the related frameworks of transition and liminality are strong threads that run through young adult fantastic realism, powerfully influencing portrayals of adolescence. In some respects developmental theory offers a hopeful and progressive image of youth. Teenagers move ever onwards to become more competent and increasingly close to the ideal of mature adulthood, and this sense of progression feeds off broader humanist impulses that value constant progression for humankind more generally. Fictional representations can actually struggle to avoid unrealistic idealism when portraying such optimism. In futuristic teen novels, for example, the narrative situation is often dystopic, with events playing out in post-apocalyptic or economically damaged worlds. In her study of fictional time in adolescent fiction, Kay Sambell argues that when such novels attempt to pursue an optimistic sense of development or progression they fail artistically. Youthful optimism simply does not succeed within dystopic narratives unless it is accompanied by knowing irony. While the evolutionary logic of a post-apocalyptic text such as Jean Ure's *Plague 99* (1989) suggests that humankind is degenerating morally into a destructive and reckless race that can create nuclear holocaust, at the same time teenage protagonists survive and presumably proceed to rebuild an ethically and structurally improved society. Sambell points to the narrative contradictions in these texts:

> Instead of reposing trust in the reader's ability to respond to the irony of these hugely undesirable scenarios [such as nuclear war], they attempt to identify the main teenage protagonist unequivocally with a saintly ideal, which is diametrically opposed to the bleakly ironic view of human nature. (152)

Her argument that most young adult fiction is inherently too hopeful for the dystopic mode can usefully be applied to fantastic realism, where positive versions of development are the ideal and texts resist an alternative representation of young people. In fantastic realist texts (rather than futuristic or science fiction ones), the hopeful improvement is less likely to concern saving humankind or effecting social advancement, and more likely to be individualistic and internalised.

Rather than portraying a wholly positive vision of social improvement, therefore, teenage fantastic realism is more likely to deal with individual advancement or its failure. After all, despite its pattern of continuous movement, developmentalism returns adolescence to certain binary positions, measuring what is normal and successful against what is abnormal or deficient. It is important to remind ourselves of the various critiques that have been made against developmental theory, particularly the fact that it provides 'too rigid a framework within which to conceptualise adolescence' (Coleman 11; Stainton-Rogers and Stainton-Rogers 178–203). This kind of blueprint or guideline for what is natural or expected at the stage of adolescence has also characterised images of childhood and has serious implications for fictional representation of teenagers; protagonists who do not succeed in completing a developmental task are represented as existing outside of usual adolescent discourses, however interesting they may be as characters. In a complex novel like Alan Garner's *Red Shift* (1973), for example, teenage Tom never manages to maintain a satisfactory sexual relationship with his girlfriend, Jan, unable as he is to evade his parents' dysfunctional marriage and his own solipsistic nature. Throughout the narrative Tom is linked (through fantastically experienced sensations) to other characters from different historical periods who suffer from madness, and the novel's 'Afterword' (in the form of a coded letter) implies that Tom is about to commit suicide. Tom's bafflement regarding social interactions and his inability to form 'normal' adult relationships mark him out as different from Jan and her healthy (that is, sane) teenage relations and sexual urges.[5]

Developing through Fantasy • 35

Although such fantastic realism does not relate wholly ordinary adolescent experience, there is still a strong tendency to assume positive developmental models. Any change of form or development of magical qualities is most often portrayed as beneficial, whereas backwards motion—for example in time-travel novels—can be problematic, suggesting as it does the danger of stagnation in protagonists who cannot 'move on'.

It is worth noting here that, as a broad discursive framework, developmentalism is located within a predominantly patriarchal context. That is, it relies on the politicised 'time of history', which is 'time as project, teleology, linear and prospective unfolding: time as departure, progression and arrival' (Kristeva, 'Women's Time' 192). Julia Kristeva claims that feminine subjectivity is excluded from this political time through its links with cyclical, repetitious or eternal time:

> On the one hand, there are cycles, gestation, the eternal recurrence of a biological rhythm which conforms to that of nature and imposes a temporality whose stereotyping may shock. [...] On the other hand [...] there is the massive presence of a monumental temporality, without cleavage or escape, which has so little to do with linear time (which passes) that the very word 'temporality' hardly fits. ('Women's Time' 191)

Adolescent development is caught between the two states. In its concern with linear progression it prioritises a masculine version of time and any diversion from the correct sequence is considered to be unhealthy (unhealthily feminised, perhaps). Nevertheless, female development at adolescence remains tied to those 'stereotypes' of cyclical time by encouraging teenage girls to embrace apparently natural roles of reproduction and motherhood as part of their maturational tasks. As such, *female* development is situated as an alternative, an other, in the general framework of development; girls, it is suggested, can only go so far on this progressive route before they slip back into matrilineal patterns of 'women's time'.

Time, and travelling through time, is clearly crucial for developmentalism, and it is not surprising that it features heavily in young adult fantastic realism. What must be questioned is whether that time-travel represents positive aspects of development or whether it articulates the dangers of deviant adolescence.

Travelling through Time

In her monograph on subjectivity in adolescent fiction, Robyn McCallum argues that fiction aimed at children and young adults is predominantly humanist in its approach to fantasy and history. This fiction portrays the past as part of a teleological process with the improvement of humankind as its focus. She argues that children's literature draws upon assumptions from humanist history, and in particular she points to 'culture epoch' or 'recapitulation theory', which claims that the history of any race can be found in metonymic form in an individual's development from childhood to adulthood. This process describes cultural development 'according to a model of child development, which thereby correlates modern western culture and moral and intellectual concepts associated with adulthood' (McCallum 168–169). Time-slip or time-travel novels for young readers, therefore, might offer a simple ideology of progression from primitive past to sophisticated present.[6]

Despite her focus on 'adolescent fiction' McCallum does not pursue this developmental context in order to consider its specific relevance to theories of adolescence. However, it is clear that such humanist concepts of history and time are pertinent to the themes of development and transition that this chapter explores. Although recent work in psychology and cultural history has questioned—and mainly discredited—the premises of recapitulation for its assumptions about Western society's innate supremacy as a cultural system, the connections between historical and individual developments are retrievable in works that are still influential. Granville Stanley Hall's seminal study on adolescence offers the following interpretation:

> Adolescence is a new birth, for the higher and more completely human traits are now born. The qualities of body and soul that now emerge are far newer. The child comes from and harks back to a remoter past; the adolescent is neo-atavistic, and in him the later acquisitions of the race slowly become prepotent. (xiii)

Echoes can be heard in one critique of Piaget, which suggests that children are like a tribe, with beliefs and ideas that derive from 'an implicit animism and artificialism with many parallels to primitive and Greek philosophies' and from which adolescents move onwards (Elkind, *Children and Adolescents* 15). Moving on, moving through time and becoming civilised seem to be key.

History Lessons: Learning to Move On

Time-slip occurs where 'the protagonist slips back in time, characters from the past reappear in the present, or both' (Cosslett 243). Alternatively, texts might be linked to the past via fantastic connections with a special, historical place or an empathic and uncanny bond with a character in the past. Susan Cooper's *King of Shadows* (1999) and K.M. Peyton's *A Pattern of Roses* (1972) employ these devices in different ways. In the former, Nat Field travels from America to Britain to act in a company of boys at the newly rebuilt Globe Theatre in London. While he is there he mysteriously becomes ill with the bubonic plague and, during his fever, swaps places with Nathan Field, a young actor from the year 1599. The two boys literally and physically swap places, rather than just entering each other's bodies, but because Nathan Field was borrowed from St Paul's school for the London production nobody recognises that Nat is a different person. Similarly, Nat's plagued body is kept in isolation and the attending nurse never discovers that she is in fact treating a boy from the sixteenth century. In his new life, Nat meets William Shakespeare and they form an instant relationship—partly based on performing the roles of father and son to each other—as a way of coping with the loss of their own family members.

At the opening of *A Pattern of Roses*, Tim Ingram has recently moved to a new home in the country and is worrying about his parents' expectations. They anticipate academic brilliance and professional success, but he prefers modest art and craft to the cut and thrust of his father's thriving advertising business. Tom Inskip, who lived over seventy years previously in the same cottage that the Ingrams have chosen to renovate, is similarly out of place because of his artistic talent; in this case Tom's drawing classes with the Reverend's daughter set him beyond his working-class status as a ploughboy. When Tim finds a stash of Tom's old pencil drawings in the chimney, he starts to research his life and discovers that he died aged fifteen. The crux of the novel is Tim's search to discover Tom's identity and fate, which reveals subtle links between the two boys. Although Tim does not strictly travel into the past and Tom does not regularly appear in the present, the connection between the two lives is made clear since Tim experiences the blacksmith boy as a ghostly presence, 'a sense that haunted him' (109).

At the outset of both novels, the protagonists are troubled and caught in a phase of inertia in their lives. Nat's mother died of cancer when he was young and his father has consequently committed suicide. To escape and shut out painful reality, Nat immerses himself in the role of Puck in *A Midsummer Night's Dream* and refuses to talk about his feelings. Tim has a more internalised lethargy and is portrayed as what could be described as 'diffused' or even 'foreclosed' in Marcia's terms of fidelity at this stage of identity:

> He was all for a quiet life; he was not aggressive by nature, not even very energetic. He wasn't very anything, he often thought, just a vessel into which a lot of money had been poured to educate, to make presentable, to reflect the achievement of his parents. He did not like this thought, but he didn't rebel against it. He would have admired himself more if he had rebelled. (4)

Tim is ill with glandular fever and puts off going back to school so that he can also defer more important decisions about his future. He considers everything about himself—including his name—to be weak and effeminate and this impression is emphasised to the reader by contrast with his vibrant new friend, 'flaming' Rebecca (and later with the stolid Tom). Throughout the novel Tim's character is tested and strengthened through encounters with typical adolescent tasks or sites of struggle: he fights with his parents and finally refuses to live his life through their desires; he realises his vocation (as a blacksmith and iron-worker); and he builds a relationship with Rebecca. These elements of the realist narrative correspond to conventional sociological theories of development in an uncomplicated manner. Changes in Tim's identity can also be found more obliquely in one of the motifs of the fantastic time-slip: fact-finding or investigating the past. This archival activity employs a variety of research methods from parish records to interviewing first-hand witnesses. Tim also relies on the dreamlike contacts with Tom that he experiences and becomes alternately invigorated and exhausted by his efforts to trace Tom.[7] For instance, he unearths the grave of the ten foxhounds that died in the mysterious accident that also killed Tom:

> Tim was happier now; the scent was keener, the accident a sharper mystery. [. . .] For the first time in weeks, Tim felt alive and interested, sharply aware of everything around him, from the threads of spiders' trails [. . .] to the shadows of emotions long expended, far away in time [. . .] the last faint breath touching him in this mysterious way. [. . .] It was very paintable [. . .] it kicked Tim with a desire he had almost forgotten, the excitement of just seeing. Oh, I will, he thought. (64–65)

This historical reconstruction becomes a project that is his own—not his parents' or his schoolteachers'—and, moreover, it focuses his energies on aspects of his life that have been neglected and yet are a crucial part of his identity: that is, art, nature and creativity. As Rebecca points out, for the duration of the novel Tom brings Tim to life.

It is the person of William Shakespeare—and his words—that brings Nat to life. Since the novel centres on a conventional humanist belief that lessons can be learnt from the past, especially the literary past, textual knowledge (that is, knowledge through literature) is given authority through Nat's experiential reality. Shakespeare is portrayed as intelligent and slightly politic, but most of all as a kindly father-figure to Nat, who happily explains, 'I liked his voice; it was soft, but pitched to carry. [. . .] I liked his face too, lined and humorous above the short brown beard' (45). Inspired by Shakespeare's performance of Oberon, Nat excels in his acting; he is also given some valuable advice that will allow him to move forwards in his twentieth-century life. Shakespeare gives him a copy of Sonnet 116 and explains that love is an 'ever-fixed mark': ' "I have no picture of what may become of us after we are dead, Nat," he said. "But I do know thy father's love for thee did not die with him, nor thine for him"' (102). Shakespeare as a 'real person' is validated as a source of knowledge or wisdom as much as his canonical texts, and Nat might as well have come to terms with his father's death through studying the sonnets in class rather than travelling through history. The movement through time itself, however, more clearly posits the past as a legitimate point of learning from which Nat must move on. Despite his urgent desire to return to Shakespeare's company and to his father-figure, Nat has to return to the present.

Developing through Fantasy • 39

Almost without exception it is the case that protagonists never remain in the past in time-slip novels. There is a clear analogy to be made with developmental theory, which demands normal progression and describes any backwards movement as regression; this point will be extended in the discussion of Robert Westall's *The Devil on the Road* below. Here, the importance lies in the way that the past functions to provide a base or a constructive educational tool to allow teenage characters to progress to the next developmental stage in their own era. Furthermore, built into developmentalism are elements of the psychoanalytic theory of individuation (and second individuation at adolescence, which will be explored further in the next chapter). This theory maintains that an individual must separate from their same-sex parent in order to become a healthy adult. Nat's psychological, physical and temporal separation from Shakespeare at the end of the novel imply that he has reached a stage where he no longer needs the father-figure to help define his own sense of self.

Pedagogic impulses—whether they relate to personal growth or knowledge of how humanity has developed over time—are rarely avoided in time-slip novels and critical readings tend to focus on the role of time-shifting as an education for the protagonist. Gertrud Lehnert-Rodiek, for instance, argues that 'time-travel generally occurs only in a specific phase of childhood, and through it children have experiences that help them to handle difficult situations' (61). There is indeed a trend for the protagonists in teenage time-slip to cluster around the age of thirteen or fourteen (although John in *The Devil on the Road* is eighteen) and this may have something to do with the centrality of educational themes, which have more relevance to slightly younger characters. It is also the case that the two texts under discussion here offer traditional representations of adolescence and of history. The past as educational space in *King of Shadows* is ideologically conservative, not only in its reverence for Shakespeare but also in its version of history. Nat describes sixteenth-century London with the kind of squalid detail that appears in school textbooks from the 1960s onwards, offering a 'living history' or 'history from below'; a history that clearly indicates how far humanity has progressed in physical terms, however much the past still has to offer Nat morally and psychologically.[8]

The 'history from below' presented in *A Pattern of Roses* is also conventional and the processes of maturation that are found in the realist aspects of the novel are mirrored by the fantastic movement between past and present. The novel is structured so that the reader discovers Tom's history in narrative episodes interspersed among the main instalments of Tim's experiences. Tim has intense visions of Tom living in the early twentieth century, and although there are only rare moments of interaction (such as an early episode where Tom asks Tim to find out his history and warns him from suffering a similar fate), the impression given by the interlacing chapters is that the present is intercut with realities and ideologies from the past. For instance, when Tim looks out of his bedroom window after an argument with his father about not returning to school, he sees 'a landscape in the Victorian style, like a long-forgotten Christmas card, an old painting in the Royal Academy' (95). This scene is brought to life with a vignette of Tom's hard labouring life and Tim experiences it vicariously: 'Tim, watching, was acutely envious of Tom's physical state, the untroubled mind, the bodily fatigue. It was simplicity itself' (96). Tom's existential ease is described later in the novel as 'perfect spiritual grace' or 'P.S.G.' and both Tim and Rebecca aspire to achieve it. The instalments from the past provide Tim with the knowledge he needs in order to develop a stronger identity and a sense of self. He understands that Tom's way of life is tough and cruel but that it is steeped in nature and primitive values of hard physical work, and through imaginative connections with the past Tim assimilates these values.

This view of the past as 'simplicity itself' is clearly a romanticised version of history that refers to what might be considered a more primitive time. This past, like a romanticised and essential notion of childhood, does not entail the difficulties of Tim's adolescent present where he must be socialised into complex modern society. But by returning to such a simple time, Tim can digest and integrate traits that are like those of an earlier childhood, and move on to the next stage of development. He and Rebecca are aware that Tom's straightforward existence had its limitations and Tim explains, '[t]here have to be openings, ambitions, even in this [blacksmith's job]. Otherwise it is back to Tom again' (167).

Ancient Danger: Trapped in Time

The fear of getting 'back to Tom again' is only partly to do with his lack of opportunities and modern fulfilment. There are also more obvious dangers in the narrative past of this and other time-slip novels. The sub-genre, in fact, is full of terrible catastrophes and hazards: in *A Pattern of Roses* Tim and Rebecca discover that Tom had died trying to save hunting hounds from drowning in the partially frozen lake; Jamie in Marcus Sedgewick's *Witch Hill* (2001) has visions of a young girl burnt in her home after being accused of witchcraft; and David Almond's *Kit's Wilderness* (1999) refers to the 1821 coal pit disaster which killed 117 child miners. In contrast to the romanticised version of history is the version in which it is portrayed as dirty, sordid, tough and hazardous, and time-slip nearly always takes the protagonist into a moment of specific peril related to the harsh conditions of life in the past. The nineteenth-century Irish potato famine slips into the present-day narrative of Ann Pilling's *Black Harvest* (1983) and in this thriller history is malevolent rather than a positive space for growth. All the symptoms of disease and starvation begin to appear to the Blakeman family. Their food turns mouldy overnight, the baby becomes emaciated for no apparent reason, and teenage Prill starts to see visions of the original victims of the famine. In this text, and more complexly in *The Devil on the Road*, moving backwards in history cannot be seen as positively educational, nor as a benign activity, comparable to assimilating the troubles or lessons of a younger self into a new identity. Instead, retreating into the past is dangerous because it exposes the protagonists to what appears to be a more primitive time, threatening to prevent any further development into maturity and futurity.

In *The Devil on the Road* by Robert Westall (1978), John Webster—who narrates the story—has just finished his first year at university and plans to spend the summer touring on his motorbike. Instead he gets caught in a storm and, when he shelters in an old barn in the Sussex village of Besingtree, he becomes entangled in the village and its history. A time-travelling kitten draws him towards the past to the Civil War in order to save Johanna Vavasour, gentlewoman and accused witch. It is only when he pulls her forward into contemporary time that John discovers that Johanna really *is* a witch with powerful 'old magic' or 'natural magic'. The seventeenth century is not glamorised in this novel and is quite specifically marked as a place of danger and discomfort. There is no sense that John admires the romance of the past, as Tim in *A Pattern of Roses* does, or that he is longing to remain a part of this historical period, as Nat wishes he could do in *King of Shadows*. Each time John travels into the past he is confronted with revolting images, sickening smells, and threats of violence and menace. He finds the rotting body of a hanged witch, meets an old hag with wrinkled breasts and hair full of lice, sees the ruthless treatment of supposed witches, and all the time the smell of the seventeenth century and of Johanna is 'of damp and mildew, lavender and cowdung' (112). This time is not merely represented as filthy and uncomfortable, but also as expressly dangerous due to the breakdown of order during the Civil War and risks of being accused of either Royalist loyalty or witchcraft.

In addition to the novel's portrayal of intrinsic danger in the past, however, there is an evident anxiety surrounding the disturbance of natural, chronological time and particularly unease over returning to the past. Johanna claims that 'a fine witch can *knead* Time' (239), folding people and events in on themselves so that they can reappear again at any point. While her analogy uses the comforting and homely image of breadmaking, the implications are more sinister. It is suggested that, instead of being in control of their own movements through time, an individual is at the mercy of a stronger force, which could at any moment return them to a point that should already be in the past. This uncertainty is unsettling in a teenage novel in terms of the ways that issues of development, improvement and maturation would usually be played out.

The anxious points of departure from normal developmental models are focused through the character of John who, as Lehnert-Rodiek explains, is 'a twentieth-century urban dweller', confident and perceptive, who is attached to modern technology in the shape of his precious motorcycle (65). His aim is to follow 'Lady Chance' to Clacton and spend the summer flirting with girls and swimming in the sea, but vicious traffic on the A12 seems to manipulate him to follow country roads into the heart of Suffolk instead:

> The side road was dreamy. Empty, shady with trees. Only the sound of my own exhaust blatting off the hedges. Rabbits lolloping out of the way; a grey squirrel streaking up a tree; harvesters in a field like a Weetabix commercial. The countryside soaked me up like a green sponge. Mile after mile of green dream.
>
> Hell, I was supposed to be going to *Clacton*! (5)

Instead of riding straight to his destination John is constantly caught up in a timeless rural idyll, dreamy but dangerous because it traps him in a web of indulgence: 'Suffolk lanes are great for dawdling, but hell in a hurry' (19–20). Later, when he accepts Farmer Pooley's invitation to stay in his barn, John discovers an even greater threat in dawdling in the past. During his stay the barn has been transformed from a modern storage space to its original state as the Vavasour's house, and it is finished off with an ancient 'four-poster in black fat knobbly oak':

> It smelt of damp and mildew, cowdung and lavender. And it was full of ghosts whispering and making love, and screaming in childbirth and poisoning and dying. That's how it felt to me anyway. Middle-aged people go on and on about how dangerous motorbikes are; they should've tried that bed. (159)

John is uneasy about living amongst the remnants of history because he feels as though the past could smother him as he sleeps. Like the dreamy Suffolk lanes the bed and barn ensnare him in the past and stop him riding off on his motorbike to grow up in his own way through twentieth-century experiences of technology and disposable leisure.

More than any of the historical relics or locations in *The Devil on the Road*, Johanna herself symbolises all that is old or timeless. Through the magic of her cat familiar she draws John backwards in time so that he is well-placed to change history, save her life and destroy the Witchfinder General, Hopkins. Then she follows him back to his present of 1977. Again, like the Suffolk countryside, the atmosphere of the past that she evokes is at first alluring, and John is tempted by her small beautiful body, her old-fashioned homekeeping ways, and her 'genius for stroking the male ego' (226). Yet there are constant traces of the cruelty and foulness that she brings from the past, such as her sly, wary posture, the smells of cowdung and mildew, and the charmed poppet in the shape of John on his bike she makes in order to control his actions. Most of all, John's growing love for Johanna is marked as unnatural and abhorrent because she belongs to antiquity. He compares a relationship with her to the carefree sexual encounters he has had with university girls:

> Johanna was the exact opposite. Making love to her would have been like a plant putting down a root. Maybe the plant would live a thousand years, and grow into the biggest tree ever seen.

But the one thing no tree can ever do is to pull up its roots and walk away . . .

If I'd made love to her, I knew I'd be part of everything for ever, rooted in the stones and bones of dead men. (227)

John's fear of being rooted, trapped, made stagnant by binding himself to Johanna in love points to a wider anxiety in the novel, concerned with moving backwards or becoming fixed and immovable. In this narrative, despite the magical possibilities offered by Johanna's witchcraft (she claims that John too could manipulate time to a degree) and her desirability, a greater importance is placed on John's potential to grow and move on, rather than be rooted in stones and bones. It is no surprise that, when he manages to escape Besingtree and Johanna at the end of the narrative, he does so on his motorbike, not only a symbol of twentieth-century progress and technology but also of dynamic momentum, not to mention masculinity and freedom.

This final section of the novel, in which Johanna and John return to present-day life, is particularly interesting because of its position in the narrative. As already mentioned above, the convention of children's time-slip means that the protagonist generally returns to their own time and does not remain in the past; and when John saves the accused witches and finds himself back in the twentieth century there is a natural sense of closure to the story. Since *The Devil on the Road* is a *teenage* fantastic realist novel, however, the pattern is complicated by more intricate problems—particularly love and sexual desire— and the crux of John's tale is not his heroic rescue scene but rather his attempt to integrate Johanna into his modern life. Furthermore, images of development and forward movement are notably gendered in Westall's text and part of the anxiety expressed regarding stasis or retreat in this novel refers to a fear of synchronic femininity overcoming diachronic masculinity. That is, while John is determined to keep on travelling in one direction and refuses to accept the potential of kneading time, Johanna, who is also known as Lady Chance or the Yarb Mother, represents a non-chronological or fluid time that works against traditional developmental theory, as well as any sense of recapitulation or progression in history. Hers is a kind of 'woman's time', as already discussed in reference to Kristeva's work, more concerned with the timeless rhythms of seasons, birth and death, and the universe than with linear historical time. Rather than celebrating this radical female version of life as an endless cycle of experience, the novel prioritises instead male-centred discourses of adolescence which refuse to allow the individual to become trapped in playful or duplicating time. John portrays himself as a salmon, caught on the hook of Lady Chance, and later complains, '[t]rouble was, once rescued, our heroine had turned into a female I now had to cope with' (212). Woman is presented as a hindrance to natural male development and setting up home with Johanna is represented as terrifyingly permanent and domestic for a teenage boy. As mentioned earlier, developmental theory is conventionally based on male experience and female versions of adolescence are represented as deviant or other. Thus 'women's time' is figured as unhealthy through tropes of stagnancy and regression, although maternal time is given due attention through the feminine trope of witchcraft and witch covens.

The complexities of time and gender revealed in a text like *The Devil on the Road* suggest that developmental drives to define the adolescent reside in subtle metaphors and abstract theories. Metamorphosis, on the other hand, can be viewed as a universal fantasy of adolescence, echoing the actual physical, mental and social changes that occur during this age-stage.

Teenage Transformations

The dilemmas of swift transition or relentless development at adolescence can partly be solved by fictional and fantastic transformation into a body that is materially, and particularly physically, 'other'. In her study of metamorphosis and identity, Caroline Walker Bynum considers ancient, medieval and modern attitudes towards shape-shifting and suggests that, despite the obvious contrasts of ideologies, they 'all imagine a world characterized by *both* flux *and* permanence' (179, my italics). According to her argument, change is an ontological problem, but where a sense of continuous identity can be retained *despite* physical or psychological transformation, selfhood can also explicitly emerge *through* change over time. Irving Massey takes a subtly different tack in considering literary metamorphosis, arguing that, '[a]lthough metamorphosis has to do with change, it tends to settle in the moments of arrest rather than development' (2). In each case, metamorphosis tests the idea of a coherent identity across time.

These two readings of metamorphosis can be successfully translated to both the discourse of adolescence and to young adult literary shape-shifting. There is a clear correspondence between metamorphosis and the physical changes at puberty, as well as more oblique metaphorical links to other developmental transformations in psychical and social realms. Yet in teen fantastic realist texts that deal with transmutation—particularly animal transmutation—it is also possible to trace disquiet surrounding unnatural changes. This reveals further anxieties about becoming the 'wrong kind' of adult, or even being trapped in a dangerous stasis that operates counter to normal developmental models, in much the same way that time-travel narratives present difficulties when teenagers become trapped in the past.

The Pelt of a Tiger: Rites of Passage

Although narratives of non-animal adolescent metamorphosis do exist (the clearest examples being cyborg selves that appear in virtual reality narratives and science fiction for young adults, to be discussed in Chapter Four), creatures of various kinds remain the most frequent object for transmutation in young adult fantastic realism. In fact, as Maria Lassén-Seger points out in her paper on metamorphosis in *children's* literature, most instances of shape-shifting in fiction for young people in general are animal in nature (1). She argues that early treatment of this fantastic theme subscribed to the Judeo-Christian tradition that regards animal states to be inferior to humanity and that sees metamorphosis as a tool of education or form of punishment (her example being Pinocchio's unhappy transformation into a donkey before becoming a real boy). More recent fantasies employ the same humanist framework in a more positive way, allowing the protagonist as animal a distinct space for developing 'higher' human traits before returning to human form. Or, in less didactic terms, 'many contemporary authors of young adult fiction use animal metamorphosis to depict teenage boys' rites of passage into manhood metaphorically' (Lassén-Seger 1).[9]

Two such rites-of-passage narratives are David Almond's *Secret Heart* (2001) and *Pictures in the Dark* (1996) by Gillian Cross, which focus on teenage boys and their fixation on—and transformation into—a tiger and an otter, respectively. *Secret Heart*'s Joe Maloney is a troubled fourteen-year-old who hears songs and sounds that nobody else does, and has visions of mystical creatures in the air. His absent father spun the waltzer at the fairground and, when a circus comes to Joe's home village, Helmouth, Joe finds himself drawn to the travelling entertainers. He makes friends with Corinna the trapeze artist but is most affected by the mythical tiger that supposedly appeared in the circus's fantastical past. In *Pictures in the Dark*, Peter is the youngest in a dysfunctional family whose father is obsessed by cleanliness and order. Peter is clumsy, provoking his father into abusive behaviour. He is also quiet and strange and so is bullied by other children at school. At night, and at times of stress, he metamorphoses into an otter and escapes to the riverside.

What is most apparent in each text is that the boys' affinity with wild creatures awakens in them a visceral and ecstatic awareness. Joe often dreams of himself and the tiger becoming one being. When he visits the circus he is given the pelt of a tiger to wear and, as he drapes himself in the skin, '[m]emories rushed through his blood, his bones, his flesh, his brain: he ran through hot grassland, with antelope running before him and the other tigers running alongside him; he prowled the shadows of forests' (152). Peter experiences similar animal pleasures. His transformed actions are focalised through an older schoolboy, Charlie, who one day watches what he thinks is an ordinary otter:

> For maybe ten minutes, while Charlie followed it with his camera, it swam and dived for no obvious reason. Enjoying itself. Then it surfaced on the far side of the river, with a fish clutched to its chest. Charlie saw its jaws clamp together in a single, killing bite [...] (118)

These active and vital vignettes are in direct contrast to the boys' behaviour during most of the realistic sections of each text. Both novels are written in the third person, resulting in the protagonists appearing to be almost silent. Almond allows us access to Joe's thoughts through indirect reported speech, which reveals the kinds of things Joe might say if he were more articulate, and in Cross's novel we are never invited to see the world through Peter's eyes or listen to his voice. Joe worries his mother by being a withdrawn loner; Peter is sullen and induces fear and anger in other people. Even Charlie's mother says of Peter, 'It's an irritating face, isn't it? [...] That boy's [...] Sullen. Secretive. It makes you want to shake him' (36). The metamorphosis is a chance for each boy to discard their uncomfortable present and develop those aspects of masculine adulthood that are perceived to be normal: physical prowess, strength and a certain amount of bestial aggression in hunting prey and employing a 'killing bite'. If this is a rite of passage, it is one gleaned from traditional male-centred communities, where a fight or hunt signifies maturity in the tribe or subculture.

Both transformations also suggest positive development in more purely physical respects. As a boy, Peter is 'small and bony' (7) and each realistic description of him emphasises his thinness, weakness and underdeveloped size. Yet the mature otter he becomes is sleek and healthy. Joe Maloney's metamorphosis is more palpably physical and pubescent (partly because he is an older character than Peter). As he dreams or experiences the change into a tiger, '[h]e felt heavy paws and lethal claws. He felt the power of his muscles, his bones. His breathing deepened, sighed from deep new lungs' (152). Muscular development and deepening voice indicate specifically male physiological development and here they are linked to power and vitality in the mythical tiger. In Melvin Burgess's *Tiger Tiger* (1996), tigers are similarly associated with developing male virility. In this fantastic realist novel, teenage Steve befriends a captive tiger called Lila who is actually a spirit tiger, able to change her shape when she needs to. When Lila's mate is killed by poachers she uses her powers to transform Steve into a male tiger in order to mate with him and become pregnant. It is in this animal form that Steve experiences his first sexual coupling. Although he does not consciously remember this sexual encounter it has a subliminal effect on his process of maturation: '[h]e had grown up overnight in a way no one had ever done before. She had left inside of him forever a streak of the tiger in his soul' (141). The explicitly physical act corresponds to a more general sense of Steven's development into an adult sexual being and the streak of tiger contributes to his specifically male physical maturity.

In each of these texts one clear implication is that the wildness and vitality of both the tigers and the otter has an affirmative and physical affect on these male adolescents. Lassen-Séger suggests that this affirmation is partly because becoming an animal forces the characters into an experiential realm that is no longer protected as childhood is, and which therefore allows them 'a temporary glance into the world of adults' (3). Her argument rests on the premise that metamorphosis in children's literature does not concern 'what it is to really be an animal' (3). However, teenage fantastic realism provides a less direct and more symbolic entry into the adult world. With the possible exception of Steve's sexual encounter in *Tiger Tiger*, the tiger and otter do not function as humans (adult or child) but are definitely and wholly wild and other. The experiences of the teen protagonists as creatures, then, are more evidently part of the *process* of actually entering that world of adults, as the transformations mirror male pubescent development. What happens, however, when metamorphosis signifies a *retreat from* rather than an *entry into* this adult world?

Unnatural Species: Retreating from 'Normal' Development

In trying to understand the animal transmutation in Kafka's *Metamorphosis* (1915), Gilles Deleuze and Félix Guattari suggest that by turning into a giant beetle, Gregor Samsa takes a kind of ecstatic flight:

> to become animal is to participate in movement, to stake out the path of escape in all its positivity, to cross a threshold, to reach a continuum of intensities that are valuable only in themselves, to find a world of pure intensities where all forms come undone, as do all the significations, signifiers, and signifieds. (13)

The movement suggested here poses a problem for conventional readings of fictional adolescence. Transformation as a form of travelling forward allows usual developmental frameworks to survive; the child develops and becomes something other, in this case a creature or insect. Crossing a threshold between human and animal also provides a metaphor for the moment of maturity or coming of age when everything changes in physical, psychical and social terms. Deleuze and Guattari echo Irving Massey's argument, however, in implying that the movement is regressive, rather than progressive. Psychoanalytic theory might be employed here to show how metamorphosis is figured as a return to a world of non-signification, before the symbolic entry into individualism or maturity and in direct opposition to the dominant developmental frameworks that have already been examined in this chapter. This aspect of metamorphosis, in fact, signals anxious tension in the conservative fabric of fantastic realism. It is striking that such an analysis of regressive transformation relies on masculinised models of chronological development as opposed to a more feminine cyclical motion, described by Kristeva as 'women's time'. Adolescence is generally conceptualised through the normal male experience, while female models are seen to deviate or are explained with explicit reference to their difference (Gilligan).

It has been argued that aspects of animality can be read as affirmative due to their association with healthy physical development and with adolescent sexual traits. For unusual protagonists, such as Joe and Peter, transformation into a creature also offers the kind of escape that Deleuze and Guattari indicate.

If Joe goes to school or attempts to mingle with other teenagers he is teased and tormented, but as a tiger he is strong and powerful and can connect easily with nature rather than society. Peter faces similar bullying at school, as well as from his father, but in his metamorphosis he transforms from a terrified and withdrawn schoolboy into a wild otter, content to swim without restraint in the river. In one respect, then, metamorphosis offers these two characters a happy 'flight' from reality, and in making a transition into animal form they can leave their wretched childhood selves behind.

The alternative interpretation of this metamorphosis (by hoof, claw or fin) involves a much more destructive movement, or even lack of movement. Massey points to the fact that transformation into an animal allows the metamorph to avoid social language for the silence or incomprehensible sounds of the bestial (28), and Bruce Clarke draws on this idea in his study of metamorphosis and writing, arguing that,

> [p]hysical transformations into nonhuman kinds are forms of self-preservation, purchased at the expense of one's proper species. [. . .] Refusing to identify with a communal body or with the given norms of a system, the metamorph attempts to escape the possession of language itself [. . .] (55)

Clarke's theorising of pre-linguistic metamorphosis suggests a feminising of the male characters, Joe and Peter. In rejecting the Symbolic 'law of the father' and refusing to enter into language the boys return to a maternal Semiotic, which either figures them as feminised or as childish, and complicates normal male and normal adolescent behaviour. Socially, the retreat into animal expression also signifies abnormality. In *Secret Heart*, Joe's voyages into tiger territory do not construct plausible possibilities for him in the realistic world of Helmouth, where the school authorities pursue him for truancy, his mother struggles to survive financially by working in an off-licence, and Joe's best friend is the transitory Corinne who will move on as soon as the circus does. Peter's ordinary existence does not benefit significantly from his escapades as an otter either. The final chapter of *Pictures in the Dark* sees Peter attacked by two girls at school and nearly drowned as a test of his supposed witchcraft. His father is forced to rescue Peter from drowning in the river and is finally persuaded to try and engage with his son. Yet, despite Peter's father's change of heart, Lassén-Seger points out that the happy ending 'feels hopelessly tacked on' (2) and certainly Peter himself has become no less awkward or out of place in his human form. Thus these two texts do not correspond to the usual pattern in *children's* metamorphosis narratives, in that they do not return the protagonist to a more competent or mature human form. Instead of acting as clear allegories of adolescent transition or as a developmental stage these animal mutations function, rather, as a point of escape, retreat or even stasis. In particular, Peter transforms into an otter but leaves his human form intact in a kind of trance, frozen as an inert and vacant body. He denies not only the normative model of dynamic male development but any development as a human at all. In these texts, developmental ideals are invoked through the positive version of change into a physically vibrant creature, but then ultimately denied in their refusal to let the protagonists move on from that animal identity. It is almost as if the metamorphosis functions as an endless liminal state, where norms are upended and not then returned to. The uncomfortable sense of non-resolution for the characters at the end of each narrative suggests that metamorphosis occurs at the expense of the proper species—that of adolescence.

Alternateens

Young adult fantastic realism offers two alternatives: a natural progression through time or physical change; and an unnatural unwillingness to develop. A third option might be found in horror, parody and more philosophical fiction for teenagers, and this option offers abjection, rebellion and rejection of the conventions of developmental theory. This is the stance of the 'alternateen', a member of the pervasive Americanised teen subculture which attempts to avoid typical mainstream teenage tastes and activities (although admittedly provoking scorn in many for subscribing to their own mob behaviour rather than being truly alternative).

Teenage Mutants: Development in Horror and Parody

The vigorous physical development implicit in animal bodies is subverted in certain texts; bodily change in horror genres, in particular, suggests aberration rather than natural adolescent maturation. Leonard Heldreth discusses sexual change and metamorphosis in horror films, and lists the ways that werewolf metamorphoses share features with puberty, including a sudden growth spurt, the appearance of hair in strange places, a loss of control over the body and awakened carnal appetites (Heldreth). Rather than—or as well as—being invigorating, these material signs of transition from human to animal are full of terror. In his essay on horror movies, Walter Evans suggests that adolescents fear the change from childhood to 'some mysterious new state', partly because horror narratives associate bodily development with 'mystery, darkness, secrecy, and evil' (146). Metamorphosis can indeed be considered a dramatic and often horrific fantasy. Massey argues that its characteristic concerns in literature are 'gross and shocking. [. . .] Metamorphosis is typically violent and flies in the face of reason' (17). The potent physicality of such transformations helps to explain why literary shape-shifting has translated particularly successfully as visual images for many horror films, and the primacy of horrific metamorphosis in film means that it is useful to consider two cinematic representations of adolescence. These films are notable not only for their portrayals of shocking metamorphosis but also because they resemble controversial teenage novels (such as Melvin Burgess's *Lady: my life as a bitch*) in their urge to undercut humanist developmental modes through parody and humour.

In John Landis's 1981 film, *An American Werewolf in London*, the link between adolescent urges and lupine desire to kill and taste blood is made explicit as the story traces teenage hero David's unwilling transformation into a werewolf. The most famous moment of the film is the dramatic mutation that occurs when David first metamorphoses, after he has been bitten by a creature on the moors. It is an excruciatingly painful experience, as his bones crack and stretch and hair appears on his body until he has become a monstrous-looking beast. Following this transformation, David goes on a series of killing sprees and wakes up back in human form in the wolf-enclosure at the zoo. Despite the horrendous effects of his metamorphosis he is initially 'hyped up' by his bestial actions and there is an explicit juxtaposition of his killing urge and subsequent sexual urges, where he sleeps with his girlfriend, nurse Alex, who has been looking after him. According to Heldreth, part of the function of representing adolescence in horror movies such as *American Werewolf* is to explore and purge Western society's obsession with—but also its anxiety about—youth, sex and violence. By portraying teenage characters as intrinsically unnatural and dangerous precisely *because* they mutate and develop uncontrollable desires and urges, Heldreth argues that films like Landis's actually display fears about the overabundance and energy of adolescence. The excessive limits of the fantasy point to the destruction and danger that these natural urges might entail if left unchecked. Evans illustrates this idea by explaining that most werewolves have to be destroyed at the end of such narratives: 'Only upon the death of adolescence, the mysterious madness which has possessed them, can they enter into a mature state where sexuality is tamed' ('Monster Moves' 152).

This pattern is more frankly demonstrated in the film *Ginger Snaps* (John Fawcett, 2000) in which a werewolf attacks the heroine immediately after her first period starts. Ginger is disgusted by the blood trickling down her leg and calls it 'gross', supporting Evans' idea that teenagers fear the onset of adolescence. The wider implication, however, is that menstruation or puberty itself indicates the start of monstrosity. Instead of developing into a woman, Ginger becomes a monster, and arguably this deviant transformation is made more unnatural through its reversal of accepted feminine norms. Ginger's menstrual blood represents an abject substance which signifies the start of a mutation that is horrific rather than desirable.

While horror will always reveal fear and anxiety surrounding metamorphosis, teenage fantastic realism does not have this primary function and takes the process of metamorphic development much more seriously. Indeed, the earnest approval of developmental frameworks is parodied in Melvin Burgess's *Lady: my life as a bitch* (2001), in which promiscuous and carefree seventeen-year-old

Sandra is magically changed into a dog. As her new self, Lady the bitch, she lives a dog's life of sensation, spontaneity and brutal hardships of existence on the streets, along with two male dogs, Fella and Mitch:

> Ok, my life could have ended at any second under the wheels of a car. [. . .] But life at the edge tastes so sweet! It's steal or starve, life or death. There's so much more to pack in. The smell of meat. [. . .] Dog shit and hot fur, spit, grass and breath! Glorious days! My pads sore, my tongue out in the cool air; the dew on my coat, the pack around me and Fella on my back. (134)

The novel plays with the idea of teenage desire gone wild and become animal. Without the restraints of society and its expectations of how bodily and hormonal changes should be controlled, Lady does everything that Sandra felt guilty about or vilified for. Visceral pleasures and the irresponsible nature of canine life, particularly promiscuous sexuality, are shocking when related to a teenage girl. Yet, instead of coming to a monstrous end—with a silver bullet through the heart—Sandra/Lady finds that she ultimately prefers the dog world and at the novel's end decides to remain in dog form. Given that metamorphosis in children's and young adults' fiction is most often presented as a temporary stage, representing a time when more adult characteristics can be absorbed and assimilated in the terms of developmental discourse, *Lady* transgresses by leaving adolescent Sandra in animal shape. This produces quite explicit anxieties in the form of moral outrage. Eric Hester from 'Family and Youth Concern in Britain' makes it clear that adolescence should not be let off the leash in this way. He discusses problems with the text:

> This is very unpleasant. It is about a girl who is on drugs, she's promiscuous, she steals from shops and she prefers in the end to be a 'bitch on heat' than to be a human being. This is quite the nastiest piece of children's literature that I have ever read.[10]

It is crucial to understand, however, that *Lady*, as well as the werewolf films discussed above, are ironic and playful in tone.[11] *Ginger Snaps*, for instance, is totally self-conscious about aligning female menstruation and animal monstrosity, and uses a heavily knowing and genre-aware heroine to point to this appreciation (the film begins with Ginger and her sister creating tableaux of their own horrific deaths). *American Werewolf* is also well aware of the conventions of horror and uses parody liberally (again, the opening sequence indicates this, allowing David and his friend Jack to get a lift on the back of a sheep truck before entering the sinister local pub, 'The Slaughtered Lamb'). The author of *Lady* refutes the censure of unpleasantness from critics such as Hester, claiming that he writes what teenagers want to read in opposition to other fiction's implicit desire to control, contain and regulate young people. Instead of figuring animal metamorphosis as intrinsically positive or developmental, therefore, he aims to playfully use the trope to write about 'irresponsibility for young people'.[12] In other words, in a comic or parodic text, fears about excesses of adolescent development are brought to the surface and do not seriously challenge the more positive images of animal transformation explored in the earlier part of this section. Because they do not subscribe to the same ideological project as fantastic realism, parodies are more likely to depict an adult reaction to adolescence than a representation of how adult discourses aim to shape adolescence through fiction. In representing metamorphosis as a fantastic invasion of serious reality, fantastic realism (unlike parody) creates a subtle tension between the valuable qualities of an animal persona, and the danger of becoming trapped in bestial form, ideologically stressing the desirability of progressing as a young—human—adult.

In direct contrast to such fantastic realist texts, but also removed from parody, Peter Dickinson's *Eva* (1988) offers another version of shape-shifting for teenagers. This novel is rigorous in its attempt to position adolescent metamorphosis as a new state that is remarkable in itself, rather than being the failure of human development. Peter Hollindale classes *Eva* as an adolescent novel of ideas, and its content is certainly philosophical, residing more clearly in the sphere of speculative fiction than fantastic realism. Eva's father works as Director of Primate Zoology and, when Eva is critically injured in an accident, he helps to reconstruct her 'neurone memory' in the body of a young female chimp called Kelly. Eva essentially morphs into Kelly, sharing her primate body but also experiencing something of the universal memories and instinct that comes with a chimp identity. Throughout the narrative she experiments with various ways of dealing with her metamorphosis, from wearing a specially made dress that reminds her of her adolescent 'girl-ness' to finally discarding all traces of her human self and embracing a new life as chimp. Robyn McCallum discusses the novel in terms of subjectivity and argues that it is about finding a way of making the various parts of this fragmented human-animal self whole and complete: 'Eva's narrative represents the psychological and social development of a child and an individual's quest for a stable sense of identity' (87). Because McCallum's concern is with human subjectivity and Eva's ability to develop the appropriate maturity to interact with others, she sees Eva's final rejection of society as abhorrent and argues that '[s]he is thus symbolically trapped in the mirror phase' (89). Eva is not trapped, however, as she goes on to lead a group of chimps away from human control to safety, mates and gives birth to a whole new generation, retains contact with her human family, and finally dies peacefully (leaving her descendants in an excellent position to evolve using her human skills and knowledge). It might be argued, in fact, that she promotes developmentalism in its broadest sense, not only maturing into roles that can be considered traditionally both masculine and feminine, but also taking part in a metonymic development of a new human race. Like Lady, she refuses to conform to conventions that dictate her role as an adult, but in addition she does so within the context of a serious narrative that does not revert to animalistic sexualisation.

Eva can be located outside of fantastic realism in the realm of 'speculative fiction' or the novel of ideas and, as such, does not share the conservative tendencies that we have found in other metamorphosis narratives. In general, fantastic realism posits animal transformation as acceptable if is temporary and if there is a guarantee that the individual will transcend their bestial form and 'evolve' into the complete human-ness of adulthood. As we have seen, a similar sense of movement is at play in time-slip or time-travel fantastic realism for young adults. I would like to conclude this chapter with a brief consideration of the chronology of developmentalism at play when adolescents travel through time.

Suspending Time: Moving beyond Developmentalism

The gendered concept of time that emerges in *The Devil on the Road* suggests that there are more complex ways of conceptualising adolescence than those offered by simple readings of developmental discursive themes. A more experimental teenage novel such as Alan Garner's *Red Shift* can help to explode some of the dominant frameworks that pervade fictions of adolescence and instead propose a representation of young people that is not essentially developmental nor even humanist. In this respect, Garner's text shares common ground with adolescent novels of ideas such as Dickinson's *Eva*. *Red Shift* is a multi-layered and dense novel, which requires a detailed criticism.[13] It is also not precisely fantastic realist in mode, in that the time-slip is generally only evident to the reader and is not perceived by the protagonists, nor is it central to their stories. However, it is useful to posit this text as an alternative type of fantasy, and one that attempts a more radical approach to the concepts of adolescence and time or history than those examined above. Maria Nikolajeva argues that Garner uses a special chronotope: 'a unity of time and space inherent to his novels' and that this unity is to do with non-linear time ('The Insignificance of Time' 129). The three main characters are all called Thomas (Tom in contemporary time, Thomas in the seventeenth century, and Mace in the time of the Romans). They play out their own dramas but appear to be connected through history by various places, objects and psychological traits. Nikolajeva follows Aidan Chambers in suggesting that these male characters are neither separate beings nor reincarnations but 'one person living simultaneously in three times, or rather in one boundless, non-linear time' ('The Insignificance of Time' 192). It is argued that all the detail and diversity of history can provide meaning for modern adolescent individuals without resorting to reactionary concern about the danger of such synchronicity as is apparent in *The Devil on the Road*. Garner's novel has spawned more critical analysis than most young adult novels, and perhaps this is due to its treatment of time within the genre of fantastic realism, which avoids the developmental frameworks that inform most texts aimed at teenagers. It is possible also to find connections with the adult fantastic in Garner's work; Rosemary Jackson's theorisation of fantastic time, for instance, is applicable to *Red Shift*: 'Chronological time is similarly exploded, with time past, present and future losing their historical sequence and tending towards a suspension, an eternal present' (47). This complete collapsing of time is rare in teenage fiction because it expresses concepts of fluidity and chaos in transition from one time to another, rather than the order of development that is considered to be crucial in discourses of adolescence.

Works such as *Red Shift*, *Lady* and *Eva* embrace a fluid and complex version of identity, selfhood and temporality, but tend to exist outside boundaries of the fantastic realist genre. Texts might be parodic, philosophical or experimental, and they most often engender controversy, but they reveal ways that fantastic genres can employ magical tropes to represent adolescence as a discrete period of distinct experience, rather than simply a stage en route to the ideal state of mature adulthood. For the fantastic realist novels examined in this chapter are shown to favour a broadly developmental framework that is humanist in its outlook and can also be said to guide readers towards an acceptable way of being adolescent. Despite their fantastical identities and situations, metamorphs and time-travellers share a remarkable compulsion to represent normal adolescence in teenage fantastic realism. In teenage fantastic realism this ordinariness is, however, portrayed as ideally dynamic and progressive, so that the metamorph succeeds if he does not treat his transition as an escape, and the time-traveller can return to the past but only in order to move forwards again into an improved future. Where novels deviate from these developmental frameworks they display an acute anxiety that materialises through unresolved closure or through negative images of refusal, captivity and/or escape, and stagnation.

What is closure, for the protagonists in these novels? The process of development takes them in stages towards the goal of adolescence: a stable and coherent adult identity. In particular, the emphasis placed on personal identity achievement manifests itself in the last decades of the twentieth century as a sense of self that is *unique*, *separate* and *private*. Ultimately, as the following chapter will propose, this is an adolescent identity born of individualism.

Chapter Two
Fantasies of Identity: The Self and Individualism

Identity achievement in teenage fantastic realism is a solitary experience. The hero or heroine is isolated from any sense of wider community by their personal experience of the fantastic, a pattern that is in direct contrast to the communal atmosphere of magic realism or pure fantasy. In my Introduction I explained that the fantastical elements in a *magic* realist novel are reported as though they are completely acceptable within the logic of the narrative and in this way fantasy pervades the whole of the textual world: *every* character in a magical realist text experiences the strange and impossible events, even if not all of them consider their experiences unusual. In *fantastic* realism the teenage protagonist alone encounters the supernatural or the impossible within a realist context and in such a space it is fruitless to appeal to society. Identity achievement here is all about an individual quest to discover a stable sense of self in the face of unsettling or decentred fantasy.

It is thus how the *individual* interacts with the *fantastic* that is most significant in the teenage fantastic realism in this chapter. Even though adolescence is shaped by the social to some degree, and protagonists are expected to engage with social roles and expectations, frameworks of individualism and introspection remain most pertinent. For some critics, the adolescent is perceived to be too introspective to warrant serious literary treatment. Writing in the late 1970s, Geoffrey Summerfield discusses teenagers and reading practices, and claims that 'with the sudden individuation, privatisation, and intensification of puberty, there can be no *satisfactory* "literature for adolescents"' (6). Summerfield dislikes the intense introspective qualities of teenage novels, and their regular focus on the interior lives of teenage protagonists through first-person and individually focalised narratives. He compares adolescent literature unfavourably with 'the constant, recurring, communal archetypes and paradigms of children's myths and fictions, the more or less clearly pre-ordained salient features of the stories of the blissfully androgynous years' (6). His critique echoes that of Dorothy Matthews, another pre-1980s commentator who we met earlier and who also worries about the state of teenage fiction when set next to classics for children. The inference is that the teenage novel's trajectory towards heightened individualism must result in acute solipsism or privatisation—figured in the image of a moody and uncommunicative Western teenager—and will therefore give rise to silence or irrelevance. To counter Summerfield, solipsism certainly does not preclude interest in a literary figure, as any great soliloquy from Shakespeare's plays might prove, not to mention the fact that the novel form itself can be said to have emerged from the condition of modern individualist societies.[1] Besides, introspective adolescents might find a release or comfort in reading of characters who display similar individualistic concerns. Of course, earlier discussion reminds us that it is not the voice *of* puberty that exists in young adult fiction but an adult voice contrived to speak *for* or *to* adolescence and so teenage fiction need not be silent; instead it articulates those aspects of individualism that prevail both in frameworks of adolescent identity formation and in the structure of the fantastic.

At the opposite end of the scale to Summerfield's dismissal is an approach to adolescent identity that focuses on the individual's growing sense of their social and ideological position. Robyn McCallum's excellent *Ideologies of Identity in Adolescent Fiction* (1999) takes this stance, examining adolescent fiction for its representations of dialogic subjectivity. 'In their preoccupation with personal growth, maturation and the development of concepts of self-hood', she argues 'adolescent novels frequently reflect complex psychological ideas about the formation of subjectivity' (McCallum 67). McCallum defines subjectivity as an individual's sense of identity as 'subject' (positioned within social discourse) and 'agent' (resisting ideology), and argues that much literature for young adults adopts a developmental progression from solipsism into social and ideological discourses. Her focus, therefore, is mainly young adult fiction that constructs 'concepts of the self as fragmented or plural, or of subjectivity as being formed through language and in dialogue with social ideologies and practices' (67). I engage with issues of agency and social expectations in the next chapter, drawing on some of McCallum's ideas, but I depart from her approach in my understanding of the extent to which this 'dialogic' process constructs selfhood in young adult fantastic realism. McCallum admits that '[L]iberal humanist and romantic concepts of subjectivity usually underpin narratives of maturation' and that this humanist ethic 'privileges concepts such as the uniqueness of the individual and the essentiality of the self' (67). While she aims to work against the grain of these assumptions, it is these very tendencies that dominate much young adult fantastic realism. McCallum's interest lies in what we have already recognised in Hollindale's terms as the 'adolescent novel of ideas', where protagonists are actively deconstructed as subjects or agents ('The Adolescent Novel of Ideas'). These texts form an important and interesting strand of teenage fantastic realism, but I am also interested in the generic form they share with more mainstream narratives of identity and the way that both types of fiction often stress the representation of adolescents as individuals. What is particularly fascinating is the fact that liberal humanist and essentialist concepts prevail in fantastic realist texts despite the use of fantastic tropes such as doubling, fragmentation and dissolution that threaten identity and test ideas of a unified self. In fact, where Rosemary Jackson argues that the 'fantastic makes an assault upon the "sign" of the unified character' (87), it can be countered that in *teenage* fantastic realism such an assault is impossible. This is because the adolescent is already theorised as being 'unfixed' or mutable (in flux or transition, as Chapter One suggested) and is in the process of achieving that unity of character. The questioning or dissolution of the self does not represent a radical reshaping of material reality in these novels but portrays conventional ideas of adolescent immaturity, where identity must yet be formed through intense attention to individuality. Permeating this discussion is a distinct problem of representation. Although young adult fantastic realism often adheres to the sense of a universal and trans-historical adolescent subjectivity that is merely explored in different ways through various fantastic tropes, this ideological representation of youth also reproduces conditions of individuality that are specific to their cultural context. In other words, it is worth examining how the individualism of fantastic realism for teenagers is a product of its historical production.

The individual in young adult fantastic realism is neither impossibly introspective nor wholly fashioned through social interaction. The fantastic realism I will examine in this chapter specifically prioritises the personal, the private, the unique and the interior in offering a framework of adolescence working towards a cohesive identity through a series of fantastic ontological 'tests'. I want to show the theoretical traffic between literature for young people and the culture of individualism that has helped to shape them. I will begin by outlining those frameworks of identity achievement and relating ideas of the teenager to the wider sphere of individualism, before analysing fantasies of individualist identity. These novels examine individuality and difference within the relative coherence of everyday experience and the humanist drive of teenage realism.

Individualism and the Teenager

Identity Achievement

According to all developmental approaches, forming identity is the foremost challenge during adolescence. Robert Havighurst's 1953 study, for instance, identifies social tasks that the teenager must complete, ranging from accepting one's physique and sexual role to preparing for marriage and family life. On the one hand these criteria are clearly dated, especially in their validation of married life in early adulthood and in their essentialist view of gender and gender roles. However, the kind of social checklist that Havighurst put forward retains a certain degree of weight, and similar schemas can be found later in the twentieth century; for example, in Susan Harter's profile of domains where the adolescent should feel satisfied or comfortable, including academic, professional and athletic competence, physical appearance, social acceptance, close friendship and romantic appeal or conduct. Psychological work in a developmental vein also examines how identity is formed through fidelity to a number of roles or beliefs in these different spheres. Thus Erikson's theory of 'identity achievement' contends that young people must develop fidelity to belief and ideology, to an occupation, and to a general sense of self within society (*Identity and the Life Cycle*).

David Elkind's research develops the work of Erikson and other Piagetian theorists by examining specific aspects of personality at late childhood and adolescence. He argues that the controlling force at this stage of human development is 'egocentrism': that is, interpersonal incompetence based on solipsism. In his early essay, 'Egocentrism in Children and Adolescents' (1967), Elkind argues that at the formal operational stage, adolescent egocentrism manifests itself as an inability to differentiate between those issues that preoccupy the teenager and those that are of concern to other people. He uses the concept of 'imaginary audience' to explain part of this phenomenon, suggesting that the adolescent automatically acts as though others are as obsessed as they are themselves with their own appearances, experiences and feelings. Although the adolescent has reached the stage of understanding that others have personal consciousness, they assume that it merely reflects their own: like an actor on the stage or screen, they rely on the assumption that everyone is absorbed in their performance. Elkind additionally uses the term 'personal fable', which he describes as a creative self-image the adolescent has of themselves as unique and as a special person, also stemming from the fact that everyone is constantly interested in their life. Although other actors (parents, authority figures and peers) feature in this fable they are not central, nor do they experience, feel or suffer with quite the same intensity as the teenager at this particular stage of life. Although we might argue that the personal fable is not necessarily a feature unique to adolescence, Elkind's terms are useful in understanding representations of teenagers in fiction as self-absorbed or at the centre of a fantastic world. They also help to explain the importance that many theorists see in other, interpersonal, developments.

Separation-Individuation

The task of achieving emotional independence from parents continues to be important for adolescence across the disciplines of psychology, sociology and psychoanalytic research. Peter Blos, for instance, employs the concept of emotional independence to stress the importance of self. Blos's work—begun in the 1960s and later advanced by Jane Kroger, amongst others (Kroger 'Separation-individuation and Ego Identity Status'; Kroger and Haslett)—

proposes four challenges that present themselves to adolescent individuals and which need to be resolved for acceptable character formation to take place. The point of childhood trauma (as outlined by Freud) must be revisited and mastered; continuity must be established between past, present and future selves; and sexual identity requires activation through resolution of the Oedipal complex. The remaining challenge is labelled the 'second individuation process' and it is this that has been most influential in subsequent psychoanalytic research. Separation-individuation refers to a stage of infancy where a young child becomes aware of the mother's existence as a separate entity and subsequently develops their own individuality (Mahler, Pine and Bergman) but Blos argues that adolescence represents a similar phase of acute individuation. The individual must disengage from their dependency on family and from any reliance on internalised parents. At the same time it is necessary to discover their individuality by opposing or questioning parental ideology and discovering their own way in life. According to Blos there is a necessary regression to childhood drives and desires at adolescence which, as long as it is temporary, is healthy and 'an obligatory component of normal development' (172). The point of this psychic revisiting is to solve previous infantile weakness and to reconstitute previous unformed positions into a stable sense of identity. Blos explains, 'One is tempted to speak [...] of an adolescent reassemblage of the psychic components within the framework of a fixed psychic apparatus' (169). At this stage, according to Blos, teenagers are likely to be argumentative and to distance themselves from the ideals and opinions of parents. This implies a normal setting out of boundaries for a new sense of self but also signals fears of being absorbed again into the needs of childhood. There is a danger, apparent to the individual at this point, that regression might result in detrimental passivity. Tellingly, Blos uses the character Hamlet as an example for this state, suggesting that '[j]ust as Hamlet [...] longs for the comforts of sleep but fears the dreams that sleep might bring, so the adolescent longs for the comforts of drive gratification but fears the reinvolvements in infantile object relations' (171). Disregarding the comic appropriation of Shakespearean poetics and the slippage once more between fictional representation and models of real adolescence,[2] we can recognise the conflict of returning and becoming trapped from previous discussion of travelling through time in *King of Shadows*, for example. Just as liminality positions the teenager in a state of temporary entropy, so second individuation suggests that regression into a kind of semiotic phase is essential so long as it is ultimately escaped.

Second individuation offers a model where the adolescent is required to make sure of their identity by reinforcing their own beliefs, attributes and behaviour when it is challenged or when regression or diffusion threatens. They also need to differentiate themselves from their childhood others (most usually parents) and realign with new relations (in conventional, normative terms, friendships, heterosexual union and occupational associations). Blos argues that 'without a successful disengagement from infantile internalised objects, the finding of new, namely, extrafamilial, love objects in the outside world either is precluded, hindered, or remains restricted to simple replication and substitution' (164).

Unity of the self is important in this framework, not only to provide the adolescent with the basis for adult identity but also to aid progression into an acceptably mature relationship with a 'significant other' or new 'love object'. In conventional psycho-social and psychoanalytic theory sexual relationships are regarded as the natural evolution from original familial security. Whereas in childhood the mother, father or the family unit generally provide an identifying object and the impression of wholeness, at adolescence the individual must separate from this comforting sphere in order to develop a discrete sense of self. The task of separation is mandatory so that the boundaries of self can then be safely traversed and merged once more through sexual love. In discourses of adolescence and in textual representation heterosexual love is considered to be a key task that follows identity achievement. Although it is structurally essential as the 'happy ending' to most narratives of the teenager the actual merging of selves is portrayed with ambivalence due to its threat to an identity that is not yet fully formed. The assumption is that the teenager should be preparing themselves for a satisfying heterosexual union (and this preparation can be done through personal fantasy, play and experimental relationships) but that their primary concern is to uncover and stabilise their own identity.

It should be noted that, as with most psychoanalytic studies, Blos's work is based on clinical research and is almost bound to speak of types of 'failure' or restrictions amongst patients. This brings to attention serious questions of what constitutes 'normal' behaviour and how far empirical work that is based on troubled individuals can describe norms of adolescence (or, indeed, how far a comparison with Hamlet, and his reluctance to sleep and dream, is useful in delineating *average* teenage fears of regression). Blos's theory certainly implies a fairly conventional image of young adult identity that relies on heterosexual relationships and is represented as male, by default. This tendency to use the male individual as the norm pervades much developmental and psychoanalytic theory, although there have been some attempts to rectify the situation. Carol Gilligan, for example, has argued persuasively that those markers of development that rely on separation do not provide a suitable model for female adolescents, as girls are more likely to function successfully through *connection* with others. The failure to separate becomes the failure to develop based on gender difference.

Individualism

Individualism suggests a range of meanings that relate not only to theories of adolescent identity but also to more diffuse representations of teenagers as intrinsically inward-looking and solipsistic. An associated sense of the term individualism refers to recent modes of liberal political and economic thought, emergent in 'second modernity' (the 1970s, 1980s and 1990s), that focus on the active individual rather than an interventionist state. According to Ulrich Beck and Elisabeth Beck-Gernsheim, within this system of thought individuals no longer unproblematically exist as part of a status-based class but actively have to *become* themselves. Although the consequences are primarily political (involving issues such as the decline of public authority and changing balances of power), there are also wider cultural implications of individualism which have a greater relevance to discussion in this chapter. Beck and Beck-Gernsheim investigate how institutionalised individualism transforms experiences and aesthetics in general. They suggest that it signals increasing personal isolation, an emphasis on individuality and self-reliance, and a culture of intimacy, informality and self-expression.[3] Significantly, a move away from what might now be called a 'nanny state' system indicates semantic links between political individualism and a teenager's shift from protected childhood to more independent adolescence. At the same time critics of an individualist society point to the 'selfish' and 'solipsistic' tendencies of the less communal public climate, using terms that are often employed in characterising teenage behaviour.

By bringing into play these applications of individualism the term can thus be employed to refer to a conceptual focus on the protagonist as individual, rather than member of a family, group of friends or institution, or part of a romantic couple. This chapter emphasises those aspects of personal growth and experience rather than social interaction and structures, and argues that such a representative framework is clearly evident in teenage fantastic realism. This framework offers an image of the teenager as inherently unformed and yet unique and in the process of becoming unified. It is significant, however, that in producing a fiction of individualism in this way fantastic realism also aids the construction of adolescence as a collective group with shared experiences and attributes. In other words, teenage fantastic realism produces a fiction of the unique individual which is then relevant and applicable to the multifaceted state of adolescence. This paradox illustrates an inevitable exchange between theory and literature; although this fiction attempts to express individual subjectivity, the genre will still succeed in re-enacting a universalised discursive field.

Narrative Implications

Karen Patricia Smith's literary-historical approach to fantasy claims that 'the contemporary period in fantasy writing has displayed an egocentric concern with the individual' (309). Her study declares itself to be an approach to British fantasy in general, but it effectively focuses on children's fantasy, and many of the texts discussed in the post-war section on 'dynamic fantasy' are in fact examples of teenage fantastic realism. For Smith, the literary child (who represents all childhood in these texts) is shaped by predominantly liberal-humanist and middle-class impulses, constituting 'a being who requires a measure of space and freedom' (314), and it is these qualities that she considers to be inherent in her versions of fantasy. Here, the personal and individual is more to do with concerns about the child (a term which absorbs the concept of the teenager too) than about features of fantasy, and it is worth developing Smith's ideas into a more specific discussion of fantasy and adolescence.

Fantasy engenders several meanings when related to selfhood and identity, and a number of these have specific significance for adolescence. On a psycho-social level the teenager is often modelled as self-obsessed and solipsistic. Elkind's model of adolescence, which highlights the solipsistic nature of teenagers and describes types of egocentrism ('Egocentrism in Children and Adolescents'), can easily filter into more informal discussions of adolescents, as we have encountered with Summerfield's assertion of 'the impossibility' of books for adolescents. Summerfield acknowledges his debt to G. Robert Carlsen who, in his guide to reading habits and appropriate fiction for teenagers, suggests that adolescents are naturally self-absorbed. For Carlsen, fantasy has a particular function at this stage of life, in that it offers teenagers 'exciting roles that relate to their hopes and desires' (*Books and the Teenage Reader* 253). By this he means that fantasy does not tie readers into the limited potential of teen realism, where boundaries and hardships exist in the same degree as their lived experience. Instead, aspects of fantasy allow the reader to project themselves into a narrative that better suits their egocentric needs. Like the mechanism of Elkind's imaginary audience, which provides the teenager with a sense that their actions are important to everybody else, the adolescent protagonist in high fantasy plays out similar desires of being the most important person in a quest that has far-reaching implications.

Carlsen emphasises pure, epic or high fantasy, where there is significant potential for youthful individual heroism or agency in secondary worlds, and he uses J.R.R. Tolkien's *The Lord of the Rings* (1954–1955) as an example, presumably correlating hobbits and teenagers as similarly inexperienced in heroics. A more recent example can be found in Pullman's *His Dark Materials* series (1996–2000) where it is prophesied that Lyra will be a hero or saviour of this world and all the secondary worlds, despite her tender years. As a fantasy of potential action, it is likely that saving the world appeals to a young teenager more than achieving high grades or successfully overcoming realistic or social problems on their own. Interestingly, fantastic tropes can also be employed to reverse this focus on the individual. Media critic Jonathan Bignell discusses the 1990s American television series, *Mighty Morphin' Power Rangers*, for instance, and describes how the teenage protagonists must put aside their individual identities in order to become a team of galactic superheroes. These team-playing superheroes are further erased by functioning as operators of huge combat machines:

> Differences between teen identities become merged in the Ranger team, and in their absorption into technologies. While the Rangers are relatively powerless as high-school students [. . .] in their Ranger [. . .] incarnations

they defeat the 'adult' alien monsters who seek to tyrannize and dominate the universe. The hopelessness of individual action, the uncertainties of social role [. . .] are present in *Power Rangers* in a coded form. (Bignell 7)

Bignell suggests that the technological metamorphosis works on a metaphorical level, showing how individuals must work together to defeat large-scale and external threats within the narrative. Less is said about the kind of internalised and private tasks that protagonists might face, as they do in teenage fantastic realism, and this is due, I think, to a difference of audience and medium. While the mass-market appeal of *Mighty Morphin' Power Rangers* (or similar fantastic cartoons) is aimed towards children and promotes interpersonal activity, the readers under consideration in this study are seen to wallow in 'hopelessness' and 'uncertainties', and moreover will read fantastic realist texts in a private and interior environment.

As a literary mode, fantasy has strong repercussions for theories of reading practice and childhood identity development. Bruno Bettelheim suggests that optimistic fantasy (in particular through the form of the folk fairy tale) is an essential tool for any child tackling new challenges and progressing towards independence and an adult identity, acting as a form of playful advice and education. Although fantasy's association with imaginative play might suggest a childishness that is communal—an indicator of childhood as subculture, or a way of socialising young people into adult roles[4]—it also links it to a state that is intensely private and personal. An individual might construct complex secret worlds that will make no sense to others, and games can therefore represent a retreat from reality into a fantastic place where the player is central.[5] Becoming an animal or playing with magic powers and invisibility relate to individualistic childhood play, offering teenage protagonists a fantasy of being out of the ordinary.[6]

In these ways fantasy provides private meanings for adolescence, acting as an intrinsic facet of identity rather than merely providing the epic scope for individual heroic actions. Elkind argues that adolescents consider themselves to be unique, and that their 'personal fable' helps to construct their sense that they see or feel the world in a distinctive and special way. By definition fantasy is 'other' to the conventional representation of experience through realism. Fantastic narrative elements, such as magic powers, time-travelling or shape-shifting, embody the idea of difference and in fantastic realism in particular the protagonist's sense of self is formed mainly through their adoption and acceptance of a magic faculty or event. For the adolescent, who is theorised as searching for identity, fantastic tropes can function as ways of differentiating a remarkable self from the mass of identities available in realist narratives. More often, fantastic realist novels represent adolescence as essentially individualist through the very aspects of fantasy that suggest difference or loss of self: the 'other', madness or erasure.

Ghosts and Doubling

Double Trouble: The Problem with Plurality

At first glance, twins, who feature in Lois Duncan's *Stranger with my Face* (1981) and Peter Dickinson's *The Lion Tamer's Daughter* (1997), seem to lead us away from ideas of essential self or individualism towards shared identities. Twins represent most fully the idea of a close social bonding between brothers and sisters—a sign of interpersonal awareness—and they provide a constant reminder that the adolescent is not totally unique or alone. Yet, as a fantasy trope, the twin functions very much as a double or doppelganger, a dangerous or sinister significant other. Moreover, that doubleness can be read as a manifestation of dialogue between an essential self and levels of internal fragmentation, as it is by McCallum, who suggests that a 'primary effect of the double is to destabilize notions of the subject as unified or coherent, or as existing outside of a relation to an other' (75). The influence of psychoanalytic criticism on this kind of reading is clear and is worth exploring a little further.

As we have already seen, Blos's work on adolescence draws on Freudian ideas of individuation which have also generated theories of psychic development in the work of Jacques Lacan and Mikhail Bakhtin. Their positions rely on the figure of an internalised other that acts to differentiate the self as a separate being. Lacan's concept of the 'mirror stage' occurring in early childhood describes a symbolic glimpse of the doubled self in a mirror, signifying the painful recognition that selfhood is an object and is constructed through external relations. McCallum compares Lacan's approach with Bakhtin's theory of subjectivity, which instead of defining the subject through lack or loss of integrity, emphasises the other as constituting 'a position of outsidedness needed to complete the self' (71). In each case, it is acknowledged that the self is not essential and unified but rather culturally constructed, fragmented and in search of a sense of unity. In my own readings I find that fragmentation can, in fact, be rather temporary in fantastic realism, since doubles and doppelgangers are never permanent fixtures and quite often they are actively resisted by the teenage protagonist.

In *The Lion Tamer's Daughter* the search for unity is embodied as a desperate need for two halves of an identity to be once more physically joined together. The novel is narrated by fourteen-year-old Keith and the story mainly concerns his best-friend, Melly. When Keith moves away to Scotland he is amazed to meet a girl called Melanie who is identical to Melly and who appears to have some kind of psychic link with her. Keith traces the history of the two girls and learns that they are both daughters of a lion tamer (to whom Melly's mother was once married). At birth, Melly and Melanie were one and the same person. The lion tamer feared he would lose his daughter because his wife threatened to leave him and so he ordered the circus clown to use a magic mirror and split the baby into two. The two girls exist comfortably without knowledge of each other until their fourteenth year when the spell wears off and they must be restored to one self.

Stranger with my Face employs a similar device of separated twins. In this case, Laurie and Lia do exist as individual twins but are separated as infants in order to be adopted by different families. Laurie becomes part of the comfortable, loving Stratton family who live a slightly isolated life on a New England island, while Lia proves to be a difficult child and remains in foster care. When Laurie is seventeen she finds herself plagued by irritating incidents where friends and family claim to have seen her in places she has not been. In revenge for their unequal childhood fates Lia has been using astral projection to appear nearby Laurie, first to befriend her but with the ultimate hope of destroying her life and taking her place.

In both novels the teenage girls feel an instant yearning to find out more about their sibling and to spend increasingly more time with them. This is not merely an inborn desire to connect with estranged family, since neither Melly nor Laurie are particularly eager to learn more about their natural father or mother. Instead they feel a bond that is simultaneously like falling in love with someone and discovering intimate knowledge of their own selves. When Lia finally reveals herself fully to her sister, Laurie describes the way she feels:

> I wish I could put it into writing, that strange feeling of being consumed and enveloped by another being ... Perhaps I could say that it was a bit like falling in love ... What I was experiencing was, in a way, like falling in love with myself. (100–101)

The overtones of utopian lesbian fantasy that emerge from these images deviate from models of normative adolescent sexual identity in early, conservative adolescent theory. Laurie focuses on the curve of Lia's lips and the 'tilt of her head' and these erotic images, along with her admission that the obsession is much like loving herself, remind us of feminist calls for celebration of likeness or completeness in same-sex relations.[7] This blissful state is engendered by sameness and the promise of a return to a state where the twins were 'two sides of a coin ... floated together in the same sea before birth' (*Stranger with my Face* 38) or 'one, like we were when we were born' (*The Lion Tamer's Daughter* 63). Tellingly though, Laurie's love affair with Lia is described in terms of anxiety and fear for the loss of individuality as she is 'consumed' and 'enveloped'. Such an intense romantic or erotic closeness is portrayed as dangerous to Laurie's individuality; ironically, when the romantic feelings are also a manifestation of the solipsism of 'falling in love with [one]self', the danger also comes from the very natural stage of egocentrism that Elkind sees as common to all teenagers. Falling in love with the image of oneself can easily be placed within the bounds of a personal fable, where all that is fascinating and lovable (or indeed all that is remarkable or threatening or important in any kind of way) can be traced to the self.

The frisson that Melly and Laurie feel when in contact with their twins is also produced through difference, however, since Melanie and Lia have distinct personalities. Unlike sensible Melly, Melanie smokes and swears and is, according to Keith, altogether more exciting and dangerous (no doubt partly a consequence of being brought up in a circus). In sharp contrast to Laurie's wholesome normality Lia is revealed to be psychologically unstable. When Laurie goes in search of Lia using astral projection herself she finds her in a mental hospital. While Laurie's spirit is out of her body in this way Lia inhabits it, refusing Laurie re-entry and trying to force her to simply fade away: to disappear bodily and ultimately to cease existing altogether. Luckily, Laurie's younger sister notices the difference and uses a lucky charm to compel Lia to leave, thus allowing Laurie to return to her own body and making sure she is not left in limbo indefinitely. The novel clearly positions Lia not only as mentally ill, but also as markedly different in character to Laurie; otherwise the younger sister would not be able to differentiate between the twins when they shared the same body. Using a Lacanian/Bakhtinian frame it is possible to analyse the doubled characters as points of outsideness and difference, to which the teenage protagonist can confidently assert 'that is not me'. Mirror symbolism emphasises this position: in *Stranger with my Face* Laurie witnesses her reflection smile back at her revealing the separate other that exists and which other people have been seeing; and in *The Lion Tamer's Daughter* the magic mirror initially splits the twins into two separate beings, independent of each other and completely different. These novels, then, set up a state of coexisting 'sameness' and 'difference' that appears at first to offer a radically diffused identity, both self-sufficient and multifaceted.

Such plurality is not allowed to continue in equilibrium, however, as the fantastic elements of the texts become threatening and the idyll of sibling companionship is questioned through ambivalent concepts of good and evil. McCallum suggests that Laurie and Lia represent these two essential positions in an uncomplicated dichotomy. She argues that horror and fantasy often use a pattern 'where the double is frequently a symbolic manifestation of a character's alterego and often represents that character's other "evil" self' (McCallum 76).[8] Certainly there are some indications of the classic dangerous or evil double in these novels. In many respects *The Lion Tamer's Daughter* is a reworking of a German doppelganger folk tale in which a wraith-like shadow pursues the hero until they come face to face; at which point the hero dies. Melly's mother is told that any attempt to get in contact with the lion tamer again (and thus with Melly's double, Melanie) will result in the death of her own child. Melanie is therefore positioned as Melly's deathlike shadow, a sinister reference to Melly's own mortality and vulnerability. A similar, if less dramatic, reading of the double is produced by critic Judith Armstrong in her work on ghosts in children's literature. She argues that ghosts are metaphorical devices designed to be 'psychological possibilities personified, placed as characters within a plot, and thus allowed development and influence which affect the protagonists, and therefore extend their perception of the possibilities of existence' (Armstrong, 'Ghosts as Rhetorical Devices' 59).[9] Her analysis of Penelope Lively's children's novel *The Ghost of Thomas Kempe* suggests in this way that the ghostly seventeenth-century apothecary who haunts young James is an embodiment of his wayward intentions and a warning of what will happen if he acts on any such intentions. Armstrong also argues that ghosts can function as a kind of 'nightmare shadow' of the haunted protagonist, which works out repressed elements of that subject's identity so that the real protagonist does not have to. This argument reflects what Jackson describes as 'allegorical readings of otherness as "evil"' that feature in traditional literary criticism of ghost stories or narratives of doubling (86). This is certainly a possible reading of many ghost or haunting novels, but teenage fantastic realism usually resists the dichotomy of a simple split self in which good is distinct from evil, and in this way it seems to me that both McCallum and Armstrong would be partly mistaken in their interpretation of twins like those in Duncan's novel. Although Lia is described as evil by many of the other characters in *Stranger with my Face* her behaviour can partly be explained by her traumatic childhood; and Laurie may be represented in generally positive terms but she is a three-dimensional character who is in no way goodness-personified. Melly and Mel likewise present two versions of selfhood that are different but not necessarily opposite.

It cannot be denied, however, that each novel positions one double as 'other', with less desirable—if not totally evil—teenage qualities. Lia's desire for the Stratton's riches and property is clearly not acceptable, particularly within a narrative that portrays Laurie as functional and secure despite her partial 'outsider' status (adopted and part of a slightly bohemian family). Lia's troubled background does not completely let her off the hook. Similarly, Melanie's difference is problematic. When she and Melly finally convince Albert the clown to perform a curative spell and return one of them to the mirror leaving a whole and complete girl behind, it is Melly who remains, while Melanie's sharp wit, rough manners and provocative behaviour reappear in hints and glimpses in the remaining twin. On the whole, however, this composite character generally acts more like the safe, sensible Melly to placate her mother and fit conventional social demands. Melanie is figured as the unacceptable other.

It is possible that there is an underlying gender-conservative thread to each of these narratives of adolescent selves which ultimately prioritises the real (figured as masculine reason) over the fantastic (and feminine irrationality) and which results in the eradication of the most troublesome twin. At the end of *Stranger with my Face* and *The Lion Tamer's Daughter* Laurie and Melly are left in an ambiguous position as they learn to live without their doubles. Both find it difficult to let the other go—Melly retains aspects of Melanie's personality and dialect, and Laurie senses Lia's 'nearness'—but there are indications that they are moving on to other, more acceptable relationships. Despite the lesbian eroticism of the body of these texts, closure comes when the teenage girls progress towards acceptable heterosexual relationships. Although her boyfriend moves to Boston, Laurie is left optimistic about possibilities for their friendship, or for a better one, announcing that '[i]n one more week, I will be leaving for college. For me, as for Jeff, a new phase of life is starting' (*Stranger with my Face* 250). Melly and Keith find something in each other that is more attractive than they ever did before Melanie appeared in their lives and the final chapter hints at a relationship between them in the future. Having assembled identities through the recognition, assimilation and disposal of their doubles, the novel constructs a traditional closure; this signals an end to the fantastic elements in the novels and shuts down possibilities of interaction with fantastic otherness, concentrating instead on a realist and conservative individualism. Once this is achieved then significant romantic relationships are made possible.

A more focused analysis of the significant other as fantastic will help to interrogate how and why conservative images of the self thrive in teenage fantastic realism. The next section considers ghosts and time-travel and offers some answers to this question.

The Ghost of a Self: Parallel Identities

Like Laurie and Melly, the heroine of K.M. Peyton's *Unquiet Spirits* (1997) forms a close relationship with her double. These two girls are both sixteen, look alike, and share the name Madeleine (or 'Mad'), but the fantastic double is a ghost who died over three hundred years before the contemporary events of the novel. This ghost is a seamstress who used to work at a local manor house, 'Good Graces', in the rural village to which Mad and her mother have recently moved. The young seamstress once fell in love with one of the previous heirs to Good Graces but could not cross the social boundaries necessary to marry the young lord, who was betrothed instead to an older, uglier and richer woman called Agnes. In an attempt to overcome these difficulties the lord and his lover tried to elope but unfortunately the young girl drowned while attempting to cross the river. With such a dramatic and tragic backstory providing the ghost with her *raison d'être*, one might imagine a character of Shakespearean calibre, but throughout the novel she is generally an invisible, benign presence that Madeleine senses in her cottage bedroom and around Good Graces (where she is given a job restoring the house as a tourist attraction). The ghost is, however, potent enough to attempt to relive her love through Mad and the modern-day teenage lord, Simon Tempest. She forces them to unwittingly re-enact lovescenes by overwhelming Mad with uncontrollable passion and physically propelling her towards Simon; at the same time, Agnes also appears to Mad and violently tries to frighten her away from him.

When examining Mad's sense of identity in *Unquiet Spirits*, Armstrong's reading of the ghost as an alternative self for the haunted protagonist is a fruitful starting point. The seamstress ghost is close enough to Mad in character, and yet distant enough in time and experience, to provide an alternative vision of Mad's destiny. They are both youthfully beautiful and, furthermore, Mad has a connection with embroidery, helping her mother to make textile art and working on those curtains at Good Graces manor that the ghost would have stitched hundreds of years before. Both girls also significantly fall in love for the first time with rebellious teenage Tempests. In the historical set of events the seamstress is penalised for acting against the social expectations of her time and her story has to end in tragedy. In the contemporary narrative, Mad encourages Simon to act against his father's wishes (by pursuing a musical career rather than running Good Graces) but here it is Simon's father, Temp, who is killed in an accident, leaving Mad and Simon alive and free to truly fall in love. The seamstress's story offers a fantastic world running parallel with reality and the real events of Mad's life exhibit elements of Armstrong's theory: individuals are 'shadowed by their negatives, which are many—all the people we might have become, and did not; all the things we might have done, and did not' (Armstrong, 'Ghost Stories: exploiting the convention' 119). The ghost is thus a 'negative' version of the protagonist, although this means a reversed or negated version, rather than an intrinsically evil one as Armstrong implies.

These parallel lives seem to suggest a certain plurality of identity and experience. The narrative implies that Mad's life has been played out centuries before in a different social and ideological context and has resulted in a different, tragic, ending. She realises that the seamstress represents a part of herself, acknowledging to a degree that she is a subject made up of various possibilities shadowing her actual self. This process is dramatised at the end of the novel, where Mad allows her own feelings to merge with the seamstress's and passionately kisses Simon. Afterwards Mad retires to her bedroom to find the seamstress sitting on her bed, appearing to her bodily for the first time: 'She came towards me with her arms out in an embrace and said, quite clearly, "Everything is all right now. We will be happy." And she came up and passed right into me, became me. She was me. Myself' (215). In spite of the radical implications for identity produced by this scene, where self and other are merged across time, class and experience, *Unquiet Spirits* ultimately resembles other narratives of doubling explored in this chapter in the way that plural subjectivity is quelled as soon as it is realised. When the ghost fuses with Mad there is only a superficial sense that the two girls are now a 'we'. Instead, Mad is liberated to love Simon in her own way, without the imposing pressure of the seamstress's passionate love, and she restores control of her own identity, no longer compelled to incorporate the feelings of another individual. Armstrong follows Julia Briggs in arguing that ghost stories most often end with the disappearance of the ghost since the spirit of the deceased has by that point served its purpose. Indeed, it is possible to read *Unquiet Spirits* in this way, since the seamstress finally gets to vicariously enjoy a relationship with the lord of the manor through the body of Mad and then happily disappears. But this is primarily Mad's story and her physical absorption of the ghost seems, in fact, to represent her ultimate return to a unified and individualistic self that is no longer haunted by an other. As the next section will argue with reference to belief and madness, any sense of split subjectivity entailed through this haunting is quickly forgotten or rejected.

Communing with a ghost—even one who died centuries beforehand—does not always entail an encounter with absolute difference. Madeleine is never obliged to grasp the profound disparity between her own twentieth-century adolescence and that of her Elizabethan ghost. She is set apart from her own contemporaries through her move away from London, and it is a character from the past that represents her point of reference for identity and experience. When Simon explains that her ghost used to work at the old manor house, Mad attempts to recreate the sixteenth century in her mind by imagining the seamstress 'working over her frame day after day' (92). This functions in some respects as the empathic heritage version of history that Tess Cosslett discusses in her work on 'history from below' in time-slip narratives. However, Mad does not really engage with the past world in order to understand its differences. Instead her continuing fantasy of the seamstress's working day develops into modern adolescent romantic and individualistic rhetoric: 'I thought of [. . .] those hours and hours of diligent, intensive labour, worked long day after long day in the twilight of the great hall by a romantic, budding young woman with no prospects, no aspirations, only dreams' (93). Mad admits she is getting carried away but her train of thought takes her further towards merging the sixteenth-century young woman with her own adolescent self: 'However many centuries back, human nature was no different, surely? Falling in love was biology, after all, the science of nature. The sewing Madeleine was myself, in essence, falling in love—dammit!—with Simon' (93).

Rather than imaginatively examining the concept of adolescence through contrasting historical contexts, the novel points instead to fixed images of female teenagers dreaming of their romantic and individualistic futures. This representation of adolescence refuses to deconstruct ideas of age and identity, allowing its fantasy elements to reinforce, rather than destabilise, these concepts through the doubling of a twentieth-century and a sixteenth-century sixteen-year-old.[10] In fact, the focus on tentative adolescent love as a primary marker of identity achievement masks other class and gender issues that emerge from the parallel stories. The text attempts—through its version of 'history from below'—to allude to the unbending expectations of wealth-transferral and marriage that shaped the lives of early modern British gentry, as Mad learns how the Elizabethan lord was beaten until he took a suitably eligible bride to continue his line. Mad and Simon are not subject to such pressures and, despite their different backgrounds, it is professional expectations (whether Simon should run Good Graces as tradition dictates) that have a bearing on their 'happy ending'. In each case, the ultimate goal is the happiness and security that a sensible heterosexual relationship will bring. Even though Mad is in control of Good Graces throughout the novel in her capacity as restoration manager, it is only when Temp is dead and there is a possibility for her and Simon to run the estate together (perhaps as a married couple) that Mad is portrayed as being fulfilled: 'I could get really excited, planning things, but it had all been pie in the sky till now' (214). As ever, prospective love and marriage are the ultimate identifiers for teenage girls.

I discussed time and history in Chapter One, arguing that in young adult fantastic realism they chiefly function in a diachronic or chronological manner, paralleling adolescent frameworks of change, progression and development. In one respect, however, ghost novels and time-travel narratives seem to favour a synchronic reading. Although the past may be represented as a strange, dangerous and less developed space or chronotope, adolescent characters from the past like Madeleine's seamstress ghost most often share qualities of individualism with their contemporary counterparts. This ahistorical essentialising of adolescence across time and cultures can also be found in some time-slip narratives and, despite the regular treatment of the past as abject and other, adolescent identity is rarely represented as completely *alien* in the past. Ruth Park's *Playing Beatie Bow* (1980), for example, constructs the relationship between contemporary adolescent and historical counterpart in a similar manner to *Unquiet Spirits*.

In Park's novel, fourteen-year-old Abigail travels in time and finds herself living with a nineteenth-century family, the Bows, who are partly foreign to her in manners and lifestyle, but with whom she also feels a distinct connection. She learns she is fated to play a part in saving the Bows' magical 'Gift' as her presence will somehow help decide which member of the family continues to see the future and have healing powers. This detective element to the novel (who is to live and carry on the hereditary Gift) is secondary to Abigail's own status and experience. In particular, she develops a bond with the Bows' eighteen-year-old sailor son, Judah. At first she notices the contrasts between him and her contemporaries: 'The difference between him and boys of eighteen in her own time was that Judah was a man' (114). But she goes on to point out how similar her feelings for him are to ordinary adolescent sentiments she has always mocked, 'all those things that old songs said, that the girls at school said. "I saw him getting off the bus and my knees went. I didn't know what I was doing. I went down the wrong street and left my school-case at the bus stop"' (116).

Abigail also recognises that her feelings for Judah in the nineteenth century have parallels with what she had always contemptuously dismissed as stereotypical modern teenage love affairs and interestingly, her realisation that adolescent first love is both intensely personal and universally experienced is reinforced by her own mother's description of falling in love as a teenager. The novel suggests that the private and emotional aspects of adolescence portrayed through Abigail can be traced back through generations and through history unproblematically, allowing a transparent representation of all teenage experience (at least, all female adolescent experience of first love). In the final chapters of *Playing Beatie Bow*, Abigail returns to the present, having saved the youngest Bow, Gilbert, so that he can go on to pass the Gift to his children. Four years later she meets one of these descendants and the connection that she and

Judah had is instantly reproduced, as if the two older teenagers have always known each other. As in other fantastic realist texts discussed in this section, the final part of the novel relinquishes any fantastic element in order to return the heroine to a state of personal unity. In this case, the fantastic time-slip is merely reversed so that Abigail's experience of falling in love is brought into her own time and replicated in the present, following a universal pattern of adolescent identity formation.[11]

In this analysis I have examined ways that doubles and ghosts provide potentially plural selfhoods for teenage protagonists, but I have also illustrated the tendency for these possibilities to be shut down by a shift towards rational individualism at the novel's closure. This pattern in part reflects conventional frameworks of adolescence as a transitional period, so that any fragmentation of identity is not a permanent questioning of individuality but an indication of a temporary and chaotic stage. I would like to elaborate on this process in the next section and suggest that rather than subjectivity being represented as *either* plural and dialogic *or* single and essential, the former model can in fact still lead to the latter ontological state. In other words, fragmentation and dissolution are powerful themes in teenage fantastic realism, but they act as tests to strengthen a distinct sense of identity and individualism. This discussion will begin by exploring issues of uncertainty and madness in terms of fantastic identity.

Threats of Madness

Unbelievable: The Loss of the Rational Self

Todorov's definition of fantasy relies on the concept of hesitation. The protagonist of fantastic realism—and the reader along with them—is uncertain of the meaning, the effects and the permanence of those incredible things that occur to them or around them. The space in fantastic realism is strange and chaotic due to its impossible aspects, and in turn it confuses and alters its protagonists. Unlike secondary-world fantasy, where heroes and heroines travel away from their reality, characters in fantastic realism do not have to journey into transformed universes because the fantastic appears in their own diurnal world, often within their own person. Jackson effectively describes this ontological position with reference to the modern fantastic:

> The relation of the individual subject to the world, to others, to objects, ceases to be known or safe, and problems of apprehension (in the double sense of perceiving and of fearing) become central. [...] The subject's relation to the phenomenal world is made problematical and the text foregrounds the impossibility of definitive interpretation [...] (49)

Perception and interpretation are marked by their ambiguity in texts where the ordinary is invaded by the fantastic. Jackson relates such ambiguity to danger for the individual subject and this can be understood in two ways. Teenage fantastic realism's focus on the individual relates it to fearful and unsettling aspects of fantasy because there is no respite to be had through sharing strange perceptions with others and the protagonist remains isolated. It is also particularly concerned with the individual's chaotic relation to the accepted world of cause and effect. Belief systems that appear to be fixed at childhood are re-evaluated and complicated at adolescence, according to Erikson's schema, which demands fidelity to a mature belief system as an intrinsic part of identity formation.[12] The invasion of supernatural or impossible elements into an apparently coherent phenomenal world therefore provides an appropriate narrative space in which to explore teenage beliefs and their effect on a sense of self.

Peter Buse and Andrew Stott explore the historical trajectory of belief in the supernatural with particular reference to ghosts, and they argue that the historical Enlightenment drew a line 'between Reason and its more shadowy others' (3). In the contemporary period, for instance, science and rationality have eradicated the possibility of the dead returning for vengeance, education, help or mischief, as it was once believed they did. Ghosts perform a different function in modern society: 'Even though it is now frivolous to believe in ghosts, they cannot shrug off the spectre of belief: it is simply that now they have been consigned to the task of representing whatever is not to be believed' (3). Buse and Stott suggest that, in most contexts, ghosts retain a connection to belief systems, but merely through rhetorical figures or metaphorical signs. As examples they proffer common phrases such as 'ghost of a chance' and 'phantom pregnancy'—sayings that cling to the hesitation between fantasy and reality, but which rest on purely symbolic understanding. This kind of reading is exemplified by a critic like Armstrong, and symbolic readings provide the dynamic for much literary interpretation of fantastic realism (and other forms of fantasy), a tendency I have already touched upon in my Introduction. Lucie Armitt discusses this dynamic as it functions in criticism of Toni Morrison's work, pointing out that 'critics go to great lengths either to explain away, render metaphorical, or blindly ignore the powerfully fantastic elements of *Beloved*' and explaining that a reading like this 'angers [her] in its almost wilfully reductive determination to transform this powerful novel into pure social mimesis' (*Contemporary Women's Fiction* 122–123). Armitt is critiquing the tradition of negating supernatural influence, partly because it is a specifically Western stance and one that does not take into account the various challenges to prevailing scientific and rational explanations of the world around us. Non-Western or alternative beliefs and practices can provide the basis for readings of the fantastic that are not purely metaphorical and which offer valuable insights into how identity is shaped. As Glen Cavaliero colourfully argues, the supernatural is a 'joker in the pack', which is unsettling to contemporary critics and should not simply be displaced onto sexual, cultural or political anxieties (13–14). There *are* sexual, cultural and political readings to be explored in the matrix of ghosts, fantasy and adolescence in teenage fiction, but it is also interesting to trace the sequence of reactions that adolescent characters display when confronted with the impossible, and to show how the progression from incredulity to belief to dismissal relates to a crisis of adolescent identity. Whilst it is commonly understood that very young children enjoy fantasy because they do not differentiate between the world of cause and effect surrounding them and the incredible fairy stories or marvellous tales they are told, by adolescence individuals are expected to accept that 'impossible' events do not occur in day-to-day life. Those developmental frameworks we examined in the last chapter set out adolescence as a kind of individualistic enlightenment, following on from the magical and less informed state of childhood, making rather uncomfortable connections between a generalised history of the human race and specific personal histories.

In *Unquiet Spirits* Mad is initially dismissive of the supernatural implications of her sweet-natured seamstress ghost, assuming that she is merely imagining her presence. When a local girl explains the folklore of the ghosts connected to Good Graces, however, she becomes more ambivalent about the possibilities: 'I had never considered ghosts in my life before, save as a joke, a game. Something you played at. I had never expected to meet one, and hadn't acknowledged that I had, until now. Not seriously' (*Unquiet Spirits* 19). This idea of playing at a game of ghosts implies that Mad's original relation to the supernatural is like a young child's relation to fantasy: a playful acceptance of the possibility of ghostly presence. Yet it is at the point of adolescence, when she is sixteen and facing a number of social and emotional changes, that Mad is confronted with more complex possibilities concerning her belief system. Throughout the novel Mad is provided with verifiable proof of her hauntings. She is physically manipulated by the seamstress into passionate embraces with Simon, and Agnes tangibly appears to her as a figure with a 'small catlike face with burning black eyes full of maniacal hate', pulling out her hair (98). In the face of such experiential validation, the narrative allows no space for Mad to genuinely deem the ghosts to be mere fancies of her imagination. In the final chapters of the novel, the historical conflict between the seamstress and Agnes comes to a climax as they battle over Mad's relationship with Simon. Both ghosts want to relive a love affair with the long-dead young lord through the living bodies of the teenage characters. Each time Mad and Simon kiss they are partly possessed by the unquiet spirits and overrun by their ghostly and ancient feelings, but by the end of the narrative the contemporary teenagers finally realise that they are actually truly in love themselves. It is at this point that the ghosts disappear and Mad and Simon can agree, 'I don't believe in ghosts anymore' (216). The progression from scepticism to belief to a final rejection of the supernatural can be read through a discourse of developmentalism using a similar method to that described in Chapter One. Originally a signifier of childhood and irrationality, ghosts enter into Mad's adolescence and coerce her into opening up to supernatural possibilities as well as other 'irrationalities' such as love. Once the transition to adulthood has been made, however (and Mad's adolescence is marked by a number of key experiences, including falling in love and a first encounter with mortality), the implication is that Mad no longer needs to believe in ghosts and can return to her senses.

Thus adolescence is perceived as a period of madness, beyond the innocent, fantastic beliefs of childhood but not yet governed by adult rationality and intellect. A number of psycho-social theories emphasise a propensity towards emotional and intellectual instability at adolescence, from Granville Stanley Hall's conceptualisation of the 'storm and stress' period (characterised by moods, conflict and risk-taking), to the work of Anna Freud and Erik Erikson, both of whom focus on the ego in crisis.[13] These two discursive fields—adolescence and madness—are often conflated in teenage fantastic realism through the collision of fantasy and realism. In some cases, this conflation is welcomed by the protagonist as a justification for their disruptive adolescent emotions: when Mad first encounters the seamstress ghost in her new bedroom, for example, her reaction is sanguine: 'I walked through into the other two rooms, and the warm feeling immediately left me. I walked back again and it returned. It was like an embrace. I thought, *perhaps I am going mad*. But I didn't mind' (*Unquiet Spirits* 6).

Yet in later parts of this text, and in other novels, madness is portrayed as fearful and represents a potential loss of an inherent rational individuality. For example, in Westall's *The Devil on the Road*, discussed in the last chapter, there is an evident preoccupation with the impossibility of time-travel that relies heavily on the main character's sense of his own rational self. John Webster is in many ways a romantic traveller who delights in the concept of 'Chance', but his own explicit self-representation is of a logical young man who is overtly 'down-to-earth', unlike his fellow university students, '[t]he rimless-spectacle types who think that just because you're studying Civil Engineering and play rugby for the first XV, you must be Neanderthal man in person' (*The Devil on the Road* 3). When he gets embroiled in the history and folklore of Besingtree village and finds himself travelling into the past with the help of the magical cat, however, the experience gives John's usual reliance on reason a knock, and makes him panic he might end up 'in the funny farm, along with women who compose new works by Mozart' (83). Not only has John's image of himself, 'with his enlightened reason and his affinity for technology' suffered 'irreparable damage', as Gertrud Lehnert-Rodiek puts it (65), but his individuality is also threatened by the intrusion of witch Johanna from the seventeenth century into his twentieth-century reality. As Chapter One explained, Johanna is dangerous because she threatens to trap John in the stagnancy of the past (not to mention the perils of femininity), but also because she begins to rob him of his sense of self, rationality and sanity.

Hysteria: Gendering the Individual

In a number of novels where madness is an issue, the self under threat is expressly female. This is particularly true of fantastic realism based in myth or history, where madness or hysteria is naturalised in adolescent girls as part of a wider pattern.[14] In *Black Harvest* (1983), by Ann Pilling, it is historical circumstance that seems to drive teenage Prill to hysteria. When incidents from the Irish potato famine fantastically seep into her family holiday, Prill starts to have visions of emaciated children, has dreams of being buried alive and literally begins to starve to death. In one scene she visits the local shop and sees a desperate mother begging the shopkeeper for food, having no money to pay for it. The woman leaves a bundle on the counter as she steals a loaf of bread and Prill discovers that the blankets hold a dead baby. This terrifies Prill and she feels nauseous and panic-stricken, but from the point of view of the local priest, who is also in the shop, the incident appears to be psychosomatic:

> She had certainly been very violent in Mooneys' Stores. It wasn't exactly a fainting fit. He had been waiting at the back of the queue and seen everything. It seemed to him that the girl had had some kind of hysterical attack. She had kept poking crazily at something a delivery man had left on the counter, a ham he thought it was. (*Black Harvest* 104)

Although her brother, Colin, and cousin, Oliver, also experience strange dreams and suffer from the fact that all the food in their house instantly turns mouldy and maggoty, it is Prill who has the most vivid connection to the suffering past and who has to be physically dragged away from the cursed holiday bungalow. Her connection is personal and empathic, experienced bodily and appealing to latent maternal anxieties about dying babies and the inability to provide nourishment. In some ways the text implies that the terrifying fantastical elements flourish because the holidaying family lacks an adult male presence. Prill's father cannot join them because he is busy with work and her mother becomes increasingly distant as she worries about her sick baby. Throughout the novel, the teenage characters regularly wish for their father's arrival, almost using his name as an incantation that would ward off the fantastic with his rational qualities. Interestingly, Robert Westall's *Yaxley's Cat* (1991) portrays a similar familial situation. In this novel, Rose goes on holiday with her two teenage children to get away from her controlling husband, but becomes trapped in a secluded country village where superstition and witch-hunts make her partly long for his logical influence. If Prill and Rose are intimately associated with the fantastic and irrational because of their femininity, the absent male figure positions them specifically as adolescent and in a crisis of identity, even if, in Rose's case, her physiological adolescence is over.

Black Harvest describes the unsettling effect of a time-slip on the perceived sanity of the teenage girl. In Alan Garner's *The Owl Service* (1967) it is Welsh myth, from the book of *The Mabinogion*, that is evoked to represent females manically possessed by powerful forces beyond their control. Garner's novel concerns three modern-day adolescents in Wales whose story reworks the *Math vab Mathonwy*, in which Lleu and Gronw vie for the love of Blodeuwedd, a woman made of flowers. In each generation, in this particular Welsh valley, Blodeuwedd returns and contemporary versions of 'Lleus' and 'Gronws' destroy each other trying to retain a hold on her. Three teenagers, Roger, Gwyn and Alison, find themselves caught up in the powerful myth so completely that the valley and its history seem to entirely control them. Alison, in particular, finds herself helplessly manipulated by the desire to 'return to flowers' and the fear of becoming an owl, attacked by other birds (which was Blodeuwedd's punishment for betraying her husband, Lleu). Throughout the novel, Roger and Gwyn must calm Alison as she gains in power but becomes more uncontrollable. In one episode she locks herself in a hut in the woods to cut out paper owls in a frenzied fit. When Gwyn tries to stop her, she resists and becomes violent, throwing plates at him, while he retorts, 'Stop that. [...] Don't play spooks with me! It's hysterics, man!' (*The Owl Service* 68). At the end of the novel, it is Roger who has to save Alison from herself as she begins to fantastically transform into an owl. He points out that she does have some agency over the myth: '"You've got it back to front, you silly gubbins. She's not owls. She's flowers. Flowers. Flowers, Ali." He stroked her forehead. "You're not birds. You're flowers. You've never been anything else. Not owls. Flowers. That's it. Don't fret"' (155). Alison is not only represented as being insanely possessed by the spirit of Blodeuwedd, losing her mind to meaningless ritual and violent action, she is also a 'silly gubbins' who can only regain any sense of real identity with the rational help of the male characters.

Louise Lawrence's *Power of Stars* (1972) is also a tale of possession, but this time the force that invades Jane Bates is extra-terrestrial. Alien cells, which draw on starlight for power and have a violent hostility towards technology, enter Jane's body and change her behaviour. Jane's two friends and rivals for her attention, Jimmy and Alan, notice the effects without realising *why* she is behaving differently. When she goes 'berserk' in front of the school computer the boys discuss whether she is mad or simply has a phobia about machines. When they see her the next day, standing in the street with her hands over her ears and her shopping spilt, Jimmy asserts his opinion: 'Look at her. [...] Now don't try telling me she's not stark raving mad' (*Power of Stars* 45). Jimmy's perspective is similar to the priest's in *Black Harvest*, although the vocabulary he has to explain his friend's behaviour is less formalised by medical reference to hysteria. Like the priest, Jimmy cannot understand that the behaviour he is witnessing is not irrational madness but instead stems from fantastic phenomena of which he is unaware. From an externalised angle, Jane appears to be strange and hysterical, but when events are focalised through her point of view her madness is explained as coming from the alien consciousness, which is terrified of becoming once more a 'cell of a mind [...] trapped inside a machine' (46).

Increasingly, the novel is focalised through the male protagonists' thoughts and actions, while Jane is described externally as gradually less rational at the same time as she becomes more attractive. A frenzied trance-like state is periodically induced when the alien infection is strengthened by starlight. Thus, when Jimmy takes her to a forbidden midnight dance, Jane is transformed from her usual 'mousy' self into a sensual and sexual teenager, moved by the rhythmic music: 'the beat pulsated through her like blood through her veins . . . She gave herself to it completely' (76). This scene locates Jane's hysteria within the context of youth subcultural activity, which initially suggests that she is actively constructing identity alongside a community of teenagers.[15] An application of Angela McRobbie's work on female dance culture might aim to argue that Jane is using her dance as a channel for 'bodily self-expression and control' ('Dance and Social Fantasy' 77), and that her rhythmic moves are 'part of a strategy of resistance or opposition; that is [. . .] marking out one of those areas which cannot be totally colonised' (134). Unfortunately, the text does not support such a reading, since Jane is never in control of her movement and therefore cannot be offering an active resistance to the constraints on her gendered adolescent life. Moreover, as soon as the star-power is drained, she is left hearing just a 'clatter of sound without any rhythm' (*Power of Stars* 77), which suggests that music and dance are not her chosen tools of liberation at all. All of this acts to construct her through an isolated and feminised sensual madness rather than through the ritual communal hysteria intrinsic to youth dance culture.

Returning to Peyton's *Unquiet Spirits* to consider its gendered representation of madness, we see that as Mad moves away from the modern reality of London she enters what is represented as a more mystical, fantastical and feminised rural wilderness. The novel foregrounds her anxiety about losing her sense of self through insanity within this 'back of beyond' space and its unknown inhabitants. When Mad first meets Simon, her feelings towards him are unusually strong, and although she has had crushes on boys before, this time she feels committed: 'It wasn't in any way a frivolous feeling, but something quite rooted and serious and disturbing. [. . .] I thought I was hallucinating, that the ghost had got me, or I was having what my mother called a teenage turn' (*Unquiet Spirits* 66). Her ghostly seamstress's feelings towards the historical Simon fuel Mad's desire for the current lord of the manor, and being haunted by both the lovestruck ghost and by feelings for Simon disconcerts her. Her fear is most intense when she is possessed by both at once:

> My ghost engulfed me with her warm scented embrace and I was in Simon's arms whether I wanted or not, and he was covering my face with kisses. It was really wild, but terrifying, because it was not of my own volition [. . .] to lose all one's power of will was literally to lose one's mind and I thought my mind was going. (139)

To lose one's mind is to lose one's sense of personal identity and, as we have already seen, for Mad this is represented in the danger both of being haunted and of falling in love. The teen ghost novel shares with other fantastic realism the exploration of fearful possibilities of a self dissolved and diluted by significant others. Unlike ghost stories, where fear originates in the horror of the supernatural in itself, haunting novels like *Unquiet Spirits* locate anxiety in the relation of the (real) self to the (fantastic) ghostly other.

Interestingly, this pattern of a protagonist being psychologically and emotionally possessed by a ghost or elements of a ghostly personality is not universal across Western cultures. Icelandic stories, for instance, are traditionally more likely to involve physical wrestling with the ghost, rather than a mental struggle for identity.[16] Such a focus on the dangers of losing one's private and internalised self in the texts considered here demonstrates the fundamental importance of a discrete individuality that is crucial at adolescence. The invasion of another subjectivity is unacceptable at an age-stage when identity is being forged and crystallised, so that even as Mad feels the comfort of the seamstress's presence and Jane enjoys communing and sharing emotions with her alien parasites, both girls have to realise that their *other/s* must be dispelled or purged. It is the threat to the self that returns the protagonist to the need for individual selfhood. This idea has been explored through the tropes of belief and madness in female adolescence, but it can also be illustrated in terms of visual images—as deceptive or invisible versions of the male self.

Dissolving Selves

Visions and Absences: The Self behind the Lens

Robert Cormier's *Fade* opens with a description of a curious photographic image. Thirteen-year-old Paul Moreaux explains that '[a]t first glance, the picture looked like any other in a family album of that time' (*Fade* 3) but at the heart of the photograph is a 'family mystery': 'In the space that was supposed to have been occupied by my uncle Adelard, at the end of the top row, next to my father, there is simply a blank space. Nothing' (3). This 'mystery' prompts endless discussion amongst the Moreaux as to how Adelard could have disappeared so quickly and soundlessly. Problems of perception and existence multiply: is the photograph that Paul sees real or tampered with; is the mystery a case of the camera's failed mechanism, as some relatives suggest; did Adelard merely duck out of the way when the shutter closed; or did he really disappear? In fact, the photograph represents the first hint of fantastic activity, indicating as it does an instance of the titular 'fade'. The fade is a hereditary ability to make the self (and any clothes or other items touching the self at the time) disappear from view, and it can be called up at will, although it finally begins to come upon the 'fader' more often and unexpectedly. The first half of *Fade* narrates Paul

Moreaux's life in 1930s Massachusetts as he discovers he has inherited the gift from Adelard and experiments with it around Frenchtown. This whole narrative constitutes a manuscript written by the author Paul Roget and discovered by his distant cousin Susan. In the second part of the novel the story alternates between Susan and the subsequent manuscript fragments by Paul that she discovers.

A similar photographic image initiates the action in Gillian Cross's *Pictures in the Dark*. In this novel, which I have already discussed in terms of metamorphosis in Chapter One, teenager Charlie Willcox has captured a strange picture of orange street-light reflected in the river, broken by ripples from the wake of something swimming: 'Whatever had made the ripples was just beyond the light. The point of the V was chopped off drawing attention to the darkness at the edges of the picture. Leaving people free to imagine monsters' (*Pictures in the Dark* 2). Although the rest of the school Camera Club cannot decipher the fantastic image and imagines the shape is a hippo, a whale or even a submarine, Charlie knows that he has captured a rare otter on film and is fascinated. He becomes even more intrigued as he slowly discovers that the pictured otter is actually one of his fellow school pupils, Peter, fantastically metamorphosed into a wild creature.

By beginning with some aspect of visual fascination—Paul's gazing at the mysterious family portrait and Charlie observing a strange human–animal transmutation through the lens of his camera—these novels emphasise challenging issues of perception and selfhood. Although *what* is seen becomes important to the themes and plots of the books, initially significance lies in *who* is seeing and what this seeing does to their sense of self. In realist terms, of course, the camera attempts to represent phenomena 'as they really are', and acts as a popular motif of literary realism. For example, Christopher Isherwood's *Goodbye to Berlin* (1939), which John Van Druten adapted into the 1951 play *I am a Camera*, features a narrator who claims, 'I am a camera with its shutter open, quite passive, recording, not thinking.' It should be noted that such objectivity is an illusion because both cinematic and photographic cameras (or their operators) *choose* what to capture and how to frame their pictures, and apparently documentary images can be vastly misleading.[17] However, both Charlie and Paul seem to want to fix the mysterious and unknown aspects of their lives through observation or image-making, as if the camera or the image provides a truthful answer to the strange fantastical experiences the boys are going through. In *Pictures in the Dark*, Charlie is an observer throughout, seeing everything via his camera lens. Initially, the images he captures through his photography are realist pictures of his domestic life—his parents, aunt, uncle and cousins all appear in various silly poses in 'funny family pictures'—but as the novel progresses he becomes more concerned with the way he can see and record the unexpected visions of the otter and Peter's metamorphosis. Christine Wilkie-Stibbs interprets Charlie's photography as a manifestation of his imaginative creativity. She argues that when Peter in his otter guise bites

Charlie, he transmits a 'dimension of seeing' that can be identified as being influenced by Kristevan 'woman's time' and expressing 'jouissance':

> [w]ith his newfound vision, the angle, and the object, and the perspective, of Charlie's photography changes; he sees the world through his transformation with greater detail, and conventional, linear time ceases to exist while he is caught up in the intensity of snapping his pictures. (Wilkie-Stibbs 97)

It is certainly true that Charlie's vision intensifies and becomes more inspired, and his photography develops maturity and artistry as well, but although Wilkie-Stibbs concentrates on the joyful rhythmic time that Peter and Charlie share within the Semiotic, her analysis does not take account of Charlie's increased alienation from friends and family, or his growing dependence on seeing *through* the camera lens rather than interacting with others. His cousin Zoe even accuses him of not taking nice pictures of people he knows any more: 'It's all trees and weeds. And you keep drifting round and *staring*. As if you were under a spell or something' (*Pictures in the Dark* 70). This is a move away from the Semiotic in many respects, and into a troubled period of adolescent absorption. Throughout the novel, Charlie uses the camera to see the natural world and other people more clearly, but as the lens is never turned upon him, the reader is left with a rather indistinct picture of the protagonist. Charlie is absorbed into the practice of watching and recording, rather than acting.

Like Charlie, Paul is an observer of, rather than an actor in, the events of his narrative, although he watches from the position of his invisibility rather than from behind a camera. The text represents Paul as a kind of naïve everyman; the unexceptional narrator of the strange events that just happen to occur around him. Paul is quiet and shy and, before he realises that he has fantastic ability, he considers himself to be much less interesting than his siblings:

> I sometimes longed to be like them, a star ballplayer who was always chosen first for a team, like Armand, or handsome like Bernard, almost too beautiful to be a boy, some people said [. . .] Most of all I envied Pete Lagniard, my best friend, who ran faster and climbed fences quicker than anyone else, knew a thousand secrets [. . .] I considered my lack of talent at schoolyard games, my thousand fears, the loneliness I could not explain. (*Fade* 11)

For much of the early part of the novel—when Paul is a teenager—he is distinctly ordinary. He is not a budding sportsman nor is he romantically successful, and even his strongest talent of creative writing is suppressed and silenced by his teachers. At first he searches for a chance to successfully construct his own identity along a masculine heroic model of cinema cowboys that is actually based on fantasies about his own uncle Adelard. Adelard has 'the dimensions of a hero' and Paul desires a similar selfhood of action and existentialist individualism: 'I felt that I, too, could become a hero if the opportunity presented itself or if I were tested' (4). However, as he works out for himself, there are few opportunities for that kind of identity achievement in Frenchtown. The other inhabitants of his hometown are much more colourful and vivid than Paul. Although many of the characters are stereotypes and one-dimensional —such as the dashing, villainous Rudolphe Toubert with his 'movie star moustache' (33) and Paul's aunt Rosanna who has red lips and wears red high-heeled shoes—they are documented keenly by Paul who has chance to study them carefully (as both faded teenager and aspiring author). At the same time, Paul himself remains visually and materially rather indistinct. Like Charlie, Paul gives no physical descriptions of himself and the most substantial references to his body occur when he fades or when he masturbates (and arguably both these activities are about eradicating the self). Before his power of invisibility becomes apparent, therefore, Paul is an observer and documenter, rather than an active hero.

Rosemary Jackson recognises the complex potential of observation, perspective and identity in fantastic literature, relating it to what she describes as 'spectral imagery' such as camera lenses, eyes and mirrored reflections. She notes a strong connection between spectral imagery and subjectivity, dependent in its nature on the narrative mode of the text. Thus, whereas in realist fiction '[k]nowledge, comprehension, reason, are established through the power of the *look*, through the "*eye*" and the "*I*" of the human subject whose relation to objects is structured through his field of vision', in fantastic literature 'objects are not readily appropriated through the look: things slide away from the powerful eye/I which seeks to possess them, thus becoming distorted' (Jackson 45–46). According to this way of theorising perception, the lucid self is powerful because it sees objects clearly, but the rational gaze in fantastic literature is gradually destroyed, along with any sense of self. Trites explores this sense of erasure when she discusses the prevalence of photography in teenage fiction dealing with death. She argues that photographs 'serve as a metaphor for death' because they capture a lifeless image and suggest our ultimate fate, although she also draws on Barthes' ontological description of the photographed individual as 'neither subject nor object but a subject who feels he is becoming an object' (cited in Trites 135). When it comes to the individual *behind* the lens, however, I think that in the case of both teenage protagonists under discussion here, the look (from behind a lens or from the position of anonymity) does not produce objects that slide away or signify death, but rather produces an eye/I that can see more clearly what other 'rational' characters cannot experience. Yet this is also an eye/I which is erased rather than powerful. We might add to Jackson's schema by arguing that in teenage fantastic realism—where the narrative is often first-person or highly focalised through the protagonist—the camera or the gaze can allow the narrator to successfully hide aspects of their own character and this elision has the effect of fore-

Fantasies of Identity • 83

grounding their subjectivity at the same time as presenting themselves as impersonal recording lenses.

Charlie's erasure from the text of *Pictures in the Dark* sets up a dynamic concern with the subject that is hidden behind his camera. To some extent this concern parallels Peter's loss of identity when he metamorphoses into the otter, which is discussed in terms of escape and stasis in Chapter One. If, as Jackson suggests, there are subversive epistemological possibilities when 'objects are not readily appropriated through the look' because knowledge of the 'eye/I' is undermined, then both Peter's ever-changing shape and Charlie's visual absence indicate fantastic foci *and* anxiety about individual identity. This somewhat paradoxical situation can alternatively be framed by appropriating the deconstructionist concept of putting language 'under erasure'. By erasing or crossing out a problematic term or idea it is shown to be inaccurate and yet still impossible to do without.[18] In the same way that a word under erasure is both there and not there—interrogated but still made use of—characters behind a camera or lens are crossed out from the visual or active parts of the narrative, but must ontologically remain fixed (as the wielder of that camera) and are in fact under greater scrutiny as individuals because of the erasure. Charlie's regular place in the text behind a camera lens posits him as a film-maker who creates with his camera, but also a spectator who is both fascinated and fascinating. Christine Metz argues that the spectator of a film is 'cast in the role of "invisible subject"' through their identification with the film camera (cited in Willeman 210) and, despite its invisibility, such a subject is still at the centre of the narrative.

A more literal kind of scrutiny of the 'seer' occurs in another of Lois Duncan's novels. In *The Eyes of Karen Connors* (1984; titled *The Third Eye* in America), the eponymous heroine gradually discovers that she has psychic powers or an 'inner eye' which reveals to her the traumatic experiences of children in danger. For example, when a young boy she is looking after disappears Karen 'sees', 'smells' and 'senses' his location in the trunk of her boyfriend's car. Throughout the course of the novel her visions become more detailed and evocative, so that the narrative evolves into one that is shared between the teenage protagonist and the missing or dead children she can sense. In particular, Carla Sanchez's final moments drowning in a local river get played out over and over again, like a looped reel of film: 'Karen threw herself down on to the tumbled bed and closed her eyes. As if on summons, the backs of her lids sprang to life like twin movie screens displaying a sequence of overlapping visions. [. . .] Icy currents closed upon her, and, tumbling choking, gasping, she was swept into oblivion' (*The Eyes of Karen Connors* 69, 71). Karen is cast as a spectator who cannot avoid watching terrible events (much like the faded Paul who, as we shall see in the next chapter, cannot close his invisible eyelids), and these events begin to take over her conscious and unconscious life, threatening to overwhelm her own sense of self and send her into 'oblivion'.

At other moments, Karen's psychic powers appear to position her as director of events, if not quite behind the camera then certainly composing what others see. When Ron Wilson—the young police officer in charge of cases of missing children—asks her to help him locate Carla, she becomes gradually aware of the route they must take in order to find her and guides him there, despite not knowing the terrain, 'issuing directions without reason' (60). She is able to reconstruct Carla's movements and tell the story: 'She fell. [. . .] Off the big rock. [. . .] She was bending over, trying to get the legs of her jeans pulled up. The rock was slippery' (64). These seemingly active aspects of Karen's personality—her ability to transform her own fantastic visions into images for others to see and use—ultimately offer Karen the chance to construct her own identity as out of the ordinary, and she eventually embraces her role as psychic. Initially, however, this power to see performs the opposite function and essentially reduces Karen's subjectivity purely to her vision. For example, her involvement in two cases of missing children (her babysitting adventure and her solving of the Carla Sanchez case) gain the attention of the small-town American press, which is enchanted by the concept of her supernatural abilities. Soon she is plagued by desperate and hopeful parents of missing children: 'Each afternoon when she arrived home from school, she was greeted by a mailbox filled with desperation. She could almost feel the agony of the contents burning her hands when she handled the unopened envelopes' (77). Although naturally compassionate and sympathetic to these heartfelt pleas, Karen is distraught by the fact that she is being defined by what she sees, not who she is: indeed, she goes so far as to say to those parents who phone her, 'I'm not what you think I am' (78). To be identified as a pair of eyes—in a way to be defined through metonymy so that 'the eyes of Karen Connors' *equal* Karen Connors—provokes an anxious descent into identity crisis.

It is surely significant in terms of general patterns of representing adolescence that Karen's fears about her lack of personality, which she articulates by classing herself as a 'nonentity', are strongly linked to memories of her early childhood, stories her mother tells her of her own childhood, and—more incredibly—visions of her future daughter. Mrs Connors continuously compares Karen's social awkwardness to her own sparkling teenage years and, not surprisingly, Karen feels pressurised to date, join the Prom Committee and generally fit in with her classmates. By the end of the novel, however, Mrs Connors' narrative of adolescent success is revealed to be false, since she too was set apart because of her psychic abilities. Karen's real site of identity achievement becomes not her internalised mother, whose adolescent identity is falsified, but her own future daughter, who appears to her in moments when Karen's (and therefore her child's) life is endangered. This daughter figure has 'hair the texture that Karen's had been in childhood' (195) and she acts as a return to Karen's own self in infancy. Thus, the connection Karen feels with this phantom little girl simultaneously enacts the kind of regression theorists like Blos see as essential in the formation of a mature subjectivity, and tests Karen's growing sense of maternal responsibility. In both cases, however, her personal identity and tangible status as adolescent are obscured by outside forces of mother and daughter: it is as if her fantastic second sight precludes her from being able to successfully look inwards for most of the novel.

Karen Connors deals with disappeared children, and Charlie disappears from his story. It is clear that forms of vanishing, including the impotent experience of dreaming, can be crucial to the construction of adolescent individualism

Dreams and Invisibility: The Self under Erasure

In Cormier's novel, Paul's actions are primarily observational and, like the cinema spectator or the narrator of a literary dream vision, he is a participant in events only so far as he wanders through a dreamscape, rather than significantly affecting the action or other characters. In the fade, Paul finds it impossible (at first) to intervene in the episodes he witnesses and, moreover, his whole body becomes inconsequential and dreamlike. When he fades so that he can spy on his friends the Emersons in their grand house, his movements are phantom-like and his capabilities based on dream actions: 'As I drifted across the lawn, the cold of the fade raced through my body but I ignored it, feeling light and airy, as if I could leap to the highest point of the house and stand on the topmost turret' (99). Several of Margaret Mahy's young adult novels, which I shall discuss in the next chapter, also evoke dreams through their strange narratives and fluid style. The sequence in which Laura becomes a witch in *The Changeover* is dreamy and hallucinogenic, and in *24 Hours* (2000) the protagonist relates a type of dream vision in much the same way as Paul. The tone is also similar to non-teenage magic realist texts such as Neil Gaiman's *Coraline* (2002), where a young girl passes through a nightmarish world mirroring her own, or Kazuo Ishiguro's *The Unconsoled* (1995), which is narrated by Mr Ryder, the ultimate passive dreamer type who is totally impotent to affect the series of events he experiences in the novel. Dream narratives partly negate the dreamer or narrator by placing them in the background of any action; but they also foreground the individual experience of dreaming that the protagonist goes through. Despite the strength of Jungian dream analysis, which stresses shared motifs that illuminate the 'collective consciousness', dreaming is also highly personal and unique to the individual dreamer. I have argued elsewhere that individual dreamtime remains inaccessible to others (Waller, '*Fade* and the Lone Teenager'), and fantastic realist texts that resemble dream narratives therefore focus on individual dreamers and their struggle for a sense of their own ethereal subjectivity. In the case of *Fade*, this struggle against insubstantiality is played out through the specific trope of invisibility.

When the fantastic trope of invisibility enters the realist world of Frenchtown, it provides a visual gap in what is already a narrative of spectral subjectivity. The original mysterious family photograph shows a blank space where Adelard should have been standing, and this represents what cannot be seen (Adelard's fantastic fade) and what Paul desires (to be like Adelard, to be invisible). It would be impossible to discuss terms of desire and erasure without some acknowledgement of psychoanalytic discourse and Jackson provides a useful point of reference. She offers explanations for metamorphosis or dissolving in fantastic literature, describing it as a modern desire for 'entropy', which has replaced religious or transcendental ideals and which offers instead 'a zero point, a space of non-being, an absence' (Jackson 78). According to Freud, entropy is the opposite of energy, and is partly a movement towards childhood solipsism where everything is fused together. If this argument were closely adhered to it would suggest that Paul's invisibility engenders precisely the opposite of adolescent individual subjectivity, and that the novel deals more with themes of early childhood and communal identity. However, Paul's position as observing eye and erased person serves to highlight the anxiety expressed over his apparent loss of identity rather than being complicit in a movement towards complete disintegration of self. Paul himself laments his own dissolving body, as well as his unravelling sense of individuality. As an adult who no longer has control over the fade in the latter parts of the novel, he explains how he has to rush from company when he feels the onset of invisibility, sometimes catching a glimpse in a mirror of his body disintegrating, and is afterwards 'left limp with exhaustion, without appetite, listless, with no direction or ambition' (166). The teenager who was resolved to become a cowboy hero instead becomes the invisible man, and this results in 'a fragmentation or dissolution of self' that works against humanist concepts of the self, according to McCallum (although she is quick to point out that 'the representation of transgressive behaviour frequently has a conservative social function', and that novels such as *Fade* breach the boundaries of adolescent fiction in order for them to be modified once more through extra-textual conservative reactions towards those transgressions, including media response, 122–123). Again, it is useful to consider Paul as 'under erasure' in deconstructive terms; he is both crossed out of the text by his invisibility, but through this uncommon erasure he is also interrogated as an individual more thoroughly, and his search for self becomes more intense. Although the fantastic elements of this novel test the supremacy of the individual self, they do not destroy it.

Images of seeing and not seeing in *Fade*, *Pictures in the Dark* and *The Eyes of Karen Connors*, then, create a complex dynamic where perception and appearance both destabilise and compose identity. The adolescent heroes are at risk of being erased—through invisibility in Cormier's work, surveillance in Cross's and engulfing visions in Duncan's—but the more these characters seem to physically disappear, the more they become the focus of narratives of individualism. *Fade* certainly sets up a more radical portrayal of adolescent identity than the other texts discussed in this chapter, because it thoroughly explores the idea of selves under erasure. And yet, in the same way that discourse cannot move beyond the essential term 'identity' and must continue to employ it to describe modern selfhood, so these novels continue to prioritise the self even as they scrutinise the very concept. While protagonists remain 'crossed out' they represent the shifting and uncertain progress of adolescence through its various stages and tasks, but as they come under the lens themselves, they are revealed as being in search of unity and coherence. The erasure is not embraced but feared.

A Rare Bird: Identity Achieved

How can the inherently isolated adolescents of fantastic realism confidently assert their identity within the context of constant threats from multiple subjectivities, dissolution into madness and erasure? The narrator and main character in *Owl in Love* (by Patrice Kindl) makes a valiant attempt. Owl Tycho is fourteen-years-old and part-human, part-owl, a condition she has inherited from her ancestors and which she happily accepts in its entirety. The novel follows Owl during her double life, in which she hunts at night and attends the local high school during the day. In particular, it recounts her first experiences of falling in love with her science teacher, Mr Lindstrom. Unlike other shape-shifting novels examined in this book, *Owl in Love* does not portray an ordinary teenager in her sudden discovery of her metamorphic ability. Indeed, Owl sees nothing odd in her condition and describes it in simple terms: 'I am Owl. It is my name as well as my nature [. . .] By day I am an ordinary girl' (*Owl in Love* 4). The only issue that concerns Owl about her duality is the fact that it might impede her imagined love affair with Mr Lindstrom; it does not entail any initial alarm about her humanity or identity (in contrast to *Pictures in the Dark*, for instance). Owl is, in fact, proud of the difference her metamorphosis produces. She describes her singularity with satisfaction and does not show any fear or loss of self: 'My fellow students at Wildewood Senior High have always thought me strange, odd. They are right. I am very different from them. My blood, for instance, is black, while theirs is red' (5). Like a number of other fantastic teenage protagonists, this heroine labels herself, allowing her fantastic traits to shape her identity. Similarly, Sandra eventually but defiantly becomes the 'bitch' in *Lady: my life as a bitch*. Instead of being produced as deviant through the negative labelling of dominant others, these characters appropriate labels to celebrate their individuality or subvert conventional representations, and relate their fantastic difference to individual excellence rather than a problematic identity.

Kindl's protagonist acts rather like Fevvers in Angela Carter's adult magic realist novel *Nights at the Circus* (1984). Both characters share the obvious attributes of being bird-women, but they also both display an initial self-confidence and self-absorption. In *Nights at the Circus*, Fevvers' fantastic independence contrasts with Walser's nervous masculinity to bring to the fore issues of female performance and power. In the context of teenage fiction, such confidence signals a specifically *adolescent* disposition. Owl dismisses anything typically human that her teenage classmates do as ridiculous, arguing that eating bread ('made of a paste of grasses and greases swollen with the gassy emissions of yeast plants', 11) is unnatural, that the majority of cosmetic companies in

America 'seemed to be unprepared for a complexion like mine' (56) and wondering why her friend Dawn takes the bus rather than walking (or flying) home. She is similarly baffled by pure owl behaviour, describing an older screech owl's mating ritual directed towards her as like 'a justice of the Supreme Court performing a striptease' (39). In other words, for most of the novel Owl considers her own conduct and composition to be ideal and of the utmost importance. Her fantastic identity is not only more interesting than that of 'normal' (realistic) teenage characters, it also appears to be unique and therefore allows Owl to presume that her problems are utterly unlike anyone else's. The inherent irony evident in certain episodes—such as when Owl congratulates herself on her human tact and restraint when she controls her desire to eat Dawn's pet hamster—implies that this adolescent egocentrism is highlighted in order to humorously encourage less solipsistic alternatives for teenage behaviour.

Eventually, Owl discovers she is not actually unique but shares her part-owl part-human nature with Mr Lindstrom's son, David, or 'Houle'. Her response to this discovery is positive: 'We're birds of a feather, and we'll be flocking together from now on. We are not your kind, and you are not ours. I take responsibility for Houle' (192). Part of her delight comes from the opportunity to share her expertise in being a wereowl with the inexperienced boy, but another reason is the prospect of a satisfying heterosexual and homosocial relationship: the satisfaction of a human boy/girl relationship and of an animal owl/owl bond. *Owl in Love* presents a protagonist at one end of the spectrum of fantasy as identity. Owl is certain of her shape-shifting nature at the novel's outset and is only forced to consider the strangeness of her individuality—and its potential to isolate her from her fellow humans (or part-humans)—at the point of closure. The narrative irony, as well as rhetorical touches such as naming the school 'Wildewood', place the text in the realm of magic realism as much as fantastic realism, and demand that the reader understand the framework of adolescent egocentrism parodied through the character of Owl.

While all the fantastic tropes under consideration in this chapter provide ample opportunities for individual identity to be fragmented, problematised and revealed to be a playful or unstable entity, fantastic realistic novels are most likely to produce a different version of selfhood. Fantastic structures and themes are employed in a manner that parallels conventional discursive frameworks of identity, and which reproduce the demands and fears that exist within existing discourses of adolescence. An individualistic identity is set up as the ideal and any attack through the threat of uncertainty or erasure cannot be sustained.

This is in direct contrast to a number of more experimental texts for teenagers, which use fantasy in a more carnivalised manner and which stress the concept of playful postmodern identities rather than a unified and individualistic self. Cultural feminism, amongst other discourses, has explored the link between fantastic literature and playful constructions of identity, suggesting that types of fiction can provide ludic space for readers to escape their material positions. Janice Radway and Imelda Whelehan, for example, both develop approaches to popular fiction that allow the exploration of pleasure as a motive for reading. They argue that reading genre novels or 'trash' can provide a kind of fantasy realm for women to reinvent their limited roles within patriarchy, as well as an active practice interacting with, interrogating, or even rejecting texts. Although these debates about readership and response are beyond the scope of this study, the trope of a fantastic playful space can usefully be applied to textual analysis of teen fiction as well. Lucy Armitt's theoretical perspective is that fantasy suggests a regression into childhood play and a carnivalesque licence to go beyond the rational bounds of realism (*Theorising the Fantastic* 4–6). In a number of teenage texts, fantasy spills over from the experience of the individual teenage protagonist into a wider context, either within the narrative or into metatextual references. Aidan Chambers' *Breaktime* (1978), Geraldine McCaughrean's *A Pack of Lies* (1988) and *Kit's Wilderness* by David Almond (1999) are examples of fantasy invading other aspects of experience within the narrative or outside the text. For instance, Kit has visions of ghosts and time-slipped people from prehistoric times, but although these visions initially appear solely to him, there is a point in the novel where they seep into the novel's material world and transform it magically. In a more postmodern version of magic realism, the characters of Ditto in *Breaktime* and Ailsa in *A Pack of Lies* are problematised through the narrative structure itself. Ditto writes an account of his week in answer to the charge from his friend that 'literature is a GAME', and the implication at the end of the novel is that he and his friend are just made-up characters in a story. Ailsa is charmed by a young man called MCC Berkshire from Reading who tells stories about her mother's antique shop. The final chapter reveals that Berkshire is a shy bookish teenager who has written himself into his own novel where his characters (Ailsa and her mother) become 'too real'.

Teenage fantastic realism resists the more radical constructions of identity that are offered through post-structural fiction like this and in feminist, queer or psychoanalytic texts or readings. Armitt follows a similar line of argument to Jackson in suggesting that fantasy assaults the unity of identity, and that fantastic tropes (such as the ghost) remind us that 'only by moving beyond the ideologically-constrained realms of patriarchal reality are new and renewing avenues opened up' (*Contemporary Women's Fiction* 106). Fantastic realism generally refuses to participate in this project, instead presenting the fantastic as a temporary test of plural and fragmenting selves that acts to *return* adolescence to those ideologically constrained realms. In doing this perhaps the genre plays a part in wider social and cultural contexts, where capitalist and individualist impulses have dominated much Anglo-American ideology since the 1980s, fetishising personal desires, success and development.

It is clear that other broadly conservative drives concerning gender roles and expectations have also shaped fantastic realism. In the texts examined in this chapter, female characters are regularly represented in terms of madness or lack of control. Moreover, as they overcome these problematic characteristics and reach a point of unified self, the natural progression is typically to enter into a conventional heterosexual relationship that will continue to 'complete' their identity into adulthood. In contrast, the male protagonists considered in this discussion do not reach a stable identity at the end of their narratives and therefore are not ultimately constructed through their projected mature sexual roles. The next chapter goes on to extend debates surrounding gender in its examination of adolescence and social agency. It asks what active potential fantastic realism provides for its teenage protagonists, and whether the genre portrays teenagers as empowered through the radical possibilities of fantasy or limited through traditional gender expectations and constrained by the conventional teenage fiction form.

Chapter Three
Fantasies of Empowerment and Agency: Gender and the Burden of Responsibility

So far, this book has followed the teenager through development and identity achievement, arguing that conservative themes found in discourses of adolescence also persist in fantastic realism. The next question is what kind of social being does the adolescent become and what possibilities do they present to the world? Is adolescence represented as a shifting space where existing social structures can be resisted and rebuilt, or do cultural conventions play a larger part in shaping perceptions of young men and women? This chapter examines the frameworks of social 'empowerment' and 'agency', and their significance for gendered representations of adolescence. It is structured through notions of social identities, resistance and reintegration, and draws primarily on the field of subcultural theory. It will also engage with critical debates on the liberatory function and status of fantasy. Fantasy can, for instance, be read as a radical and resistant genre that challenges the dominant ideologies represented through realism. Its fantastic tropes (such as magic powers and gifts) might represent allegories for the material and psychological opportunities available to teenagers. Alternative forms of criticism have found fantasy to be less successful in portraying subjective agency, and it can be argued that fantastic metaphors are as likely to *encode* prevailing anxieties over age or gender or fragmenting identities as they are to *question* them.

The main body of this chapter traces the transitional and temporary aspects of adolescent identity formation that have already been established, but considers them in new contexts. The first context relates to psychoanalytic dynamics and concerns the teenager's interaction with adult power, particularly in the shape of parent/child relations. Discussion then turns to two specific fantastic tropes that portray more symbolic aspects of adolescent empowerment. The superhero offers idealised forms of masculine agency while witchcraft represents a glamorous and empowering fantasy for teenage girls. In each case it is necessary to ask whether these fantasies are as empowering as they first appear, in exploring the potentially radical and volatile nature of adolescence.

Social Theories of Adolescence

Social Agency

According to Simon Frith the social is crucial when discussing young people: 'The task of the sociologist of youth is to show how particular societies organise the process of growing up. For us, youth is not simply an age group, but the social organisation of an age group' (2).[1] Subcultural theory is one way of describing this social organisation. It examines how teenagers respond to the adult public world and how they form a sense of their adolescent selves through negotiating space and performing or playing with identity. Early American work in the field, particularly that emerging from what became known as the Chicago School, set out the theory that modern adolescence forms an extended and drawn-out period between childhood and adulthood, resulting in disaffectedness amongst individuals who then attempt to find solutions to their anxieties and uncertainties in youth culture and gang life. Theorists including S.N. Eisenstadt, David Matza and A.K. Cohen are therefore primarily concerned with groups that are explicitly deviant and that offer 'inappropriate' expressions of 'subterranean' values. Such approaches locate adolescence as a 'problem' and concentrate on aspects of the spectacular, such as extravagant fashion, music and lifestyle identities (punk, goth and skater, for example), outsider status, delinquency and violent gang behaviour. Labelling theory is a useful entry into understanding these methods of dealing with adolescence. Successfully applied to social theory by Howard Becker in the early 1960s, the idea of social labelling argues that deviance is created by society and its explicit and implicit rules, and that '[t]he deviant is one to whom that label has successfully been applied; deviant behaviour is behaviour that people so label' (9). Teenagers are caught up in a complex web of behaviour and labelling, so that what is described as delinquent is partly fixed as such due to its subcultural status and position outside of the normal rules of society. It might be argued that at adolescence individuals are less concerned by mainstream adult judgement and more interested in the labels they invent or appropriate themselves.

Certainly a major strand of subcultural research would argue for this active appropriation of labels. The publication of Stuart Hall and Tony Jefferson's *Resistance through Rituals* in 1976 brought together working papers from Birmingham's Centre for Contemporary Cultural Studies (CCCS), which examined British youth culture and its subcultural basis. It has been described as the 'classic radical text on youth cultures from the 1970s' (Griffin 9) and its overarching assertion is that subcultures and the rituals of style, leisure and behaviour are ways of expressing identity, as well as challenging existing ideology and power structures. Subcultures provide increased agency for adolescents in the cultural sphere (as part of a group and as individual participants), where more often there is little or no power to be had. A number of British sociologists and cultural critics have followed Hall and Jefferson and produced work on the subcultural patterns of young people (sometimes referred to as teenagers or adolescents but mainly subsumed under the broader term 'youth').

Like the majority of early sociologists in this field, Mike Brake focuses on style and leisure, arguing that these arenas reveal more about how teenagers organise themselves than family life, education or occupation. Brake maintains that subcultural forms are more than a mere adolescent phase of rebellion, instead claiming that they 'arise as attempts to resolve collectively experienced problems arising from contradictions in the social structure' (vii). In other words, subcultures act to produce ways of being for young people that are more meaningful than the dominant culture of their parents and of institutions such as schools, the legal system and mainstream media. Frith agrees that subcultures provide a solution to the problematic gap between conventional society and the relatively new cultural figure of the teenager, although he prefers a reading that prioritises class disparities rather than age difference, stressing the differences between a working-class sense of solidarity and a middle-class individualism and casualness. Frith points out that everyday economic matters (such as unemployment, particularly in the 1970s and 1980s) also encourage aspirations of cultural power that can be played out in subcultures. While he argues that sociologists have exaggerated the extent of deviance among young people he still retains the concept of adolescence as a 'social problem' of sorts, but for him: '[t]he youth "problem" lies [. . .] in young people's marginal status' and 'youth culture eases the resulting anxieties and uncertainties' (Frith 21).

Theoretical interest in teenagers deviating from cultural norms in a problematic and very public way is echoed in those media representations of youth that worry about the state of modern youth. Stanley Cohen's *Folk Devils and Moral Panics* (1972) provides an interesting account of media reactions to youth subcultures in the 1960s, but panicked responses to youth culture are still very much current, as demonstrated by continuing media coverage of gun crime and violence amongst adolescents, and surveys which demonstrate rising teenage pregnancies, alcohol and drug use or weapon ownership. One newspaper editorial serves as an example, offering as it does a knowing comment on the results of a survey about teenage behaviour: 'These [statistics] will be seized upon and slotted into a narrative of gang culture and lawless teenagers which has already been widely publicised' (Bunting 15). A counterpart to these professional and popular anxieties can also be found in the concerns of early teenage fiction. As outlined in the Introduction, realism has been the prevailing genre for young adult fiction, with the 'problem novel' being particularly successful in relating stories based around topical issues of concern for teenagers and the adults involved with them: delinquency, drugs, pregnancy, and social or familial crises such as divorce and death. While the CCCS was developing a critical interest in *youth* subcultures, this form of literature became commercially viable, putting some of their key areas of research into narrative form. The two discourses appear to arise from shared socio-cultural concerns with adolescence as a new and energetic social 'class'. S.E. Hinton's *The Outsiders* (1967) is a classic example of how fiction to some extent mirrors the anxieties at the forefront of critical research as well as general public perception. It is narrated by Ponyboy, who is a member of the 'Greasers', a gang of young men who follow strict style and behavioural rules which isolate them from both adult authority and the privileged classes represented by the rival gang of 'Socials' or 'Socs'. Their language, fashions and leisure activities can happily be read as a form of 'resistance through ritual': a rejection of the conventions of the dominant ideology and a proud display of subcultural belonging. Ponyboy explains:

> We're poorer than the Socs and the middle class. I reckon we're wilder too [...] Greasers are almost like hoods; we steal things and drive old souped-up cars and hold up petrol stations and have a gang fight once in a while [...] we wear our hair long and dress in blue jeans and T-shirts, or leave our shirt-tails out and wear leather jackets and tennis shoes or boots. (*The Outsiders* 8–9)

The gang culture appears to provide a useful way for Ponyboy and his brothers or friends to act out a shared identity and to empower themselves in a world that does not offer its young people much in the way of opportunity. The novel ultimately results in conflict, however, when a fight with the Socs ends fatally and Ponyboy has to go on the run, questioning his role as a segregated Greaser. The subculture gives Ponyboy confidence but it is dangerously delinquent, and this representation of the dual nature of subculture reflects, confirms, and to a certain extent helps to produce a social theory that focuses on the spectacular and problematic aspects of adolescence. The fact that *The Outsiders* was written by Hinton when she was sixteen years old and was published a year later further links the realist novel to contemporaneous theory of adolescence, as it offers what can be seen as an 'authentic' voice of youth and can be used (anomalously, perhaps) as empirical evidence of what it is like to be a teenager.[2] Of course, adult authors create similar voices and characters.[3] It might be argued that sociological interest in youth subcultures and youth problems emerges from the same discursive field that produces teenage social realism narrating subcultural experiences.

Subcultural theories of youth are partially aware of their own fictivity and the imaginative nature of their adolescent subject matter. To begin with, the concept of a youth subculture itself both draws on and creates film, pop music, fashion and literature to provide images and labels for the punk rocker, the biker, the hippy, the goth, the raver, the skater and so on. Entry into one of these groups is an artificial process of becoming a character in a fiction and it is also performative; teenagers consciously decide to assume a particular group identity and act that identity out in order to challenge the conventional power structures that partly control them. The process involves what anthropologist Dick Hebdige would term 'bricolage';[4] that is, youth subcultures adopt cultural items from the mainstream, such as fashion and music, and break them down in order to reform, reorder and recontextualise them into new meanings. According to Brake, this 'vibrant montage' 'reveal[s] much of the interstices and hidden space of the "underside" of youth and its problems' (158). It also confronts the conservative culture of powerful adults by using its own terms and inverting them.

Theorists attempt to describe this sense of personal invention, recreation and defiance using notably creative terms. Both Brake and Frith follow Hall and Jefferson in describing subcultures as a kind of 'magical' solution to social problems, a 'magical resistance' and a way of 'casting spells' against the dominant social structures. While these details of terminology are not critical, they do point to developments in subcultural theory which posit adolescent identities as a *performative solution* to inequalities in society, rather than as a manifestation of traditional youth *problems*. Such a shift might also help to situate teenage fantastic realism as part of a wider consensual attempt to understand adolescence through fantastic and imaginative frameworks. Teenage realism that focuses on social problems or gang identity is not quite able to represent the magical possibilities of performative agency through subcultural forms. Fantastic realism, however, offers a number of metaphors and tropes such as magic, special gifts and witchcraft that portray teenagers as empowered and dynamic.

Gender and Society

These fantastic roles also allow space for a specifically *female* potential, issuing in a concern with gender issues that emerges in later work in the field of subcultures. Such work challenges the early paradigms in subcultural models and searches for alternative ways of describing teenagers' interaction with the social. Influenced by feminist, postmodern and deconstructivist impulses, cultural critic Angela McRobbie questions subcultural theory's emphasis on male experience in the public sphere. McRobbie suggests that girls have been ignored in most subcultural theory, and that while boys can make temporary 'flights' from boredom or the 'romance trap' through their subcultures, girls find it more difficult to escape. Female cultural space is as essential in resisting existing ideology and McRobbie claims that girls create it in their much more restricted sphere of domesticity, through role-play, fantasy and ephemeral interaction with the public through magazines, film and music. Indeed, according to her, the expression of cultural identity 'happens as much around the breakfast table and in the bedroom as in the school and the workplace' (McRobbie 'Settling Accounts with Subculture' 22). Constructing fantastic selves and fantastic spaces in this way returns discourse to concepts of liminality, which I have touched upon in previous chapters. McRobbie argues that the magazine-based subculture that is prevalent amongst girls allows teenagers to experience adult romance, sex and relationships vicariously through pin-ups and problem pages. It is a safe stage, where power can be manipulated and ideologies resisted without recourse to the material world of power relations. Feminist critics, including McRobbie, indicate the powerful potential of fiction as a strategy for escaping patriarchal systems. McRobbie argues that private fantasies or daydreams are as much part of reality as any more obvious act of resistance, such as political action. Her study of female subcultures in the 1980s develops this view, arguing that the fantasy life of teenage 'teeny-boppers' negotiates a space for them to construct their own identity without having to participate in the street life of other, more male-orientated subcultures (McRobbie 'Dance and Social Fantasy').[5]

Brake's theory of leisure-based subcultures further supports the idea that youth subcultures are simply a liminal or indeed developmental 'phase'; he not only argues that participating in a subculture is a way for teenagers to enter into the social world, but he also suggests that any radical attempt to move away from the dominant culture will soon be redundant. Either the subculture itself will become part of the mainstream (as extreme fashion items move into the high street, for example) or the adolescent participant will return to more conventional modes of behaviour; according to him, subcultures are 'nearly always a temporary solution' (Brake vii). Frith also notes that his theorisation of youth subcultures as ideological tools may not tally with teenagers' own ideas about their experiences. He admits that members of a youth subculture might not see themselves as 'winning cultural space', being much more accepting of their ultimate place in society than he might wish (*Sociology of Youth* 45–47).

In this respect it seems that after a brief period of experimentation, fantasy and individuality, the adolescent is likely to *return* to much more conservative modes of behaviour and mainstream social and cultural patterns. Rather than continue to exert power through challenging dominant ideologies, adolescents are perceived as eventually subscribing to mainstream adult concerns, such as jobs, stable relationships, conventional social and gender roles and style and conduct. Adolescence, evidently, is the last valid space for fantastic empowerment before the responsibilities of adulthood commence. This sociological insight supports work in both psycho-social and psychoanalytic models, where development is always towards successful completion of adolescent tasks and the progression into adulthood. These dominant models rarely construct adolescence as being a legitimate, stimulating or sustainable state in itself, nor do they suggest ways that teenagers can be represented without reference to their future adult selves.

Teenage Power

Power is political. The terms 'empowerment' and 'agency' are most often found in politicised discourses of minority or disadvantaged groups: feminism, postcolonialism or gay and lesbian studies, for example. Children and teenagers have more recently been located alongside such minorities by advocates whose demands for empowerment range from a relatively modest request to recognise that young people constitute a discrete and generally weak subgroup within society (James, Jenks and Prout 30–31), to more radical 'emancipatory' theories that are committed to 'understanding the situation of babies and children from a first-person point of view, exploring the contingent forces that block children's full emergence as expressive subjects, and discovering how these forces can be overcome' (Galbraith 188; de Mause). For young children, such emancipation must take place through the actions of understanding adults, but in the case of adolescents it might be argued that individuals are able to find their own way of taking control or resisting dominant systems of power.

The concept of resistance is crucial in discourses of adolescent power, being most visible and most clearly critiqued in those discussions of teenage subcultures I have just outlined. Ideas of resistance also indicate some of the problems inherent in using the term 'empowerment' in a political context. Many feminist scholars, in particular, argue that it is increasingly rare for the term 'empowerment' to be associated with concepts of resistance to existing ideologies; instead it connotes individual, interpersonal and relational levels of power. For instance, Ellen Riordan suggests that when 'empowerment' is employed in reference to teenage girls and third-wave feminism, the 'rhetoric of empowerment can unwittingly advance an individual sense of entitlement rather than pose a challenge to patriarchal and capitalist structures' (282). She explains that the use of the term in popular discourses such as self-help books (and, we can extrapolate, girls' magazines) helps to locate the act of empowerment in consumerist and individualist practices that encourage women and girls to concentrate on their own desires and well-being, rather than push for collective action to change the way all power is structured. Riordan prefers the term 'agency', which implies individual action and resistance that can work on a collective and political level.[6]

With this distinction in view, in this chapter I am concerned with both empowerment *and* agency as they are represented through fantastic attributes and actions. Does fantastic realism provide an arena for adolescent *agency* in its politicised sense, and does the use of fantasy subvert or question ways that teenage protagonists interact with the rest of society in the realist elements of the novels? It can be argued that adolescence is not politicised in the same way as race, gender, class or sexuality, and that because it is a temporary state rather than a label for life, it is hardly necessary to seek out large-scale structural changes in social attitudes towards young people. Adolescents, moreover, may be represented as *empowered* precisely because the term has connotations of the private, the individual and the popular. As Chapter Two indicated, fantastic realism often prioritises personal relationships over the wider social realm; and personal empowerment is clearly part of this individualistic discourse, but the form might also offer much the same magical and temporary space for adolescent agency that sociologists have recognised as functioning in subcultural practice.

What, then, are the possibilities open to contemporary adolescents in fictional worlds, and in what ways are teenagers *dis*empowered? Clarke, Hall, Jefferson and Roberts argue that youth serves as a metaphor for the workings of society:

> 'Youth' appeared as an emergent category in post-war Britain, one of the most striking and visible manifestations of social change in the period. [...] Above all, Youth played an important role as a cornerstone in the construction of understandings, interpretations and quasi-explanations *about* the period. (Clarke et al. 9)

This approach to adolescence not only suggests that young people become the central public, political and creative figures that shape and run the world of tomorrow, but that their behaviour and status is also crucial in economic, cultural and social spheres today. Lucy Rollin's cultural history of the teenager points to the huge potential for spending by adolescents, and the inevitable attention this generates in a capitalist society:

> With the increased spending power of teens in the affluent Eighties [...] major industries, such as clothing, cosmetics, music, automobiles, and sports, fastened their attentions on the teen market with greedy enthusiasm, hiring marketers to poll them endlessly to determine their tastes and habits. (271)

Not only are numerous elements of modern life directed towards adolescent consumers, Rollin suggests, but those adolescents are also powerful in being able to sway popular or mass culture through their desires and demands. On the other hand, on an individual level such power may not be immediately evident and, in practical terms, the adolescent is constrained by social, educational, political and legal expectations. Physical changes at puberty also mean that the teenager's body is often represented as 'out of control', trapped by hormones and defined by gender and by sexual or emotional needs.[7]

Similar conflicts between power and powerlessness reside in the site of fiction itself. Peter Hunt astutely recognises that '[w]hatever the tone or the voice, children's literature cannot cease to be a site of power imbalance' (*Children's Literature* 15). Fiction for young people is indeed fraught with unequal power relations, due to the nature of its production (controlled by adults) and its inherent ideological content, which most often reflects the position of relative disempowerment that children and teenagers inhabit as citizens in Western society. Barbara Wall, Jacqueline Rose and John Stephens, amongst others, have scrutinised the author/reader relationship and noted some of these naturalised hierarchies that exist in children's literature. The adult creates and controls narrative, constructs and positions the child character and implied narratee, and imparts information to the compliant reader. Literature for children and young people differs from other fields that are defined by a shared positioning in their political and ideological intent. Whilst women's fiction, black poetry or working-class drama on the whole aim to speak through, or on behalf of, their chosen subjects, and are often characterised by politicised agendas of recognition and self-representation, children's and young adult fiction is produced *for* that readership with an external sense of what is good or useful or entertaining. In other words, teenage fiction is most likely to portray *adult* impressions of adolescence that are shaped by prevailing discourses and which perhaps dictate that power and agency reside in experience and wisdom rather than youthful instability. Even discourses produced directly out of youth cultures, such as rebellion or nonsense, are in danger of being undermined as forces for power. Mike Brake argues that subcultures are limited because they only ever offer temporary and symbolic solutions; ultimately '[y]outh groups [. . .] do not seek to change society, but to re-enter it' (26).

Despite their radical appearance, subcultures can thus be described as reactionary in their adhesion to existing social and cultural expectations. Teenage fantastic realism employs aspects of subcultures through an explicitly fantastic mode, constructing social identities as fantastic gifts or powers, but it is possible that, as a way of representing adolescent agency or empowerment, subculture can remain restricted. I would like to now turn briefly to fantasy itself, and consider the subversive or limiting nature of fantastic representation.

Fantasy as Agency

Lucie Armitt points out that most writers and critics of fantasy feel the need to defend their chosen genre against accusations of 'mere escapism', and of being low-brow, infantile or irrelevant (*Theorising the Fantastic* 1–2). Fantastic fiction is often dismissed as overly stylised, guilty of locking characters and readers into binaries of good and evil or masculine and feminine, and remaking existing social inequalities in other worlds or bodies. In addition, fantasy is charged with wilfully evading concerns that are central to the everyday world, unacceptably championing the personal and apolitical, and offering easy 'magical' solutions to complex literary or social narratives. As a counter to this position, John Fiske upholds the case for fantasy, complaining that too often it is excluded from considerations of power or dismissed from a cultural or social agenda: 'Underlying this is the notion that *representation* has a social dimension, whereas *escapism* is merely personal flight into fantasy' (317). He points to the fact that, all too often, realist representation is seen as a way of making sense of the real world and acting as a site of struggle for power, while fantasy is considered to be too far removed from the everyday to be political in any sense.

By classing fantasy as 'mere escapism', critics actually stumble upon a crucial emblematic function: escape can provide an important point of resistance or a method of denying power to the pursuer. Indeed, in Chapter One I explored the ways that metamorphosis tropes, for example, provide teenage characters with strategies for evading normal adolescent growth and resisting the dominant discourse of developmentalism. This view, which acknowledges fantasy as an alternative way of making sense of reality, finds support from the fantasy writer Ursula Le Guin, who claims that 'the fantasist [. . .] may be talking as seriously as any sociologist—and a great deal more directly—about human life as it is lived, and as it might be lived, and as it ought to be lived' (3). Author Jill Paton Walsh argues even more forcibly that because the reader is required to work hard in order to apply metaphorical meanings from the fantastic text to their own material position, there must be an explicit and robust link between fantasy and real experience. Fiske interrogates these notions of the 'personal flight into fantasy' by asking what is escaped *from* and what is escaped *to*. Flight can often be towards a private space representing possibilities for resisting dominant representations of power through control of the local. In teenage fantastic realism, which the last chapter suggested is a literature that focuses on the individual and the private figure, personal experience of fantasy sets the protagonist (and by extension, the reader) apart from a more general realist interaction with the world, instead reserving for the protagonist a position of knowledge and power beyond the ordinary. The space provided by fantasy can also be structurally subversive. Armitt argues that discussion of fantasy should not be confined to genre theory, but that it is 'about opening up subversive spaces within the mainstream' (*Theorising the Fantastic* 3). In this she draws on the work of Rosemary Jackson, who argues that the modern fantastic provides openings and gaps in the veneer of the real:

> Structurally and semantically, the fantastic aims at dissolution of an order experienced as oppressive and insufficient. [. . .] By attempting to transform the relations between the imaginary and the symbolic, fantasy hollows out the 'real', revealing its absence, its 'great other', its unspoken and its unseen. (180)

In other words fantasy can challenge the accepted norms of reality through its very structure; and once challenged, those norms can be resisted.

To see the fantastic as a site in which power relations are enacted, then, is also to recognise the fact that fantasy may equally fluctuate between empowering and disempowering, or at least that subversive fantasy can still be bound by the 'reality' of cultural norms and social expectations of age and gender.[8] Fantastic realism sets up these conflicts between everyday reality and 'flights of fancy' that might challenge existing structures. If adolescents are empowered through a sense of special status or through resistance to existing social or familial structures, then fantasy motifs fittingly represent adolescent power; pleasures are found in exerting power or in evading or opposing it. Yet fantastic realism also plays a part in weakening teenage characters, ultimately figuring fantastic abilities or gifts as elements that alienate them from the normalised world of teen realism and that act as a burden of social responsibility.

Before these patterns are explored I would first like to consider the familial sphere, which is not only crucial because it is seen to be the origin of adolescent resistance and identity-making, but also because mothers and fathers—even those who exist within the fantastic—help to shape the gendered expectations that continue to constrain forms of adolescent agency. Alongside specific ideas of separation-individuation, more general psychoanalytic discourse is most useful in explicating these relationships.

The Fantasy of Family

The last chapter introduced the theory of separation-individuation at adolescence, where individuals socially detach themselves from their parents (specifically the mother) in a process that parallels psychological separation at infancy. The concept of subcultures relies on a similar premise of asserting independence from familial structures; Leo B. Hendry, for example, argues that for teenagers in the confusion and fluidity of modern society 'it may be easier to deflect and separate than to adapt and converge' (160). In other words, there is a strong theoretical tendency to portray adolescence as a time of rupture from parental control, although it must be noted that more recent work suggests complete separation is not essential, and that autonomous maturity can be achieved from within family relationships.[9] As it clearly provides possibility for conflict and narrative drama, this rupture regularly appears in teenage fantastic realism as some kind of battle with a magical parent figure or dynamic interaction with parents through fantastic experiences.

The Mother: Witch and Ally

In their discussion of C.S. Lewis's *The Lion, the Witch and the Wardrobe* (1950), Margaret Rustin and Michael Rustin argue that Edmund's unhealthy alliance with the White Queen of Narnia rests on the illusive promise of a nurturing mother/child relationship. Edmund is tempted by this cold and undeniably evil woman because part of him is 'feeling hungry for mother's love and care' (45). When he is 'mothered' by the witch he expects to find further traits that are characteristically associated with the conventional mother figure: domesticity, nourishment and caring tendencies. According to the Rustins' psychoanalytic reading the White Witch's negation of each hoped-for quality represents the frustrated desires of Edmund who is separated from his own mother. C.S. Lewis's fantasy series is aimed at a pre-adolescent readership and Edmund is still positioned in the latency period, requiring a continued connection with a nurturing parent. As an adolescent he may have played out a slightly more ambiguous role, since when the anti-mother is confronted in teenage fantastic realism, sexual desire and fantasies of control are also at play. Louise Lawrence's *The Earth Witch* (1982), is a good example of the way a mother–son relationship is constructed and deconstructed through a fantastical trope of myth and witchcraft.

The Earth Witch focuses on seventeen-year-old Owen Jones and his relationship with Bronwen Davies, a figure drawn (as in some of Garner's stories) from the Welsh *Mabinogion* who 'has many names but it is all one woman' (*The Earth Witch* 22). Owen's mother deserted him when he was a child and Bronwen emerges as a surrogate, offering him comfort and support although she is bitter and hostile to other villagers. Owen increasingly spends all his spare time with her, abandoning his guardian aunt and uncle, as well as the siblings Kate and Jonathan who form his peer group in the remote Welsh village. Bronwen, in turn, admits, 'I have always wanted a son like you' (66) and at one point holds him so that 'all the lost years of his childhood were [. . .] crammed into one embrace' (105). She performs classic nurturing actions, tenderly applying ointment to Owen's back when it is sunburned and cut from working in her garden and, more crucially, feeding him with enchanted spring water and oatcakes that satisfy him completely but destroy his appetite for any other foods, including the dinners his Aunty Glad provides. These victuals have a significant role in cementing the power balance in this unnatural relationship; not only does Bronwen encourage Owen's dependence on her own mothering at the expense of alternative female characters such as his aunt or his friend Kate (who, incidentally, is positioned as an appropriate romantic partner in the text), but she also binds him to her through the sinister magic spell cast on the food. Diane Purkiss links motherhood with food provision in her discussion of images of witchcraft, claiming that providing the child with its first sustenance is crucial to the identity of the mother (99). If that mother figure is instead a witch—an 'anti-mother'—then, the significance of food changes:

> Food has significance for women because it is a means of nourishing, sustaining and protecting—and therefore controlling—the bodies into which it is instilled. The witch's food reverses this positive charge; instead of sustaining it destroys. The witch's gift of food to a *child* puts her in the place of the mother. (108)

Accordingly, as a 'mother' Bronwen proves to be a great threat to Owen and, in offering the comforts of mothering, is actually aiming to control, trap and kill him. Her final meal of stew, rye bread and cider is poisoned to paralyse so that she can sacrifice Owen to the spirit of Cerridwen, a Welsh goddess of Nature who endlessly consumes and gives birth.[10] Lawrence's novel also engages with traditional narratives of a cannibal-witch to be found in fairy tales and folk tales such as 'Hansel and Gretel' and 'Black Annis'. Purkiss argues that the 'devouring witch' acts as both a 'bad' mother and as incarnation of a good mother's fear of not providing enough for her children (278–279).

Part of the menacing power that Bronwen exerts is linked to concepts of innate witchcraft and femininity that I will consider in more depth later in this chapter. A similar pattern appears in Westall's *The Devil on the Road*, where the 'Yarb Mother', or young witch Johanna Vavasour, manipulates teenage protagonist John. Chapters One and Two argued that Johanna represents a specifically feminine power, but in addition it can be identified as peculiarly maternal. When she and John return to the present from the seventeenth century she sets up home for him in a manner that, on one hand, suggests patriarchal visions of a wife's duty but, on the other, implies a mothering, nurturing purpose. She complains about his poor housekeeping and hygiene: 'But there was no real anger in the muttering; just the eternal female complaint that men were babies to be cleaned, fed and scolded from cradle to grave' (*The Devil on the Road* 213). Like Bronwen, Johanna represents this fully cyclical reproductive role which takes the teenage characters dangerously close to danger and an early death. Again, the implication is that the desire for a close relationship with the mother at adolescence is treacherous because *separation* from familial ties is essential for safe and healthy maturation. While both Owen and John find it comforting to be looked after and to submit totally to their respective mother figures, surrendering completely means that they become trapped or destroyed and their own power is drained.

This pattern is complicated further by the protagonist's status as adolescent and as a newly sexual being. Bronwen's character changes with the seasons and is linked to natural cycles of fertility and sterility. During the spring and early summer she becomes a beautiful maiden, presenting an idealised version of feminine virginity as the village's May Queen. The power she wields slips from parental authority and motherly care to sexual influence and control, and Owen is now seduced by erotic desire rather than the comfort of latent childhood. This slippage indicates a complexity in power relations that is perhaps exclusive to teenage fiction, and particularly to fantastic realism. For however powerful a mother or anti-mother may be, the teenage child is close to the status of adult or parent themselves, and where Bronwen magically shifts from mother to maiden, Owen's status also changes from child to fully sexualised teenager. Once more though, the adolescent boy is warned against female power, as Bronwen's sexual charms prove to be as debilitating as her maternal ones. Owen becomes as addicted to her love as he has been to her charmed food, and both sap his power in the everyday world outside of her cottage. This blurring of relationships allows Owen to play out the potentially destructive desire for his mother in a clearly sexualised—but also wholly fantastic—arena. That is, although he is robbed of agency, fantastic elements of the novel do at least permit him to enact fully the classic psychoanalytic narrative of male adolescence.

Whilst such a confusion of relationships does not provide Owen with any distinct agency, the situation shifts when a teenage character is the same sex as the threatening adult. For female characters, this power struggle is much more intricate. When the cycle of mother–maiden–crone has been completed within Bronwen, the narrative suggests that Kate will take over the mantle of 'Earth Witch'. During the final scenes of a Halloween night, Bronwen finally attempts to kill and consume Owen by drugging him and turning herself into a vicious and ravenous carnivorous sow. She is thwarted by Kate, however, who arrives in time to destroy the creature and rescue Owen. By killing Bronwen, Kate fantastically absorbs the spirit of this figure who 'would walk forever in the flesh of woman' (201) and she tries to comprehend the change:

> It was power Bronwen had, power to enchant and destroy, power without conscience: and Kate could feel that same power in herself, the small stirrings of an embryonic thing that had yet to be born or given way to [...] an instinct of blood sacrifices and fertility rites, ancient rituals of birth and death, a woman wanting to come free [...] sensuous, savage, uninhibited, earthy and sexual as nature, beautiful as Bronwen, cruel and gentle as the land. What Kate saw, loved and feared and hated in Bronwen were the secret parts of herself. (133–134)

This extraordinary passage suggests that all the maternal and sexual power that Bronwen possesses is passed onto Kate as she reaches adolescence and indicates her sexual interest in Owen. The danger Kate faces is clearly no longer external but becomes inherent in her own power as she reaches the state of potential motherhood herself (that is, becoming sexual and fertile). That her attitude towards this power is obviously ambivalent, incorporating fear and hate as well as love, is significant. Bronwen's version of womanhood is portrayed in seductive terms, but ultimately she symbolises danger and the destruction of 'normal' male youthfulness. She also represents those aspects of femininity that are revealed to be inappropriate for adolescent girls in most fantastic realist texts. Kate's 'secret parts' are only secretly celebrated; in essence her new 'power without conscience' does not form an acceptable discourse of female adolescence.

Surprisingly, in many teenage fantastic realist novels the real mother/daughter relations are mostly untroubled and unproblematic. Despite concern amongst some critics that mothers are regularly absent, already dead or killed off in contemporary children's literature,[11] a number of teenage fantastic realist texts offer the image of a close-knit unit of mother and child or children. *Forests of the Night* (1995) by Geraldine Kaye, *Playing Beatie Bow* (1980) by Ruth Park, and Margaret Mahy's *The Changeover* (1984), each focuses on a teenage daughter and single mother, with a younger brother or surrogate brother completing a triad. Penelope Farmer's *Thicker than Water* (1989) appears to have a similar domestic set-up although, in fact, the father in this novel is merely overworked and too busy to impinge greatly on family life. What remains constant is the productive bond between daughter and mother that works against frameworks of separation at adolescence and it is possible to trace this phenomenon to the fantastic aspects of the novels. These benign power dynamics are particularly evident in *Playing Beatie Bow* and *The Changeover*.

In *Playing Beatie Bow* Abigail's father has left the family home, so adolescent Abigail and her mother, Kathy, live together alone and display a cheerful family portrait: 'although they were such different characters [they] had fought and hugged and scrambled their way to a close friendship' (*Playing Beatie Bow* 6). Abigail is often responsible for looking after small children for a next door neighbour, and she is often represented as more mature and reserved than her mother. When they argue, Abigail retreats to her bedroom and '[a]fter a while her mother gave the door a ferocious kick. The girl could not help grinning; Kathy was such a child' (21). A similar pattern emerges in *The Changeover*. Laura's life with her mother, Kate, is chaotic but loving. When Kate rediscovers a picture drawn by her young son, Jacko, it illustrates a positive family portrait:

> a happy, family drawing, for that was all he could draw. There they were— Laura, Jacko and Kate, wild yet geometrical, with huge heads and little legs and smiles so wide that they extended beyond their faces on to the paper around them. (*The Changeover* 5)

Like Abigail's family, Laura's is missing a father because he left them when she was young, but Laura's relationship with her mother is affectionate and mutually supportive. Kate is portrayed as rather inept, struggling to find a lost shoe, start the car and get to work on time, and she refuses to let Laura stay in bed on the day of a fearful supernatural premonition because she needs her to child-mind her brother: 'It's late-night tonight, and who'd collect Jacko, take him home, give him his supper and read him a story?' (*The Changeover* 5). In both *The Changeover* and *Playing Beatie Bow* the roles of mother and daughter, adult and teenager, or carer and dependent, become almost interchangeable, and the traditional balance of sexual knowledge is also modified so that, at times, the teenage daughter gives advice or admonition rather than receiving it. Laura rages against the fact that her mother sleeps with a new boyfriend during a family crisis, and Abigail berates Kathy for considering a return to her ex-husband, accusing her of having no 'self-respect'. In these novels the mother figure is not an adult source of order, authority and wisdom, but a partner in a relationship where responsibilities of childcare and domestic duties are shared, and behaviour is monitored both ways. Such a situation implies equality that is not evident in conventional conceptions of motherhood but which is relevant to late twentieth-century family structures, where traditional roles and relationships are shifting and diverse. It also makes sense in the context of adolescence, where girls become more like women themselves. In her feminist critique of Freudian developmental psychoanalysis, Jessica Benjamin explores the fact that the dominant paradigm of psychoanalytic theory involves separation and individuation from the mother. She argues that '[t]he problems with this formulation is the idea of separation from oneness; it contains the implicit assumption that we grow *out of* relationships rather than becoming more active and sovereign *within* them' (18, italics in original). Benjamin's point is that, in demanding separation from the mother in order for (adolescent) individuals to achieve identity, existing theory disallows the mother's subjectivity and denies an alternative development that could rely on interaction with, and recognition in, the mother.

It is interesting, then, that the teenage girls in fantastic realism appear to have reached this point, and it is partly due to the space allowed by the fantastic (although, as I shall show later, this cooperative pattern does not necessarily break down the constraining expectations of femininity). In *Playing Beatie Bow* Abigail is distraught because her mother plans to return to her ex-husband and move the whole family from Australia to Norway. After a fight, Abigail storms away but instead of ending up in the park she is transported into the nineteenth century where she is taken in by the Bow family and falls in love with their sailor son. The months she spends in the historical world allow 'the kind of growing up she could never have experienced in this one' (164), involving as they do violence and intimacy in greater quantity than in the contemporary time, where her mother works all day and where they inhabit a rather clinical apartment in Sydney. When Abigail returns from the past, no time has passed in the primary chronotope and her mother is still angry from the argument. However, she notices some difference in her daughter: 'It's amazing . . . you do look different . . . I suppose I just haven't looked at you properly lately . . . Just for a moment there I could see what you'd look like in a few years' time. It was sort of—eerie. I forget you're growing up, you see?' (167).

Not surprisingly, a 'change' is also at the heart of Mahy's novel. *The Changeover* is a quest novel located simultaneously in fantastic and realist spheres. The heroine is Laura, whose five-year-old brother, Jacko, has a strange encounter with an evil spirit in the shape of a shopkeeper called Carmody Braque. Braque sucks the life force from Jacko and leaves him in a coma: it is left to Laura to save the boy by becoming a witch and battling with the dangerous spirit. While Jacko is ill, Laura's mother is understandably preoccupied with this family drama, as well as with a new romantic and sexual relationship of her own, but Laura's change into witchhood and the supernatural or spiritual elements this brings to her life bring the two female characters closer together. Christine Wilkie-Stibbs points out this phenomenon, which appears strongest at the point at which Laura goes through a metaphorical journey in her transformation into a witch:

> the changeover has also brought with it a new, and unexpected, maternal dimension to Laura's experiences in which, for example, she shares in Kate's memory of Jacko's early breastfeeding as if it were her own: 'his

nose pressed into her breast [. . .] Laura's mind was so mixed with Kate's that the memory seemed entirely her own' (175). (112)[12]

The fantastical experiences that both heroines go through change them significantly; each one is closer to adulthood afterwards and although they return to the domestic, collaborative mother/daughter relationship at the end of the narrative, both Laura and Abigail have also taken a step towards leaving that environment. Abigail, in particular, is eighteen at the novel's end, and has no interest in how her mother and father redecorate the flat because she will not be there much longer. She has met Robert—who is descended from the Bows—and the implication is that she will form a new relationship with him. Fantastic realism potentially encourages a mutually supportive relationship between mother and daughter rather than a struggle of separation by locating the essence of 'growing up' outside of maternal influence and transferring it instead to the inherent power to be found in the state of fantastic adolescence itself.

Teenage fantastic realism offers scenarios of growth and maturation for teenage girls without explicit social rupture or conflict with the mother in the material world. However, there is a clear sense that this stage of fantastic adolescence eventually gives way to the reproduction of previous versions of the mother. That is, Laura and Abigail are set up to enter into heterosexual relationships that are likely to result in the 'happy ending' of marriage and motherhood. Kate more explicitly follows in Bronwen's footsteps to adopt typical feminine roles of lover and mother. Mother/daughter relationships maintain those admirable feminine qualities that the texts seek to endorse: caring, nurturing motherhood. When that relationship concerns a mother and son, however, such feminine qualities are expressed as seductive and dangerous, and as a threat to young manhood; more likely to sap energy and ability than to empower.[13] Sons, therefore, are urged to look to more masculine role-models.

The Father: The Law and the Wolf

In her examination of fatherhood as a form of masculinity, Lynne Segal points out that 'the father as God, God the father, may be one of our most powerful mythologies' (28). Indeed, the concept of the father as authoritarian, powerful and always right maintains its iconic potency into the late twentieth century. There are other cultural types, including the 'new' nurturing father (Lupton and Barclay 14) and the dynamic heroic father, recently expounded by Francis Spufford in his autobiographical account of reading Ian Fleming's 'James Bond' novels as a boy—these provided him and his friends with a fantasy lens through which to view their fathers, and a glamorous promise about their own future male adulthood (Spufford 160–162). The father's status as 'godlike' emerges out of psychoanalytical and social discourses of masculinity. Theories of adolescent psychological development are heavily shaped by the concept of entry into the social world through a Symbolic (Oedipal) relationship with the father. In this context the father can be desired *and* feared. Alternatively, in social discourse the sex-role model identifies fatherhood as the clear version of masculinity provided for a male offspring to imitate. In other words, the teenage boy should be able to find both approval and guidance from his father or father figure in order to develop satisfactorily, and to construct his own masculine identity, developing in the image of the father. It is important to note, though, that a reliance on sex-role models serves to 'present a fixed notion of masculinity and femininity as "a kind of laundry list of behavioural characteristics"' (Kimmel 12, cited in Lupton and Barclay 45) and, moreover, these characteristics may be valued in different ways. In fantastic realism the value is ambivalent.

In *The Changeover*, the villain Carmody Braque resides somewhere in the uncanny space between anti-mother and anti-father. Like the Earth Witch or the witch in 'Hansel and Gretel' he entices his prey with promises of luxurious treats and material pleasures. He tempts Laura's brother Jacko into his enchanting *Brique O Braque* shop and offers 'little nonsenses' to satisfy the young boy. Instead of a toy or sweet, however, Jacko receives a stamp of the shopkeeper's image, which Braque uses to transfer life and energy from the boy to himself. Braque marks the intersection between the ordinary everyday experience of Laura and Jacko's walk home from school and the supernatural world in which Laura magically transforms herself into a more adult—and more dangerous—individual. He also acts as an aberrant mother figure, first using terms of endearment such as 'pet' and 'wee lambie' for the siblings, and later disguising himself as the parody of a respectable and feminised neighbour, performing such domestic tasks as pruning the roses and hanging out 'immaculate underwear and shirts on his washing line' (*The Changeover* 157). These indicators of conventional feminine nurturing and domesticity are made sinister because, rather than caring for them, in fact the shopkeeper absorbs or consumes the vitality of his various youthful victims. Moreover, in displaying conventionally feminine qualities, Braque is exposed as perversely 'unmanly'.

Braque's role as anti-mother contrasts sharply with the other mother figures available to Laura (her biological parent Kate, the witches she befriends and even her own developing and future maternal qualities). But Braque's abhorrent portrayal of femininity also highlights the apparent absence of an appropriate father figure in *The Changeover*. Laura's father, Stephen, is no longer a part of the Chant nuclear family because he and Kate were incompatible in the domestic sphere. According to Kate, he was 'a better housekeeper than I was' and was, moreover, a martyr about the domestic work, vacuuming the carpet 'as if he were St Peter being crucified upside down' (26). This perhaps indicates Mahy's attempt to complicate normal gender roles and characteristics, allowing Kate to perform the roles of both mother and father in Laura's upbringing, and focusing on the feminine processes of development that are inherent in the form of witchcraft produced in this novel. Nevertheless, Stephen Chant is later described as Laura's 'dark, powerful father' and, however feminised her environment has become, his status is still crucial. The Freudian family romance, which dictates that the daughter desires the father, is produced here as conflict because Laura is determined to hate Stephen for not loving her and Kate enough to stay with them. Yet she also hates her mother's new boyfriend, Chris Holly, for attempting to take his place. These multiple clashes are finally resolved via Laura's fantastic powers. In gaining powers as a witch she is able to confront Braque and destroy him, finding an outlet for her own familial frustrations at the same time: 'Laura was offered a unique chance to discharge her own burden of human anguish and to strike at the powers of darkness, and no one would know' (*The Changeover* 184). By despising Carmody Braque and forcing him to suffer the 'full force of all the fury she had ever felt' (184), Laura directs her hatred away from her father and from her mother's new partner. By the end of the novel she finds she can forgive Stephen and accept Chris. Her change of heart is not directed by the actions of two men but proceeds from the knowledge of her own new power in adult relationships. As a witch she can deal with an incubus like Braque, and as a maturing teenager (almost a woman) she learns to manage her interactions with the men in her family life.

Fantastic realism also portrays a more palpable power struggle between the adolescent protagonist and a father figure, where the father represents order, discipline and rationality in the face of the fantastic or incredible. In two of Gillian Cross's novels—*Pictures in the Dark* (1996) and *Wolf* (1990)—the teenage characters are forced to re-evaluate the relationships they have with their fathers, and in each case fantasy provides the appropriate site for the realignment of these potentially destructive bonds.

An abusive relationship between Peter Luttrell and his father is central to the novel *Pictures in the Dark*. Mr Luttrell first appears as a dominant patriarch of the home, expecting order and discipline from his wife and children, and not tolerating disruption. As the discussions in Chapter One and Two made clear, Peter is an unusual boy, clumsy and absent-minded, and it is partly this early adolescent awkwardness that antagonises Mr Luttrell to the point of violence. In addition, Peter regularly metamorphoses into a wild otter, leaving his human body behind as an empty shell, and the utter impossibility of such a phenomenon enrages Mr Luttrell further. Peter's father is the embodiment of rationality, logic and, in Lacanian terms, the Symbolic, and as such he refuses to accept the wild and imaginative identity that his son adopts. It is difficult to tell whether Mr Luttrell's excessive anger (expressed through routinely locking Peter in the garden shed, for example) occurs because he cannot accept the fantastic in any form, or whether Peter's metamorphosis into the otter is a fantastic response to paternal pressure that already exists. The text is ambivalent on the subject, but there are elements of psychological discourse in evidence that suggest the otter-form is an escape route that Peter has developed as a solution to his familial problems. The sex-role theory of fatherhood and adolescence, which traces how the interaction (or absence) of fathers affects and influences a child's cognitive, social, moral and personal progress, informs the way that others regard Peter's situation. Charlie, the older boy at school through whom

Pictures in the Dark is focalised, claims that Mr Luttrell's strict and obsessive behaviour is to blame for Peter's status at school as the 'weird' one, implying that more competent fathering would result in a more normal teenage son. He compares Mr Luttrell's cruel treatment of Peter with his own father's good sense: 'I thought he [Mr Luttrell] was going to explode. [...] But he didn't. He just... looked. I'd hate it if Dad looked at *me* like that [...] he wouldn't look as if... as if he hated me' (*Pictures in the Dark* 29–30).

Wilkie-Stibbs theorises from a feminist psychoanalytical stance instead and stresses Peter's agency: 'Peter's escape into the body of an otter is his *resistance* to submission to the Father's Law in the Symbolic that is embodied in the overbearing presence of his father' (94). Wilkie-Stibbs's focus lies in the way that Peter embraces the feminine 'jouissance' available to him through the identity of a wild, fluid, river-based creature and how this works against the system of the father. In reading the novel's conclusion, where Mr Luttrell is forced to save his own son from being drowned in his otter form, Wilkie-Stibbs argues that:

> although the novel is ostensibly a quest for father/son reconciliation, a reading in *the feminine* reveals it as a story of *maternal* reconciliation expressed in changed relations, and achieved through the resurfacing of the Semiotic in the Symbolic and the newly realized capacity of the male figures to communicate in the language of *le parler femme*. (99)

This analysis suggests that both Peter and Mr Luttrell are finally free to commune within the sphere of the feminine fantastic, but in Chapter One I showed there is no real evidence that the father is more receptive to his son's imaginative persona or that Peter is less awkward than before. Realignment does occur, but it is tentative and partial, and leaves the reader in an uncomfortable position, uncertain as to whether the metamorphosis is now an accepted part of the father/son relationship, or whether that fantastic ability has been shut down forever, in preference for the law of the Father. This hardly represents real resistance.

The relationship between father and daughter is abandoned to similar ambiguity at the end of Cross's *Wolf*, although several critics of the novel again argue that it is in any case more concerned with thirteen-year-old Cassy's growing understanding of her mother, with whom she no longer lives but who she goes to visit whenever her grandmother (Nan) mysteriously wants her out of the way. Adrienne Kertzer proposes that 'it is the very quest for the maternal voice and story, the maternal pretext, that empowers the heroine' (20) while Wilkie-Stibbs's reading of the novel argues that 'Cassy struggles through an Oedipal drama to reconcile herself with her deserting mother by working through her Oedipal attachments to her estranged father' (133). While the content of the narrative bears out this approach to some degree, the fantastic elements of the story indicate a considerable interest in the details of that very Oedipal attachment with the father.

Cassy is understandably curious about her father as she has not seen him since she was an infant and her grandmother refuses to tell her about him, reiterating a series of sensible mantras such as 'It'll be time enough when you're grown up' and 'Never trouble trouble till trouble troubles you'. Through the story, Cassy learns that Mick Phelan left their family due to his involvement in the IRA's terrorist programme and returns to Nan's house periodically for shelter. While the facts of his existence and nature remain cloudy to her, at the age of thirteen she begins to experience uncanny premonitions and memories of him through her dreams. These fantastical sections of the novel give her the psychological freedom to explore her feelings about her long-absent father through the narrative of 'Little Red Riding Hood'. Mick features as a menacing wolf with 'large and luminous' eyes and 'stained, curving murderous teeth' (112, 127) and, as Cassy approaches him through a dark wood in her visions, he is also near in the external world, searching for some plastic explosive that Nan hid in Cassy's bag. By the time the dreaming Cassy (as Little Red Riding Hood) has reached grandmother's cottage in her fantasy sphere, in the waking world her father has actually left a note for her explaining that he will kill Nan if the explosive is not returned.

Mick only represents the law of the father at this point of conflict at the end of the novel. Until then, his role is displaced onto Nan, who provides those qualities of discipline and rationality that characterise conventional understandings of fatherhood (Wilkie-Stibbs 157, 162). Like Mr Luttrell, Nan closes down the protagonist's imaginative and fantastic world, as she states that 'Of course Cassy never dreams' (*Wolf* 2) (she does) and that fairy tales are nonsense (they are not, in this story). Throughout her childhood, this rational ideology has kept Cassy from wondering about her mysterious father, but his presence in her newly awakened dream world provokes a guilty desire to know him, or know more about him: it is the guilty desire to listen to the wolf in the fantastic narrative, and let him stop her on the path through the forest to ask 'Shall I show you the path? We could play a little game' (34). Wilkie-Stibbs reads these lines as a sexual enticement and links them to phallic imagery (of a bottle neck and a basket handle) in order to argue that Cassy projects her Oedipal desires onto her visions. Although this is certainly credible considering the Freudian undertones of dreams and fairy tale narratives throughout the novel, an explicit psychoanalytic reading seems laboured and does not examine the specific father/daughter relationship on offer in this text.

Wilkie-Stibbs compares *Wolf* to Freud's case of the Wolf-Man, in which the dreamer conflates feelings of fear and desire in the object of the wolf itself, that actually represents the father. On one hand it might be argued that Cassy uses the fantastic space of her dreams to play out the Oedipal drama, much in the same way as Owen enacts his desire for his mother through the fantastic figure of Bronwen in *The Earth Witch*. On the other hand, while Mick is being constructed as a wolf, the image of the wolf is simultaneously *deconstructed*. Cassy's mother is involved in a drama group that performs a piece called 'Wolf!'

to schools, aiming to educate them about the endangered animals and their inherently noble and nurturing nature. When Cassy is finally confronted with her terrorist father, therefore, she appeals to his connection to the wolf: 'Wolves don't forget about their children' and 'You wouldn't have done that if you were a *wolf*.' (136, 137). It is here that the norms of gendered parent/child relations could be broken down and reordered. Kertzer persuasively suggests that Cassy's mother takes on the role of protective wolf and/or heroic woodcutter when she intercepts and saves Cassy from Mick's gun, but Kertzer fails to note that Mick's role as father is left unexplored. Instead of being deconstructed into a caring wolf, he is reordered as the wolf of nightmares, the werewolf. At the text's realist closure Mick is arrested and taken to prison, but in the fantasy dream world he remains at large, and in the final paragraph an infantilised Cassy asks '*Dear Wolf, Don't vanish into the dark forest again. I still need to know about you. Perhaps I can come and visit you, or . . . or . . .*' (140). The interesting questions of how she might actually relate to this violent father now that she knows him remain unanswered.

Possibilities for adolescent agency in Cross's novels and in Lawrence's *The Earth Witch* break down when the teenage protagonists aim to meet parental expectations or integrate themselves into the ways of being that have been set up by mother or father figures. Real agency might be expected to reside in those spaces where mainstream culture—as epitomised by parents—is properly resisted and reshaped. Subcultures provide the opportunity for young individuals to distance themselves from familiar power structures and construct new fantastic identities, and in the next two sections I will consider two fantastic tropes that offer protagonists new social roles and active powers to resist or defy dominant adult structures within the everyday world. Superheroes and witches each have specific historical, cultural and archetypal qualities that teenage characters absorb, manipulate and restructure into positions of fantastic power within the texts. They can be read as fantastic subcultures, magical solutions to real conditions of powerlessness. Yet it is important to question how far this practice goes in producing any real sense of adolescent agency. These close readings of fantastic realism explore how far superheroes and witches exist and function within parameters of acceptable social roles and responsible, 'adult' actions. They consider how naturalised gender difference is portrayed and maintained through the superhero and witch trope.

Superheroes

The superhero figure displays many of the features of masculinity that are expressed in male subcultures. Significantly, there is a large male adolescent fanbase for comic books and their characters, surveys suggesting that comics are particularly popular amongst boys between the ages of ten and fifteen (Pecora 61–77). The traditional comic book superhero can be most clearly represented by DC Comics' Superman. Introduced to the American comic book market in the late 1930s, Superman embodies those themes that ultimately became the epitome of male heroic fantasy: good versus evil, the fight for truth, violent battles against obvious villains, incredible (and virtuous) power, the endless rescuing of helpless female characters, and the mandatory 'wimpy' alter ego. Although he may represent quintessential American masculinity, Superman is also an *external* force from the planet Krypton where his powers originate. As such, his precursors can be found in classical heroes and gods such as Hercules or Apollo, who were also distinct from earthly men. Many critics argue that comic books provide an excellent social critique of society, particularly American society, reflecting political and ideological trends (Sabin; Richard Reynolds). It is interesting, then, to consider how the figure of the superhero has transformed alongside the comic book. While early comics presented a single complete story in each issue, the 1970s saw the introduction of multi-part stories, crossover storylines and long-running serialisation. Alongside this practical development came the possibility for increasingly complex superheroes, as well as the space for more female characters, although these remain remarkably limited. The archetype for a new type of hero can thus be found in Marvel's Spiderman, a human mutant who never wanted special powers and who is plagued with doubts about how to employ his abilities. Other new characters fight against evil despite physical or mental flaws—Marvel's Daredevil is blind, for example—and new versions of problematic masculine power emerged. Most recently the trend has favoured anti-heroes whose understanding of good and evil is shaped by psychological uncertainty and ambivalent notions of justice. Perhaps the most popular character in this mould is DC's Batman, but we might also include Judge Dredd (Fleetway/IPC). According to the author of *Knightfall* (a novelisation of a series of Batman comics), 'we have co-opted the grimmer archetypes, embraced them, declared them, with all their ferocity and relentlessness and inhuman competence, our allies' (O'Neil 40).[14]

Peter Dickinson's *The Gift* (1973), Robert Cormier's *Fade* (1988) and *The Giver* by Lois Lowry (1993) are not comic books by any means, yet their heroes have the kind of abilities that might be found in a comic book narrative and they face the difficult challenge of integrating these strange powers with their ordinary teenage experiences.

Superman: Heroic Masculinity

The superhero is traditionally located in the role of the 'good guy', using his powers for the common good and battling with extreme enemies. The figure of the traditional superhero also solves certain issues of masculinity and power, in effect offering the protagonist an escape from an unacceptably weak adolescent role through a fantastically empowered alter ego. Teenage fantastic realism shares some of these strategies in portraying male characters, but it also draws on more recent comic book fiction which humanises, complicates and deconstructs the superhero image, never allowing the alter ego absolute freedom and dictating instead that real (adult) responsibilities and burdens play a part in shaping identity.

As we have seen, *Fade* narrates the story of thirteen-year-old Paul, and the adventures and troubles he faces when he discovers he can fantastically become invisible. At first Paul fades without realising what is happening, but during his early adolescence he learns to control his ability and use it to escape, spy or commit forbidden acts. The last chapter discussed Paul's inherited ability to 'fade' as a visual (or invisible) metaphor that indicates anxiety over the potential loss of a teenage selfhood. There is an alternative impulse in the novel that conceptualises this talent for vanishing as a potential superpower, one that enables Paul to evade adult control and to fulfil adolescent desires of voyeurism and revenge. Special powers provide a common theme amongst male protagonists in fantastic realism. In *The Gift*, Davy Price's unusual power is mental rather than physical. When he is a young boy, he sees one of his grandmother's memories appearing as a picture in his own mind and he learns that the men in their family often have this ability to see visions of other people's thoughts. Although he learns to ignore the invading pictures most of the time, a series of events that occur when he is a teenager force him to connect with his gift. He begins to see manic, aggressive thoughts of a man he calls Wolf, who is part of a criminal gang. By piecing together the visual clues Davy realises that his father is caught up in an attempted wages heist with Wolf and the rest of the gang. Davy and his sister Penny persuade their father to go to the police and inform on his colleagues; the heist is stopped and the gang are all arrested. Davy continues to see Wolf's disturbing mental pictures, however, and he realises that Wolf has escaped custody and followed Davy and his family to Wales in order to exact revenge.

Visions like Davy's also appear to the protagonist of *The Giver*. The novel is set in the future and describes a new kind of choiceless society where citizens are organised by 'the Elders' into family units and designated jobs for life. As such, the novel falls into the category of speculative fiction or science fiction, rather than fantastic realism, but it shares with *Fade* and *The Gift* a protagonist who has an extraordinary power and who experiences strange occurrences that the rest of his community do not, and it will help us draw conclusions about the ambiguous nature of masculine superpowers in the context of teenage fantastic fiction. It has also provoked a great deal of debate over its intended readership and so offers a useful case-study for thinking about ambiguous endings and adolescent readers. In the narrative, each child is assigned a career at the age of twelve and protagonist Jonas is not sure what his will be. He does know that he has developed a strange ability to see some objects in a different way, which he eventually learns is the 'Capacity to See Beyond'. Due to the Capacity he is assigned 'Receiver of Memory', a unique position which means that he must absorb all of the memories that have previously been removed from the community's collective psyche for their own good. Unlike the rest of his society he can see colour, recognise pain and joy, know love, and remember cultural items such as family, music and war.

In each novel, the adolescent protagonist is represented as one in a long tradition of men with special powers. The titular 'Giver' in Lowry's novel trains Jonas in his task, literally passing on memories through the power of his hands as those memories had been passed on to him previously when he was the Receiver, and as it has always been since the conception of the Community, 'back, and back, and back' (*The Giver* 99). In *The Gift*, Davy learns about his inherited talent for mind-reading from his Welsh grandmother, but it is also recorded in an ancient poem about the Welsh hero Owain Glyndwr, who passed on 'the sight of the hawk' to one of his faithful captains as a gift. It locates Davy in a long lineage, as a player in mythological narratives which focus on widespread magic and heroic deeds. There is a sense that Davy himself must continue the heroic deeds of his Welsh forebears, using his gift to overcome such modern enemies as a fractured family, psychological illness and crime. Paul's gift has no such literary legacy but it is similarly passed on through the paternal line of his family, and has historical longevity which suggests a kind of myth that stretches '[b]ack to the time of Christ, maybe' (*Fade* 63). Each boy receives proper knowledge of his fantastic ability at the first stages of adolescence, and the passing on from one generation to another suggests the kind of rite of passage that can also be found in matrilineal witchcraft, discussed below. In this case, however, rather than representing initiation into a network of female witchcraft, the fantastic powers are transferred from one man to another as the inheritance of individual male power.

The fade, which comes upon Paul alongside puberty, is accompanied by the promise of heroic possibilities that appear to far exceed his potential as a developing young man. As noted in Chapter Two, Paul possesses a deep conviction that he could be a hero 'if the opportunity presented itself' and when it does he recognises his prospects at once: 'I can do anything, I thought, go anywhere, cross oceans, reach mountaintops' (*Fade* 63). It is possible to note in this excited declaration some shared rhetorical features with the tagline for Paramount's 1940s Superman cartoons: 'Faster than a speeding bullet. More powerful than a locomotive. Able to leap tall buildings in a single bound. Up in the sky. It's a bird, it's a plane, it's Superman!'[15] Certainly, Paul links his invisibility to other superhuman abilities, such as flight, bionic speed and invincibility. His new sense of self is one of indestructibility, aligned with the idealised image of superhuman masculinity in the figure of a Superman.

Fantasy heroes permeate the adolescent leisure-time of Paul and his friend Pete, who both 'loved drama and movies and mysteries' (12) and who are captivated by *The Ghost Rider* film (whose main character was later transformed into a comic book regular). The superhero represents an enticing fantasy, forming a literal escape from the material world in terms of losing oneself in a comic book or film, but also a metaphorical flight from everyday restrictions of power relations and status formed through age, class or intelligence. This is particularly pertinent considering Paul's actual status, which is marginal in many ways. He is just thirteen-years-old and has no material power to influence social and political events, such as the strike at his father's comb factory, or to control his own relationships, particularly his sexual desires for unattainable women like his own aunt Rosanna. Paul is also excluded from the dominant group of boys at school because he is regarded as sensitive and artistic. Even teachers strip away his self-confidence by attacking the one natural talent he displays in creative writing. When he submits a story about his father's poor working conditions to the school magazine his teacher tells him it is not suitable, and a warning that his cousin once gave him comes back to Paul: '*You're a Canuck, Paul, and nothing you write will ever be good enough*' (91). Being a poor French-Canadian in New England completes Paul's powerless position in the reality of Frenchtown. Any tangible and pragmatic means of overcoming this position through education, money or improved status appear to be closed to Paul; the only way his experience of the 'real' world can be changed is through fantastic empowerment.

In a discussion of the Superman myth, Umberto Eco argues that fantasies of superhuman ability provide 'the power demands that the average citizen nurtures but cannot satisfy'. Eco's argument contends that, like Paul, the average man, consumer or reader is disempowered: 'In an industrial society [...] where man becomes a number in the realm of the organization which has usurped his decision-making role, he has no means of production and is thus derived of his power to decide' (107). Thus, where there is no hope for any identification with a normal human hero, power demands take a fantastic form instead. While it is unwise to compare adolescence too closely to the position of a proletarian caught in a capitalist system, Eco's comments are useful in theorising the concept of empowerment and agency in *Fade* and other fantastic realist texts for teenagers. For, in certain discourses, the adolescent *is* represented as powerless, either as subordinate to adult control or as a 'number' in the system of gangs and status at school and on the street. Moreover, cultural readings of the comic book hero stress the specifically gendered implications that such a figure represents, traditionally endorsing an image of masculine strength and control that corresponds to dominant gender and power relations in society. For invisibility also provides the opportunity for active and heroic agency. In the most potent demonstration of his fantastic power, for example, Paul kills Rudolphe Toubert, the town's successful but corrupt gangster figure. As well as fathering a child by Paul's adored aunt Rosanna and continuing to 'touch her up' when she needs more money, Toubert also creates trouble by providing strike-breakers when there is industrial unrest at the factory where Paul's father works. When Mr Moreaux is injured in a fight between the workers and the 'scabs', Paul is able to exact revenge and rid Frenchtown of the man he sees as his evil nemesis. He constructs this as a social action, imagining that every other man would want to kill Rudolphe if he had the fantastic power to make it possible. Norma Pecora's gendered summation of the figure of Superman has a similar tone: 'Superman is the quintessential male role model. He is a success, he has power and control—he is a man' (63). Paul's invisibility, then, not only empowers him as an adolescent, it also allows him the opportunity to perform an ideal, male, adult role, although, as we shall see, this concept of masculine success, power and control is somewhat limited in the context of teenage fantastic realism.

In *The Gift* and *The Giver*, superpowers of psychic visions set Davy and Jonas in place to perform as superheroes of a different kind, since their roles are arguably far from idealised masculine ones. Davy does, however, use his fantastic sight to actively save his father from getting further embroiled in criminal activities. His gift allows him to see Mr Price's ludicrous secret daydreams of illegally gained wealth and the envious pictures of other people's 'fat wallets', as well as memories of the shady deals he is taking part in. Since Davy's father is usually keen to exclude his children from the details of his unlawful acts, the gift directly contributes to Davy's sense of agency and his ability to make a difference in his own small familial sphere. The Welsh poem that describes his gift explains that, in return for his good deeds in battle, his ancestor was bestowed with the ability to 'peep through the eyes of others':

The gift that is given for your fight at the ford,
The gift of Glyn Dwr. You cannot refuse it.
By a deed of like daring may your last son undo it. (*The Gift* 40)

It appears that Davy, as the last son, must act heroically, although, curiously, this bold act is ultimately necessary in order to *dispel* the power of the inner eye, rather than to use it for further noble purposes. Davy's act of courage comes at the end of the novel when he faces an enraged Wolf who is desperate to find and destroy Davy's father. Rather than being the evil adversary that his name and outward actions suggest, Wolf is a troubled man called Dick, who shows evidence of mental illness. Davy uses the images projected into his own mind to recognise Wolf's situation and his need for patient help rather than violent action. Just as Davy is learning how to interpret the terrifying 'furious black squiggles' that infest all of Wolf's thoughts, his own brother arrives with a gun, recklessly scaring Wolf away to fall to his death down a slate quarry. At this dramatic point Davy's gift disappears. It is significant that his 'daring deed'—stopping Wolf's revenge—involves empathy and kindness rather than action and strength: 'the gift helped, allowing him to feel and share Wolf's exhaustion and hunger as well as his despairing rage' (154).

A similar pattern of empathic heroism emerges in Lowry's novel. Jonas's role as Receiver of Memory is considered to be 'the most important job in the community' and one that has 'enormous honour' (*The Giver* 86, 98). Most citizens are unaware that Jonas's role encompasses even greater ethical connotations and that his act of controlling their unmanageable memories can, in fact, be compared to a superhero's task of 'saving the world'. In his Foucauldian reading of the novel Don Latham suggests that the Community represents a system of power structured through discipline and punishment that controls each individual and shapes them into functioning social and economic players. Jonas's role is to provide a 'radical rupture in the social fabric of this society' (Latham 146) so that its citizens can return to a life of choice and individual subjectivity instead of a world of sameness. Jonas's ability to see more than the rest of his people at first endows him with the task of keeping them in ignorance, like a gatekeeper or protector of the whole community's mental peace. Although he performs this task heroically for some time, Jonas discovers that he is shielding others from the memories that would enrich their lives. Ultimately, he decides that these remembrances should not be denied the wider community and he escapes to 'Elsewhere', leaving his fellow citizens to reclaim their cultural memories and deal collectively with the problems they might bring. This is his heroic act and the final act of desertion is possibly more conventionally heroic than it first appears. The final chapter sees him starving and exhausted, sledging down a hill into Elsewhere with the sound of a new and joyful community ahead. It is possible to read this as an act of unconscious suicide, in which Jonas hallucinates an optimistic destination but is, in fact, required to die to set the memories free for the rest of his people. The ambiguous ending leaves this interpretation up to the reader, and is part of the reason why Lowry's novel has been so successful and controversial.

Davy and Jonas perform as superheroes but their fantastic powers do not emulate the strident masculinity that Pecora allocates to Superman. In fact, their abilities of mind-reading and seeing the past, along with Paul's invisibility, can be regarded as essentially passive. It is the female superheroes or heroines who are most likely to possess such mental and empathic powers, along with the ability to avoid trouble and physical contact, in most traditional comics. They often function more like romantic heroines waiting to be rescued than as powerful agents. The Invisible Woman was the 'token female' character in Marvel's superhero group, 'The Fantastic Four'. She was originally called 'The Invisible Girl', indicating her rather subordinate and ineffectual role, and early plots in the 1960s and 1970s often involved her being captured and held hostage. Bearing in mind these feminised roles, before moving on to explore the lack of agency that invisibility and other passive superpowers might engender for a male teenage character, it is necessary to examine further the different types of power that the fade, the gift and the Capacity to See Beyond do actually bring Paul, Davy and Jonas.

Superpowers: Knowledge and Power

Paul's attitude towards his fantastic invisibility is at first marked by what he can tangibly *do* with it and what power it might bring. His initial thoughts are boundless in scope, but he soon discovers there are '[n]o mountains to scale in Frenchtown' (Cormier, *Fade* 63). Superhuman feats of physical energy and bravado are soon replaced by more modest ambitions of using the fade to improve his sense of empowerment or personal control over everyday life to some degree. He realises he can look at the bodies of girls and women without censure, he can play tricks on the local shopkeeper, and he can evade the town bully who inevitably tries to give chase. His uncle Adelard shared similar small-scale fantasies when he first discovered the fade in his adolescence, claiming '[I]t gave me wild desires. Made me feel as though I could do anything' (167). In fact, Adelard's power trips were always restricted to spying on girls and robbing stores. Despite the universal comic book potential of invisibility, Paul and Adelard become locked into standard adolescent desire.

The fade offers its teenage protagonist more than a fulfilment of teenage daydreams, however. In Chapter Two I discussed how far Paul's position *behind* the lens of the fade allows him to see rather than be seen and, certainly, being invisible means that Paul is able to move amongst people who do not know he is there, and thus he is able glean information and knowledge that is usually unavailable to him. Foucault's familiar remarks on the nature of power are pertinent here:

> We should admit [. . .] that power and knowledge directly imply one another; that there is no power relation without the correlative constitution of a field of knowledge, nor any knowledge that does not presuppose and constitute at the same time power relations. (*Discipline and Punish* 27–28)

With a number of avenues of knowledge opening up as he spies and eavesdrops on other people, Paul shifts the normal pattern of power relations in French-town, which usually rely on deeds performed in secret and which, furthermore, prioritise the knowledge of experienced adults over the relative naivety of a teenager. In Foucault's model of power and discipline the most effective form of control exists in the Panopticon, a surveillance structure in which the observer remains invisible to the observed, and thus where power relations are implicitly rather than explicitly or violently maintained.[16] As we shall shortly see, the height of Paul's power comes when he is able to act like the Director of a Panopticon, indicating to a terrified Toubert that he is watching and yet remaining invisible and unknowable to the captive man. In general, though, Paul's power is more secretive; it comes from underhand knowledge rather than official power. Film theorist Laura Mulvey's discussion of Freud and voyeurism is useful in framing how this situation specifically affects an adolescent subject. She explains that '[Freud's] particular examples centre on the voyeuristic activities of children, their desire to see and make sure of the private and forbidden' (Mulvey 114). Translating this desire to a teenage context increases its potency as the adolescent not only covets information about the private and forbidden, but is also eager to know what the future self might do and become. Paul is intent on invisibly watching adult interactions, particularly in physical or sexual zones, because he is uncertain of his own developing adolescent body with its treacherous urges and mysterious changes, and hopes that the sight of other people and how they act will help him gain control of his physical and social actions.

Further insights from film theory's treatment of voyeurism suggest that Paul's superhuman invisibility can also be read as the apparatus for expressly *masculine* empowerment. In his study on cinematic voyeurism, Norman Denzin cites a number of categories that the watcher might fall into, including 'the erotic, violent gaze of Peeping Toms, usually men looking at the bodies of women' (5). Denzin's work intersects with theories of the male gaze, which stipulate that in patriarchal visual representations the female form is constructed as passive (a spectacle) and is regarded through the active and powerful gaze of the hero, the director/camera and the male spectator (Doane 74–87; Mulvey). Similar critiques have argued that Cormier's novels tend towards a 'reductiveness in his references to sex in general and to females in particular' (Knowles and Malmkjër 150). The descriptions of Paul's aunt Rosanna and of his female classmate, Page Winslow, certainly offer an exclusively sexualised gaze on female bodies, concentrating as they do on breasts 'round and full and white as milk' or causing 'gentle roundnesses in her sweater' and on Page's girlish underwear when she undresses. Mastery over these women occurs on the level of fantasy, through Paul's visions of them as mere sexual objects; in reality he is helpless to confront or interact with them. In contrast, the gaze that *The Giver*'s Jonas directs towards a girl in his age group called Fiona is a direct employment of his fantastic power within a community that is kept ignorant of anything disruptive, including sexual difference. When Jonas dreams of bathing a naked Fiona he tells his parents about the unsettling feelings this engenders during their 'dream-telling' session. It is at this point that he—like other young people reaching puberty—is given medication that will eradicate the 'Stirrings' of adolescent hormones. However, his Capacity to See Beyond provides him with knowledge of human desire and love, as well as the freedom to stop taking the pills. He is free to give in to the 'wanting' that characterised his dream and to summon further images of washing Fiona in a bathtub; Fiona, on the other hand, remains a powerless object for his desires, trapped as she is in the controlling system of their community.

In *The Gift*, Davy's sister Penny plays a much more active role in the narrative and yet possibilities for action remain bound within gendered positions that correspond to the fantastic power in the novel. Davy's power, like the other protagonists', is concerned with *seeing* more than others and, crucially, Davy can penetrate the mind of his otherwise impenetrable father. The gift is difficult to interpret at times because it shows people's thoughts skewed or embellished by their mental state or weaknesses, but it still provides fantastical access to Mr Price's desires, plans and anxieties and this, in turn, helps Davy to understand his father and to change the course of his actions. Davy discusses his gift with Penny and even proves it to her by reading her mind. In this way the novel has a more communal and potentially carnivalesque feel to it than some other teenage fantastic realist texts, promoting shared knowledge and social grouping. Davy's gift remains exceptional and isolated, however, and the novel never completely reverts to the status of children's collective adventure. Despite being included in the knowledge of Davy's powers, Penny is left out of the connection, although she is desperate to understand why her father is constantly endangering their quiet lives with scams and criminal forays. She does not have a fantastic gift to help her to see her father clearly; instead the focus of her abilities is on her emotional skills. First, she is 'Dad's girl', and this implies that her feminine and daughterly qualities provide an alternative power to Davy's, one that is based on realist and interpersonal, rather than fantastic, abilities. Furthermore, Penny is identified as having empathic abilities which act almost like a magic power: 'Davy was used now to Penny knowing so much about why people did what they did, and were like what they were like. He himself always found people quite mysterious' (*The Gift* 28). Penny's intuitive knowledge links her to the feminine powers of witchcraft that will be discussed in the following section. Interestingly, Davy's fantastic gift aligns him with this conventionally feminine talent for empathy, understanding and interpretive skill, making his heroic power both more complex and less overtly masculine, and possibly suggesting that intimate and interpersonal wisdom wields as much power as clearer instances of controlling knowledge. Where knowledge, power and control do come together in teenage fantastic realism, the outcome is not necessarily straightforward. Despite the balance of power resting with the seer rather than the seen, there are inevitable aspects of growing up that reduce and problematise this power for the teenage protagonists and these are complicated further by gendered expectations of male agency that are not always reproduced in these novels.

Spiderman: Superheroes and Moral Dilemmas

Paul's most crucial act as a superhero is, at first glance, masculine and active in the most stereotypical way: killing the 'bad guy' involves violence, force and machismo, as well as superior or tactical knowledge. When Paul decides to kill Toubert he knows where to find him and how to get revenge by terrifying him, invisibly wielding a knife:

> I laughed.
> Not exactly a laugh but a giggle, a giggle of delight and triumph, enjoying not only the sight of Rudolphe Toubert sweating with fear but knowing also that my laugh, my chuckle, would hurl him into further horrors. (*Fade* 170)

Paul displays all of the superpower potential discussed above: he employs his fantastic gift in an extreme context, appearing simply as an eerie and threatening knife suspended in the air; moreover, he can observe Toubert—and the terror he is instilling in the man—while remaining hidden himself; and power and knowledge combine to place Paul in the position of superiority over Toubert that he has been desiring throughout his whole childhood. Paul's giggle, however, is significantly childish. There are Oedipal undertones in Paul's murder of Toubert (who sleeps with the desired aunt and who exerts power over the whole of the Moreaux family) and the killing scene itself, which compares Toubert's bleeding to that of Paul's father's, suggests a sense of unease in destroying what might be described as an 'anti-father'. Paul even convinces himself that the natural death of his little brother, Bernard, is some kind of cosmic revenge for his murderous act and it is possible that he is subconsciously aware that his hatred for Toubert is not completely rational. Indeed, it is later revealed that '[w]hile hardly a paragon of virtue [. . .] [Toubert] was not the vicious persona Paul depicts' (136). Guilt, confusion and desire that is fixed at Freud's Oedipal stage, limit Paul's fantastic power. The extensive and adult knowledge that it bestows is restrained by Paul's adolescent status.

Guilt is not a regular emotion for the traditional superhero. The original Superman of the 1930s is noble and untrammelled by any thought that his actions might be wrong or have negative consequences: 'He is the embodiment of society's noblest ideals, a "man of tomorrow" who foreshadows mankind's highest potentialities and profoundest aspirations but whose tremendous power, remarkably pose no danger to its freedom and safety' (Andrae 125). Later incarnations of comic book heroes embrace the complex ethics of their roles, however, and are often traumatised by their actions in much the same way as Paul is in Cormier's novel. Both Davy and Jonas also question the purpose and possibilities of their magical powers, both discovering that their abilities are not without limits. When Davy is first told about his gift at the age of seven, he hopes it will be like having a bright new toy to play with. His father also wants to restrict the gift to childish fantasy, claiming that it is a family myth and a 'silly story' that Davy should have grown out of by his age. Davy goes on to learn that his visions are neither toys nor a fairy tale. He confides to Penny that he is afraid the gift will not be able to help them understand their father any better, explaining: 'It's not like that . . . It doesn't tell you anything you want to know—only just enough to make you worry or feel afraid' (*The Gift* 87). Rather than being a plaything, his visions are disturbing and introduce unsettling knowledge and moral dilemmas that Davy has not had to manage before.

It seems reasonable to argue that the fantastic power of insight provides a fictional representation of developmental frameworks for morality at adolescence. Lawrence Kohlberg's influential model of moral development, expounded in *The Philosophy of Moral Development*, suggests that at adolescence most individuals have reached a stage either of conventional or post-conventional morality. That is, adolescents are generally understood to have moved beyond self-interest and doing good merely for reward, to a position where they can understand the need for social order and duty, or even beyond that to a kind of utilitarianism and desire for the greater good. Davy's second sight pushes him towards a more developed sense of ethics and, although he primarily uses it as a lever to force his father to go to the police and 'shop' the other criminals, the gift then allows him to see inside the mind of one of these criminals, recognising Wolf's mental illness and need of help. When Wolf appears at Granny's cottage with the intention of brutally killing the whole family[17], Davy is able to see into his thoughts: 'His mind was full of the swarming squiggles, whose abstract rage was as much a hatred of himself as of the world that had made him like he was. Poor Wolf' (*The Gift* 156). Davy's growing sense of responsibility is, in effect, spurred on by his fantastic power: because he has insight into Wolf's mind he feels he has an obligation to act upon it to help and to understand, however dangerous this might be for him. This offers a different model from Superman's noble civic ideals, which merely represent an individual's duty to maintain law and order in society. Instead we might turn to Spiderman, whose more complex morality suggests a reluctant sense of responsibility. Spiderman is a mutant and, according to critic Mel Gibson, shares with other mutants the status of outsider. He is neither wholly and magically alien (like Superman) nor is he an ordinary human. Gibson also suggests that the concerns of mutants correlate to teenage angst, insecurity and feelings of coming to terms with adulthood.[18] Part of this maturation concerns the moral reasoning that Spiderman has to employ in using his special powers, as his tag-line indicates: 'With great power comes great responsibility'. This stance points to a higher level of ethical awareness (in Kohlberg's hierarchical terms), and a more complex version of masculine power and morality. Davy's weary acceptance of his duty as the holder of a special power reflects the changes in ideology that can be read through comic book superheroes.

Paul also begins to develop a sense of ethical awareness through his voyeuristic power. This does not primarily affect his feelings about the spying or the murder he committed—although he regrets these to an extent—but instead chiefly forces him to protect or save the next hereditary fader, his nephew. When the adult Paul realises that his gift has been passed on and that another adolescent will have to deal with the dubious gift of invisibility, he is determined:

> I would find him.
> Warn him, protect him.
> I would try to do for that poor fader what my uncle Adelard had never been able to do for me. (*Fade* 178)

Paul is determined to help his nephew Ozzie resist the fade, rather than use it for personal gain or violent satisfaction. The novel clearly reveals that invisibility is not a gift in any positive sense but rather that it is a burden. Although my discussion above stresses Paul's initial identification with the superhero and his realisation that invisibility equates to more personal aspects of power (such as voyeuristic knowledge), the scenarios that Paul witnesses due to the fade represent the underbelly of adult experience and illustrate types of human deception and depravity. His uncle recognises this aspect of the fade immediately and is also contrite about passing it on through his genes, saying to Paul, 'I'm sorry you have to carry the burden of the fade' (88). Returning to the concept of voyeurism, then, it is possible to align Paul with the position of passive victim rather than active gazer. Denzin's taxonomy of voyeurism includes a further category of the voyeur as a troubled individual, referring to 'the accidental, unexpected gaze of innocent by-standers, including children who happen to see what others don't want to see' (5). Rather than learning from the experience of observation, the voyeur is damaged; and instead of being in a position of active power through seeing everything, like Foucault's Director in the Panopticon system of surveillance, the spectator is powerless to intercede or interact. Paul's helplessness is at its most obvious when he encounters sexual activities which he had never before imagined, and which he considers depraved and incomprehensible. One of his first experiences of the fade takes him to the back room of shopkeeper Mr Dondier. Paul considers playing a trick 'among the fruits and vegetables and canned goods' (65) but instead ends up discovering that Mr Dondier pays thirteen-year-old Theresa Terrault money so that he can secretly burrow 'between her thighs.' Paul's response is fear and disgust, vomit rising in his throat and his heart pounding. A similar event occurs later in the novel when Paul invisibly enters the house of Emerson Winslow—his elegant classmate—and discovers that Emerson is enjoying an incestuous affair with his twin sister, Page. As the twins kiss, Paul tries to shut his eyes:

> But, astonished, still saw them clutching each other, having forgotten that my eyelids, too, were in the fade, and could not prevent me from seeing [...] I clamped my hands against my ears, sank down to the floor, crouching, my ears filled with the distant echo of a seashell's roar, but I was not at the seashore, I was in the bedroom with Emerson Winslow and his sister, Page. (102)

In both cases any power gained through visual knowledge and sexual mastery is immediately renounced because Paul cannot actively participate in these bodily pleasures. Instead he is left impotent. Although the fade satisfies Paul's adolescent and voyeuristic desires, it then imprisons him in a position of observing that which he is not ready to see. He is also forced to cope with his new knowledge in isolation, as the only person he can talk to about the fade is his uncle Adelard, who shares the gift but who also knows the burden of it and who soon leaves Frenchtown. Rather than provide him with an active or heroic wisdom about worldly matters, Paul's observations destabilise his own sense of knowledge and morals, and his ability to act with positive agency.

Of the three novels discussed in this section Lowry's makes most explicit the moral responsibility that a fantastic gift places upon the protagonist and reveals how the superhero trope can rob them of individual agency. While Jonas is being taught his duties by the current Receiver, the older man explains, 'I have great honour. So will you. But you will find that that is not the same as power' (*The Giver* 107). In fact Jonas learns very quickly that his Capacity to See Beyond and know more than his fellow citizens—and not being able to tell them about this knowledge—is lonely, frustrating and disempowering:

> He didn't want the memories, didn't want the honour, didn't want the wisdom, didn't want the pain. He wanted his childhood again, his scraped knees and ball games. He sat in his dwelling alone, watching through the window [. . .] ordinary lives free of anguish because he had been selected, as others before him had, to bear their burden. (151)

In this novel, more overtly than in *The Gift* or *Fade*, the possibilities evoked by a fantastic power are linked to adolescence through an explicit loss of childhood, an increased sense of responsibility, and an awareness of the burden that adult power can be. It is difficult to read absolute agency through the superhero trope in *The Giver* as the text denies Jonas those possibilities to *transcend* a very limited and structured society, even when he rebels and escapes the Community in his act of resistance and rupture. Latham attempts to interpret the narrative optimistically, arguing that Jonas represents an agent of 'positive social change' and that the novel itself avoids the tendency of the 'typical' adolescent novel to tell stories about uncontrollable teenagers being taught how to conform (134). Jonas does not take control in a powerful, adult, functioning society, however, but is simply the most responsible citizen in a community that is cosseted, immature and innocent; he takes on adult responsibility in a childish version of the state. In this way, Jonas hardly rebels against the norms of dominant ideology nor does he assert any kind of radical adolescent power. Instead, he develops the very qualities that would reintegrate him into a conventional adult world of power relations. Even Latham admits that:

> *The Giver* is ultimately a socializing novel in the sense that, through reading it, adolescents experience vicariously what Trites describes as their 'capacity to disturb the universe' [. . .] while simultaneously being reintegrated into the power structures of that universe in which they will enact their own power. (150)

The superhero trope offers adolescent protagonists a way of taking on a powerful identity in a world that is more usually controlling and constrained. The superhero in fantastic realism is a way of finding agency through magical means, but there is always a threat that this magic ultimately returns the teenager to an appropriate position as adult in society. A more recent novel by Matt Whyman called *Superhuman* explicitly spells out the links between male adolescent agency and superpowers by creating a character who is part of a painfully cool subculture of skateboarders and graffiti artists but who is also the son of a real superhero. Like subcultural teenagers, who adopt a temporary identity, the protagonists of teenage fantastic realism soon realise that their superpowers are limited by certain expectations of age and gender. They cannot change the world or escape from it forever, and ultimately their powers are a magical way of reintegrating them into the adult world. Teenage superheroes are constrained by changing narrative conventions which force them to 'grow up' into modern men. Female superheroes may not yet have reached that state. According to Sabin, 'when [women] appear as characters [in comic books], they are invariably either plot devices (there to be rescued) or sex symbols (all plunging necklines and endless legs)' (221). It is not surprising, therefore, that an alternative subcultural identity has materialised in the less male-dominated realm of magic and witchcraft. But are witches any more desirable as figures of empowerment for young girls?

Witches

In contrast to the superhero—a fictional character created to reflect ideas of power and masculinity—the witch has the status of mythical being, real historical figure, fairy tale character and modern icon. Through these identities she offers complex and hybrid versions of femininity, and her powers are also more ambiguous. In certain epochs, especially when Christianity is ideologically dominant, witches are viewed as anomalous, malevolent and dangerous, although a modern-day, anthropological interpretation might describe witchcraft rather as a specific practice employed by humans with extraordinary powers (Sanders). Christina Larner, for example, argues that the witch is 'by definition, an abnormal person' (45). Secular societies treat supernatural abilities with greater scepticism but also imbue the image of the witch—particularly the teenage witch—with more positive and glamorous powers. Much modern paganism, for example, draws on the rich history and mythology of witchcraft to form its benign worldview, and a number of cultural critics have pointed to the way that witchcraft has been appropriated as a signifier of the adolescent in recent television series such as *Sabrina the Teenage Witch* (1996–2003), *Buffy the Vampire Slayer* (1997–2003) and *Charmed* (1998–2006). P.G. Maxwell-Stuart astutely points out that US television series such as *Sabrina* indicate the fact that 'the twentieth century appears to prefer the youthful image' when it comes to witches (141; see also Moseley 403–422). Thus the figure of the witch is one of a fearful outsider and yet she also holds an alluring and potentially dangerous power that is incomprehensible to those (adults) around her. Witches are mostly, although not exclusively, portrayed as female, and in fantastic realist texts protagonists are constructed and construct themselves using the elements of witchcraft that are most appropriate to female adolescence. The process is not dissimilar to that of subcultural identification, where teenagers build a sense of self through a bricolage of styles and through experimentation with beliefs, behaviour and image. The following discussion of witches in teenage fantastic realism will consider how far the various strands of witchcraft offer active power to contemporary adolescence. Does re-invention through a magical identity radically empower teenage heroines or problematically bind them to certain conventional notions of feminine abilities?

From Myth to Political Stance: Images of Femininity

Ronald Hutton's *The Triumph of the Moon* attempts to disentangle the way that witchcraft as a recent movement has drawn upon ancient roots. Although he argues that many of the symbols and stories that writers and occultists have used to describe ancient witchcraft rituals and traditions have mainly been shaped since the late eighteenth century, it is nevertheless clear that supernatural frameworks were in place before the advent of Christianity in the Western world. These include fertility rites, pagan deities, magical processes and an investment in the spirituality of nature, as well as a number of figures that appear under the guise of the witch. How far early beliefs have worked their way into later systems is difficult to tell. Hutton follows many recent historians, for example, in disclaiming Margaret Murray's theory that modern witchcraft emerged from an extant and coherent pagan religion that had survived covertly in British rural areas (Hutton 194–201). The witch arguably has her most distinct origins in both pre-Christian paganism and in the classical world. Kathryn Hoffmann finds precursors for early modern women accused of witchcraft in the goddesses Medea and Ceres (459–470)[19] and these mythical characters continue to contribute to feminist narratives of empowered female sorcerers. They also appeal to modern conceptions of a true pagan witchcraft religion that worshipped a goddess figure, and they remain potent symbols of witchy femininity in various guises. It is impossible to ignore the most enduring image of the witch as a historical figure, either as a benign healer or malevolent devil-worshipper. Originally there were two types of witchcraft across Europe: white magic, which was healing, and black magic which was malevolent. In the fifteenth century the Canon Law of the Church introduced a theory that witches were in a demonic pact with the Devil. Consequently all witchcraft was viewed with suspicion, as even a white witch could be corrupted and 'turn bad'. During the early modern period at least 40,000 people are supposed to have been executed in Europe through witchcraft laws and there was a distinct shift from 'the isolated harrying of individuals to a widespread crusade against witchcraft, to a recognisable mania and persecution' (Larner 3). Although it is not true that all accused witches were female, the majority *were* women from all parts of society. Feminist historians highlight the historical misogyny that sees women attacked when, for instance, they display professional abilities to threaten male-centred economies (such as healing, in place of the doctor). More recent forms of witchcraft celebrate the least menacing elements of practice and belief. Wicca is the best-known religious movement of its type in the Western world and its tenets stress the importance of benevolent Pantheism, ritual and an ancient festive calendar. Wiccans also worship a Mother Goddess (sometimes with a male consort) who is a product of combined concepts of classical goddesses, Mother Nature, wise women and an empowerment of the female spirit. Wiccan groups are not all feminist in nature but clearly there is an exchange of ideas between the two movements, especially in terms of female autonomy. For contemporary readers, therefore, the witch is equally likely to be evoked as an aged and despised hag of myth and fairy tale, a female victim of early modern history, or a compellingly sexual teenage seductress in television and film. The figure of the witch evokes ambiguous responses and in this respect it is relatively easy to understand the attraction of creating teenage witches in young adult literature. Both the female adolescent and the witch are viewed with a mixture of awe, envy and fear, and with desire to contain and control.

Before moving on to a reading of specific images of witchcraft in teenage witchcraft narratives, it is worth bearing in mind that, despite a continuing focus on the individual in these texts, becoming a witch at adolescence is also a social act. In Margaret Mahy's *The Changeover* (1984), for example, the heroine, Laura, is told how she will be initiated into the craft by her friend Sorry and his mother and grandmother: 'As you know, you're what we call a sensitive, my dear. You stand on the threshold of our condition, and we can invite you in —Sorry, Miryam and I. We could help you to make a witch of yourself' (102). The act of initiation combines individual will—making a witch of yourself, and all the implications for individual development this entails—with encouragement from within a shared magical community that is often expressly female. Initiation into a coven most clearly uses imagery and ideology from modern witchcraft practice, neopaganism, or Wicca religions, since the concept of covens is historically suspect[20] and, like female subcultures, covens offer a fantasy zone for disempowered adolescent girls as well as a chance to shed fears of being different or abnormal and to embrace a shared identity instead. As we have already seen, this shared social space can often include mothers and daughters as well as peers, since modern witchcraft often encourages the passing on of knowledge and destiny through maternal lines. In *The Changeover*, Laura is invited to join a 'feminine magic' by Sorry and his mother and grandmother; in Marianne Curley's *Old Magic* (2000), Kate is taught the powers and restrictions of growing up as a white witch by her grandmother, Jillian; and in the historical novel *Witch Child* (2000) by Celia Rees, Mary is protected on her journey to Puritan New England by her mother's coven:

> All along the coast, I saw women in high places, on craggy headlands and jutting promontories, keeping a watch for our passing. [. . .] I knew that they had been sent there by my mother. Word had gone out to protect me. I am her daughter and she is a most powerful witch. (*Witch Child* 47)

Becoming one of the 'imaginary creatures' (*The Changeover* 134) of a female coven, or 'connecting with the rhythmic time/space dimension of *the feminine*

Imaginary' (sic) (110) as Wilkie-Stibbs puts it, is only part of the initiation process. Teenage witches are also initiated into *practices*, which indicate their membership in a subcultural body. This process can also function as a 'coming of age', setting protagonists aside from their previous selves and offering a new, mature subjectivity. Jean Thesman's *The Other Ones* (1999), for example, tells the story of Bridget Raynes, a socially dislocated teenager who has witchcraft powers but hopes to ignore them so that she can behave like any ordinary adolescent and avoid being teased by the school bullies. Unfortunately for her, her maternal aunt is a witch who is determined to welcome Bridget into her culture.

> One day Aunt Cait had simply asked, 'Do you remember the earth spirit in Seattle, the one you knew when you were five?'
> When I nodded, she asked me if I ever saw beings like that in Bayhead.
> Of course I had. I knew the earth spirits in the fields and the tree spirits in every tree I saw.
> I had shaken my head in a lie that day, but Cait had brushed back my hair and said,
> 'Don't deny your powers. You're special. There are reasons . . . .'
> But I'd cried and said, 'I don't want to be different. I want to be like everybody else.' (*The Other Ones* 16)

Wanting to be like everybody else indicates a crucial strand in social theories of adolescence, as peer acceptance offers a relatively safe space in which to affirm identities. The peer group at Bridget's school consists of 'competing cliques' who have 'more fun excluding people than including them' (2), and Bridget struggles and fails to gain approval from her aggressively popular classmates. She finally submits and attends a night meeting where she is welcomed by her 'threshold guardian' (a comical spirit called Xiii) and the community of witches known as the 'Other Ones'. She is introduced to their practice: ' "From the beginning," a tall young woman said, "each of us has been a threshold. Gifts pass through us. Healing, compassion, and safety flow into the world. We create. We build" ' (174).

Bridget's status as 'threshold' is significant since it has connotations of the liminal space between one state and another and so signals a concern with her transitional nature as teenager and as witch. Bridget becomes a witch through her actions, however, which become increasingly mature and responsible and which stake out her position in the society of witches. She goes on to use her powers to release those suffering from the 'bad dream' of reality by sending them into a fantastical existence beyond bullying, poverty or grieving. Interestingly, Bridget's initiation is also symbolically marked by the disappearance of Xiii who is replaced by a cat familiar called Nimuâ, a true emblem of witchcraft. (A similar transition to the adult state occurs to all characters in the secondary world of Philip Pullman's 'His Dark Materials' fantasy trilogy

[1995–2000], where animal daemons become fixed in a certain shape at the point of puberty and sexual maturity.)

The following readings examine selective images of witchcraft in order to construct female adolescence as *acceptably* empowered on a personal level in Marianne Curley's *Old Magic* (2000) and in Margaret Mahy's witchcraft novels, *The Haunting* (1982), *The Changeover* (1984) and *The Tricksters* (1986).

In *Old Magic* fifteen-year-old Kate has been raised as a witch by her grandmother, Jillian. When a mysterious new boy, Jarrod, arrives at school she spends weeks trying to convince him of his own powers of sorcery but he stubbornly refuses to believe in any supernatural phenomena that might disrupt his reliance on logic and reason. Jarrod finally realises that he needs Kate's help because his family has been cursed by an ancient and powerful sorcerer. The teenagers travel back in time in order to change history and deflect the hex, as well as to help Jarrod discover and accept his innate witchcraft. Kate is an outsider. She and Jillian literally live away from the rest of the community, halfway up a mountain. Socially too she is an outcast, but is content with this alternative status. She and her best friend describe themselves as the 'weirdos' and are happy to be shunned by the more popular group at school: 'we're different, we don't conform to strict society rules. Hannah is simply too poor... and of course, she hangs around with me—*Scary Face*' (*Old Magic* 56). Kate's tolerance of her social position defies the stereotypical adolescent desire for acceptance that the other teenage characters in the novel display. Her behaviour is structured through an alternative framework of adolescence that sees subcultural identity as a way of reclaiming power from the dominant social group. Kate uses her witchcraft as a form of resistance, defiantly setting herself apart from the rest of her community and proudly defining herself via a modern version of paganism, in which she is training to be a healer and spell-weaver. Representing Kate in this way aligns her with the 'outsiders' who are constructed as such according to labelling theory. Kate knows that the term 'witch' is often employed as an insult or threat because witchcraft practice is outside of the norms or rules of general society, in the same way that drug taking, 'anti-social behaviour' and sexual experimentation are perceived to be activities that place adolescents beyond the boundaries of accepted conduct. Kate's awareness illustrates the theory that labelling is a cultural action rather than a natural classification of what is normal and what is deviant. She and her grandmother have always been viewed with a certain amount of fear because of their status, but Kate resists the stereotypical labels employed by their neighbours: 'Sure, [Jillian]'s a witch, but most people have stupid preconceived ideas of what a witch is. Jillian's not "typical" in any way' (12). Kate's implication is that the witch is not necessarily a fixed identity that has to be feared or despised. Careful historical study of the persecution of witches in the Middle Ages would support this view, pointing to the fact that witchcraft's connection to deviancy is cultural and political rather than inherent. Maxwell-Stuart points out that before changes in Christian dogma rendered magic suspect, versions of the witch were an everyday part of society and types of enchantment were practised by all kinds of individuals, from village healers to clergymen:

> We should [. . .] put aside the modern habit of drawing strict boundaries between magic, religion, and the natural sciences. [. . .] Magic, it should be emphasized, was not an exotic recourse to which people turned when religion or 'science' in the form of medicine had failed. [. . .] It was a perfectly valid extra or alternative way of seeking to exercise power. (47)

Kate welcomes the label 'witch' because it provides her with an identity that allows her to feel empowered without having to subscribe to the mainstream behaviour or concern with appearance that other girls in the novel embrace unthinkingly. Initially, in fact, Kate's magic is portrayed as naturally attractive and powerful precisely because she does not approve of expectations of 'normal' feminine adolescence. Her own genuine charms (of the non-magical kind) are compared with Tasha's. Tasha is one of the 'trendies' and portrays herself as a 'blonde airhead' despite being the cleverest girl in class. Kate explains:

> she acts like a bimbo, pumping out feminine charm by the bucket load. And the guys love it. I think of a spell that will make her body create a flush of testosterone. I colourfully visualise her delicate flawless cheeks disappearing beneath a layer of bristly dark facial hair. The thought makes me dizzy. (106)

Kate is represented as a rebel against the kinds of prescribed femininity that conventional discourses of adolescence advocate, but as such she also comfortably resides within actively resistant subcultural frameworks. Although she does not go so far as actually de-feminising Tasha, she possesses the powerful knowledge that she has the spell at her fingertips; and, although at the end of the novel she has not radically re-ordered the factional social structure of her school community, she *has* managed to educate Jarrod in the superficial nature of the trendies and convince him to be her boyfriend on a more meaningful basis. Kate's witch identity is both defiant and empowering on a personal level despite, or even because of, its marginal status. She might be compared to other fictional witches who are aligned with additional marginalised identities in an attempt to empower the female teenager. In the television series *Buffy the Vampire Slayer*, for example, Buffy's friend Willow is witch, lesbian and Jew, but each minority identity provides her with a powerful sense of difference.

The Haunting tells the story of Troy, a quiet and seemingly unremarkable girl who inherits the status of 'Scholar Magician' from her maternal uncle, Cole. The title 'Scholar Magician' is somewhat ironic, as it implies the kind of sorcery earned through book-learning that is more often associated with masculine forms of magic. The Scholar Magician, however, displays innate witchcraft rather than learnt magic. At first the story revolves around her younger brother,

Barney, whom Cole presumes to be the next magician because he is the only male child of his generation; but towards the end of the novel Troy reveals that she has always hidden her witchcraft ability in an attempt to remain normal. In another of Mahy's novels, *The Tricksters*, Harry Hamilton develops strange witchy characteristics while she is on a summer holiday with her extended family at their holiday house, 'Carnival's Hide'. She innocently conjures up three ghostly spirits—the Tricksters—who join the family and cause havoc. Harry falls in love with the most sympathetic Trickster, Felix, but by doing this she gives him more power over his brothers Hadfield and Ovid. In revenge, Ovid stage-manages the Hamiltons so that older sister Christobel humiliates Harry by publicly reading her unfinished romantic novel. Harry responds by telling the family secret—that her father Jack had an affair with Christo's friend Emma, and that Emma's baby is his child. The Tricksters disappear, leaving the Hamiltons to mend their fractured family.

Like the heroine of *Old Magic*, Harry and Troy both consider themselves to be outsiders, lost in their own thoughts and in many ways ignored by their relatives. In each family dynamic the teenage girls are initially silent and relatively inactive. In an interesting twist on the usual pattern of witchcraft's matrilineal lineage, Troy is actually not recognised as a plausible candidate for Scholar Magician because she is 'just a girl', and is completely overlooked. She also appears to have little effect on the power structures that weave through her complicated family. Her father remarries after his first wife, Dove Scholar, dies giving birth to Barney. Consequently Troy and her siblings are left with an extended family, including a pregnant stepmother and three sets of grandparents, as well as a Great-Granny Scholar, 'a terrible old lady, a small, thin witch, frail but furious' (*The Haunting* 11). The family is mostly controlled by this old lady, who refuses to accept that any magic flourishes in her blood and, to counteract it, has 'clipped and pruned [her children] as if [they] were a family of standard roses' (64). In opposition to this ordered upbringing, Troy's younger and more outgoing sister Tabitha tries to organise the family through her self-imposed role as 'family novelist', searching out facts and details and recording them in the novel she means to publish when she is twenty-one. Troy, in contrast, is neither vocal nor controlling, and goes so far as to avoid any conflict or manipulation. She is notably almost voiceless throughout the novel, and when there is a tense argument she wanders off 'to lean against the wall in a forgotten corner of the room' (22). Likewise, Harry is the third child in a family of five and, as such, is positioned as the awkward teenager, mostly outshone and overlooked by Christo, who teases her for being like 'something from out-space' or as having puppy fat like 'a mature St Bernard' (*The Tricksters* 37). Harry tries hard to feel important in her own right but is disappointed to realise that she desperately craves Christo's approval.

Both witches embrace the opportunity to construct a new adolescent self that is powerful and mysterious. Once Troy acknowledges her fantastic abilities she revels in the fact that she can finally flaunt her magic and reorder the power structures in her family. Tabitha is subdued by her older sister's sudden transformation, complaining that now it seems everybody in the family is special in some way except her, while Great-Grandmother Scholar is undermined when Troy exposes her as a witch who is endowed with the very magic and creativity she seeks to repress. Troy takes control of the workings of family life, using her supernatural knowledge to bring out into the open family secrets that need discussing, such as Barney's fear that his stepmother Clare will die in childbirth like his own mother did. At the same time she gains specific freedoms that are relevant to her status as teenage girl. When her stepmother warns her to be careful when going for a walk at night, for example, Clare corrects herself, saying 'I don't suppose I'll ever need to worry about you again, will I? I don't suppose I've ever needed to worry over a magician' (*The Haunting* 124). Harry also changes from being quiet and seemingly unremarkable to controlling the balance of power and knowledge at Carnival's Hide. In her new witchy identity she can change the dynamics of her family with one word about her father Jack, much in the way that she evokes the Tricksters through the story she tells about them in her romantic novel. Although distraught that she has revealed her father's secret infidelity to Christobel, Harry realises that she had always wanted to be the one to deflate her sister's self-involved attitude and she performs this liberating domestic feat 'wearing her enchantress face' (*The Tricksters* 230).

Harry uses her 'enchantress' self in much the same way that Kate employs her reputation as witch, adopting it defiantly when the situation determines. This new self also entails an element of performative identity. Harry calls her inner witch into being through rediscovering her original name, Adrienne, and re-christening herself as an individual 'who could make people think she was beautiful simply by declaring herself so' (172). She becomes like a classical goddess, in control of her powers and the fate of those around her. Elsewhere I have argued that Harry can be compared to Medea, a goddess who kills her children in revenge for Jason's fickle love. On a less dramatic scale, Harry also turns against her family when she is betrayed by Christo and partly destroys it by revealing Jack's affair.[21] Troy is similarly demonstrative and, in a reversal of her old silent self, confidently asserts that she is the Scholar Magician, desperate to flow into her new identity: ' "Oh, let me!" begged Troy. "I'm not going to be the same Troy again, anyway. Let me be free! No nightmares, promise!" And she held out her arms, became a flowering tree, a flying bird, a burning girl, a creature made of stars' (121). These shapes visually express her status as witch illustrating various forms of witchcraft: growth, freedom, defiance in the face of persecution and natural cosmic power. Alongside the image of a historical witch being burnt at the stake[22] these fantastic metamorphoses link Troy to the mythical goddess Daphne, who changes into a laurel tree to escape Apollo's sexual advances. Troy's witchcraft is thus represented through anomalous versions of the witch, although each portrays resistant forms of femaleness. Indeed, each fantastic realist text under discussion here incorporates elements of witchcraft that serve the representation of their empowered teenage witch rather than form a coherent account of historical events or modern religions. There are some witchcraft novels that employ more unified pictures: Cate Tiernan's *Wicca* series (2001–), for example, acts as a fictional introduction to the contemporary pagan belief system and Katheryn Lasky's *Beyond the Burning Time* (1994) is a purely historical novel that presents a fictionalisation of events during the Salem witch hunts but does not incorporate any fantastic elements. Yet in *Old Magic*, *The Haunting*, *The Changeover* and *The Tricksters*, myth, history, religion and feminist rhetoric exist concurrently in an amalgam of images and connotations.

Diane Purkiss argues that contemporary witches, particularly those with a radical feminist agenda, have taken up disparate images of witchcraft and reorganised them to serve their purpose, highlighting the historically oppressed nature of womanhood but also putting forward a claim that specifically feminine witchcraft has its own possibilities and agency. This new 'myth' of witchcraft combines the oppressed and marginalised woman who struggles against dominant power play in a patriarchal world, the matriarchal Goddess Mother who represents eternal cycles of life, and the timeless image of woman as 'midwife-herbalist-healer' in an ideal feminised society. What Purkiss describes is a 'bricolage' of attitudes, iconography and representations that can be compared, without too much of a stretch, to the phenomenon of bricolage amongst teenage subcultures. The discourses that adolescents are perceived as borrowing from and reshaping in subcultural theory also range from the historical and mythical to the contemporary and political. In employing an eclectic mixture of witchcraft images to portray female adolescence, fantastic realism selects those aspects that appear to be most liberating or empowering for its protagonists. One very clear arena where this process takes place is that of teenage sexuality.

The Hag and the Temptress: Power and Sexuality

In the discursive fields of adolescence and of witchcraft, female sexuality is a key site of potential repression and empowerment. Witches are represented as sexual beings, not through the binary of wife/whore, but through opposing figures of 'hag' and 'temptress'. The first of these figures originates in Christian fears of the demonic and is represented most forcibly in the *Malleus Maleficarum* or 'The Witches Hammer', a treatise published by two German clergymen and inquisitors in 1486 and meant to guide and encourage the identification and treatment of witches. Here it describes the vision of witches copulating with the Devil's creatures:

> the witches themselves have often been seen lying on their backs in the fields or the woods, naked up to the very navel, and it has been apparent from the disposition of those limbs and members which pertain to the venereal act and orgasm, as also from the agitation of their legs and thighs,

that, all invisibly to the bystanders, they have been copulating with Incubus devils. (Kramer and Sprenger 114)

What is stressed throughout the text is the unnaturalness of this act. Sexual union with the Devil is described in terms of perversion, disgust and excessive sexual appetite. With the dogmatic link between witchcraft and Satanism came this picture of the lusting hag whose desire for the Devil or one of his spirits (in the form of an animal 'familiar') continues into old age and thus signals an unnatural (that is, non-reproductive) sexual hunger. If aged sexual perversion is one stereotype that has retained its power, an alternative version of excessive sexuality maintains a youthful image. Highly sexual and alluring goddess witches or temptresses have their roots in classical narratives of beautifully dangerous enchantresses such as Circe or Medea, or in biblical figures such as Eve or Lilith.[23] These women aid the gods with magic potions and spells, but can turn men into swine; they bear life but destroy man through weakness and rebellion. Here sexualised witchcraft is not abhorrent but seductive and yet remains couched in terms of danger and excessiveness. Both the hag and the temptress have unnatural libidinous natures that threaten traditional sexual power relations. In *The Virago Book of Witches* editor Shahrukh Husain collates fifty-seven tales of witchcraft originating from a variety of folklore and mythical traditions, of which a remarkable number involve a seductress or a narrative imbued with sexual elements. Husain explains part of the reason for this: 'Young men were in constant danger of the witch's lust which, sharpened by the expert sex-play of Old Nick and his virile imps, threatened to strip them of their vitality—or make them redundant' (xvi–xvii).

Radical feminist critics have appropriated this excessive witch as a liberatory figure, persecuted because of her marginal status but politicised through her subversive sexual desires. Catherine Clément's and Hélène Cixous' witch is associated with the hysteric and provides a wildly imaginative paradigm for femininity that will not be controlled. Their witches attend sabbats where sexuality is carnivalised through laughter and a 'mingling, a mixing of bodies' (Clément and Cixous 37). Teenage fantastic realism is more likely to borrow selectively from sexualised discourses of witchcraft, offering a sense of personal empowerment to its teenage witches rather than representing them as actively defying existing sexual hegemony.

In *The Tricksters*, Harry's witchy abilities develop alongside a burgeoning sexuality. At the beginning of the novel she unsuspectingly evokes the Tricksters through her storytelling and through a pact with the sea: 'She slid the white ring on to her finger. It was rather large but looked convincing on her brown hand. "There! I've married the sea. I'm Mrs Oceanus," she said. "Everything comes out of me"' (23–24). Later she realises that she 'had crumpled things up by wishing to be the sea's wife' (26). Descriptions of Harry in the sea throughout the novel are sensual. At the end of the narrative she repeats her wedding vows to the ocean and experiences an ecstatic sense of oneness with the natural elements: 'In the end she was indeed possessed by the brute blood of the air so powerfully but so delicately it was like no possession she had ever imagined' (263). These descriptive passages are fleeting reminders that Harry's magical summons of the Carnival triplets have opened her up to sensuality in a new way. Her old self, 'sexless as a tennis racquet', is threatened by the appearance of Trickster Felix (who closely resembles Belen, the winged man she has created for herself in her secret writings) and they become lovers. But Felix is not real and Harry worries that she has 'made love with a ghost' (220). Their liaison represents only a slightly more substantial version of Harry's romantic imaginings about the dashing villain Belen and both represent a form of adolescent sexual fantasy. Her writing and her magic conjure up Felix to fall in love with; in a way Harry is a seductress, a siren or a spell-weaver alluring and binding a man to her as the enchantresses seduce Odysseus, or as witches have traditionally done throughout history using 'binding spells'. Sexual identity and power is tested within the safety of the fantastic and, in this way, the evocation of Felix can either be seen as the whim of a powerful erotic sorceress or as the extended practice-run of a sexually curious teenager, mirroring the kind of fantasy a girl might really perform using magazines, TV and film, or music as her props.

In *The Changeover*, Laura's transformation into a witch is also marked by a recognition of her sexual power. Distraught by her little brother's magical illness, she tries to decide whether she should make the permanent change from an 'ordinary' girl into a witch in order to save him. Her mother is also clearly upset and, as we have already seen, seeks sexual comfort from a new boyfriend. Being starkly confronted with her mother's sexuality acts as a catalyst, first for Laura to think about losing her virginity as an emotional outlet, and then to persuade her that she should take power into her own hands and embrace her magic identity. The journey from being a 'sensitive' to becoming a witch takes her through symbolic landscapes of menstruation and the possibilities of reproduction, and this crossover also awakens the latent sexuality in Laura's teenage body. The preparations for this journey involve being dressed up in an expressly feminine and sensual costume: '[Miryam] hung chains of silver around Laura's neck and then dropped over her wet head a white, silky shift laced across the breast so that the chains showed beneath it' (136). When she wakes she finds Sorry, her fellow witch, transfixed by her breasts and awed by her changed state, which is powerfully appealing and yet terrifying to him. Miryam explains that all women have this charm whether or not they are witches:

> Sometimes I think all women are imaginary creatures, as Sorry chooses to put it. He doesn't mean that we're simply imagined, you know, but that our power flows out of the imagination, and that's the faculty that makes magicians of all of us. Witches just act upon it with such conviction that their dreams turn into reality. (134)

Magic allure in this context does not merely function to attract men but is part of the empowering experience of being female.

This ostensibly empowering sexuality requires more careful consideration as it is easy to equate it with a version of female power that is in fact complicit with existing patriarchal frameworks. Rachel Moseley has examined a similar emphasis on feminine allure in her reading of teenage witchcraft films. She argues:

> In the way in which it brings together conventional ideals of femininity and female power, 'glamour' can be understood as figuring a postfeminist identity which, whilst informed by second-wave feminism, rejects the feminist identities associated with it, instead celebrating and understanding conventional modes of femininity as *not necessarily* in conflict with female power. (Moseley 419)

Moseley's analysis suggests that teenage witches in television and film illustrate a contemporary urge for teenage girls to embrace images that are both powerful and still acutely feminine. Like the teenage witches in fantastic realism, they can possess active magical prowess and yet continue to celebrate expressly teenage and feminine qualities such as non-reproductive sexuality. Moseley warns, however, that the terms 'allure' and 'glamour' are 'double-edged', and that wanting to 'have it all' exposes tensions and problems in this iconic form of postfeminism. The concept of 'having it all' is nicely complemented by Purkiss's disquiet with the bricolage effect of modern paganism or Wicca: 'The problem for witches who want to assert creativity and control is that witchcraft remains, on the whole, tied to an historical narrative which is well-nigh inescapable as a male fantasy about what femininity should be' (39). She claims that the image of the witch employed by modern practitioners and by radical feminists is not based on any real or feasible version of womanhood, but on a mistaken fantasy of having it all:

> There is more than a passing resemblance between the witch-herbalist and the fantasy superwoman heroine of the 1980s and 90s, professional women who have beautiful country gardens, bake their own bread, make their own quilts, and demonstrate sexuality at every turn. (20)

Purkiss's point illustrates a valid concern that a bricolage approach to identity may ultimately serve to hamper women—and teenage girls—by constructing an image that simply combines a number of gendered expectations in an impossible fantasy rather than challenging any of them. In teenage fantastic realism that identity is particularly confused through the conflicting discourses of adolescence and witchcraft.

The sexualities on offer through images of the witch are modified by frameworks of female adolescence. Teenage witches may not resemble the persecuted and unnatural hag, but they are also some distance from the sorceresses of feminist discourse such as Cixous' and Clément's witches. Harry, Troy, Laura and Kate are not represented as wholly liberated and independent women. Laura and Sorry both struggle over their desire to go to bed with each other, finally deciding to defer the moment of consummating their relationship until Laura gets older, Sorry returns from occupational training, and when they might 'get married' or 'live together somehow' (*The Changeover* 203). Laura is actually relieved that Sorry is going away for three years so that she can have 'a little longer to be [her mother's] daughter and Jacko's sister' (205). This waiting time not only highlights conventional concern with feminine restraint but also the concept of adolescence as a pause or stage on the route to adulthood and a stable relationship.

In *Old Magic*, the magic that Kate inherits from her grandmother is shaped by a classic concern of social discourses of the teenager. Both her grandmother and her mother became pregnant when they were fifteen and Kate is terrified of following their pattern. In the second part of the novel she uses her witchcraft to transport her and Jarrod back in time to visit his ancestors and stop them being cursed by an evil sorcerer. In this more magical society she is freer than ever to actively use her powers to protect herself. Yet, instead of feeling liberated, she remains bound by the social and sexual concerns of her developing relationship with Jarrod. When they pretend to be married and have to share a bed, she deflects his advances, explaining to herself: 'I'm wary of taking a major step towards intimacy. If we kissed or anything, would it stop there? I don't quite trust myself' (*Old Magic* 202). Kate's witchy sense of empowerment declines in a number of ways in the second half of the novel, where traditional versions of female magic override her initial defiant resistance. Although she is the dominant character in the first part of the novel—in control of her gift and concerned to help Jarrod recognise his own witchcraft—Kate is overpowered by the medieval sorcerer Rhauk when she travels into the past. He captures, drugs and paralyses her, leaving Jarrod to accept his own magical power in order to rescue her. The final showdown between Jarrod and Rhauk positions them as villain and hero while Kate is reduced to a romantic heroine whose abilities are stripped away and who can only act in typically feminine and vulnerable terms: ' "Hurry, Jarrod" I urge softly, curling into his chest, knowing a horrid death is only seconds away' (299). Even when they return to the present, where Kate is at home with her witchiness, versions of feminine magic return her to conventional gender expectations. During their travels Jarrod has finally discovered that he can control the weather. This is a talent that Kate has always coveted and he instructs her on what to do: 'Keep your eyes closed and concentrate on something you really want. Go with your heart, Kate' (315). This episode exposes two features of young adult witchcraft fiction: first, it points to the tendency to link female magic to the heart, to emotion and to innate ability rather than book-learning or skill. In a similar manner, Laura is advised by Sorry to enchant her 'mark' (the magic token that will defeat Carmody

Braque) and is told to follow her senses rather than any formal spell: 'You *do* know what you want it to do. Make up the words!' (*The Changover* 153). Second, it illustrates that, although girls are more likely to be witches, real power must be surrendered to male characters if a satisfactory sexual closure is to be obtained. By reining in any suggestion of excessive sexuality the heroines of teenage fantastic realism will achieve their romantic happy ending. In addition, they must avoid any association with the darker side of magic.

Black Magic: Appropriate Power

Sexual restraint is only one indication of the limits of witchcraft as a feminine identifier in teenage fantastic realism and, like the constraints of social responsibility attached to superhero powers, conventions of ethics and morality also affect the extent of personal empowerment for the teenage witch. Purkiss's claim that identification with the witch is selective is most clearly illustrated in the aim of modern Wicca movements to avoid any connotations of demonic or fearful practice, despite the fact that the wicked witch is key in historical and fictional discourses. In history, witches were accused of communing and forming pacts with the Devil himself and were ascribed with the power of 'black magic' or 'maleficium', the conscious intent to do deliberate harm. The figure of imagination most available in traditional narratives aimed at young children, such as classic children's fairy tales, pantomime, playground lore and Halloween iconography, is also the terrifying haggard old woman. In myth and folklore the witch is amongst the '*Kinderschreck*' or 'frightening figures' that are evoked to frighten or threaten children. John Widdowson collates stories told by real children in Newfoundland about witch figures, which suggests that a frightening threat is the primary association, although more contemporary and media-aware children may be influenced by alternative witch images, such as *Sabrina the Teenage Witch* or characters from J.K. Rowling's *Harry Potter* series. The wicked witch features in a number of novels for young adults, but in these cases she is always a threat to the protagonist rather than being an identity for the hero or heroine themselves. In Marcus Sedgewick's *Witch Hill* (2001), for example, Jamie is haunted by a typically old and haggard supernatural figure, with no teeth, rotting flesh, claw-like hands and a hobbling gait, who terrorises the village of Crownhill throughout history and comes to claim the lives of those who dream of her. Fearful witchcraft also appears, perhaps self-evidently, in popular genre fiction for young adults such as horror. The Scholastic Point imprint produces a range of horror, thriller and supernatural texts and series, and one of its titles, *The Bearwood Witch* by Susan Price (2001), features a witchy spiritualist woman possessed by a dangerous demon. Mrs Beckerdyke attempts to help the teenage protagonist to contact her deceased boyfriend but a malign spirit takes his place and enters into the woman's body. Elizabeth Beckerdyke becomes a terrifying embodiment of the *Kinderschreck*, threatening teenage characters with possession and annihilation. As we have already seen, there are also examples of less conventionally horrific witches who nonetheless threaten young male protagonists in young adult fantastic realism. Novels such as Louise Lawrence's *The Earth Witch* portray the female witch, not as a terrifying aged crone, but as her youthful, maidenly or motherly counterpart, all the more dangerous because of the sexual or maternal love she promises, and for the beauty that masks her power.

On the contrary, the adolescent witch as heroine is never truly wicked, and in some cases she acts to categorically deny the links between witchcraft and evil. In *Old Magic*, Kate recognises that most of the community is fearful of her and Jillian and their mystical lifestyle, but is outraged when she hears Tasha explaining to Jarrod that they partake in a number of stereotypically terrifying practices: 'Jillian's into live sacrifices, you know. They drink blood and hold black masses [. . .] they've been seen dancing naked in the rainforest. It's disgusting—pure devil worship' (63). Tasha is not only rather scared but disapproves of the inappropriate nature of these rituals, which are dangerous and 'disgusting'. Kate is quick to deny this kind of behaviour and defend her style of witchcraft from any such connotations of Satanism or lasciviousness. At most, the newly empowered sorceress of fantastic realism finds herself tempted by potentially possessive and controlling magic. Like Paul and his initial excitement about what powers the fade might bring him, teenage witches are tempted by the world of possibilities opened up to them. After Troy has unmasked herself as the Scholar Magician in *The Haunting*, the heroics of her actions in standing up to Great-Grandmother Scholar are soon forgotten and she becomes bored with the restrictions of being a *teenage* witch. At one point she starts to neglect her homework in order to conjure a miniature solar system, which she spins faster and slower. This is, as her stepmother points out, a 'dangerous game', projecting the rather gentle witchy powers that Troy has so far displayed into much more significant, cosmic and metaphysical realms. When she is admonished Troy immediately agrees that it would be '[a]wful to overbalance now' (133). In *The Tricksters*, Harry's magic begins with the stories she wrote in private, as her fictional characters transform into the Trickster triplets. At the end of the novel she begins to write again, but recognises the implications of her power and is more thoughtful and careful with her actions: 'Once the first words were written she had plenty to think about, for they might lead in any direction' (266). *Wicca*'s Morgan is introduced to a form of witchcraft by the new boy at school, Cal. In the first novel of the series Tiernan goes out of her way to deny her protagonist the possibility for evil power. Morgan defends her interest to her parents, who claim that witchcraft goes against their religious beliefs. She explains, '[b]ut it's not like . . . black magic or anything. [. . .] It's just people hanging out, getting in touch with nature' (*Wicca* 101). Much of the plot revolves around her finding out how Wicca works in positive ways and how it should not be misused; for instance, trying to help her friend get rid of his acne by casting a spell is out of bounds, according to Cal, because 'You're not allowed to perform a spell for someone without his or her knowledge' (144). Instead of being an entry point into boundless possibilities, witchcraft here is posited as a practice with distinct rules and relations which limit the magic power. Moreover, a sense of personal responsibility and restraint is emphasised, so that Morgan cannot simply do what she wants with her new powers.

In *The Changeover*, the personal battle between using magic for good or for evil is carefully worked out. When she uses her enchanted powers to defeat Carmody Braque and rescue her brother, Laura is left in the position of having Braque at her mercy:

> With her commands exploding in his mind he would howl like a dog, fling himself in front of earth-moving machinery, bite pieces out of his own arm or tear off his clothes and dance naked outside the school gate [...] Laura was offered a unique chance to discharge her own burden of human anguish and to strike at the powers of darkness. (183–184)

This punishment seems, at first, to be acceptable, especially if a simplistic model of a battle between good and evil is lifted from children's fairy tales or from their more gruesome predecessors. Grimm's story of 'Snow White', for instance, punishes the wicked witch by making her dance in red hot slippers. Yet Laura's boyfriend and fellow witch, Sorry, points out his own theory of power: 'There are always two people involved in cruelty, aren't there? One to be vicious and someone to suffer! And what's the use of getting rid of—of wickedness, say—in the outside world if you let it creep back into things from inside you?' (185). Sorry's admonishment expresses a naturalised sentiment that runs through these witchcraft novels: that the power available to female witches must be carefully monitored and kept in check. In other words, while the heroines may profitably adopt and adapt the identity of 'witch' in order to negotiate a potentially powerful identity and a space to perform it, these powers must not be used indiscriminately or without bounds. In fact, most teenage witches function within an expressly domestic sphere. Even when maleficium threatens to infiltrate from an external source, the girls' respectable behaviour, and some ironic rhetorical touches, save the day. Mahy's narratives, in particular, switch from supernatural coming-of-age narratives to romance or comedy, with all the elements of the plot settled back into recognisable forms, only subtly changed by the heroines' experiences and new powers. Furthermore, the magic is sharply undercut by a return to domesticity which refuses to allow a darker side to the witchcraft. This may be directly related to the fact that the subcultures that Angela McRobbie and others identify as being expressly female directly relate to received emotional and sexual adult roles and are often played out in a domestic setting rather than on the street or in other public spaces. In each novel the climax of magic and danger is followed by a final scene of normality. In *The Haunting*, Uncle Cole attempts to impress Troy's family with a display of black magic but he is swiftly deflated by Troy's own magical power and then is offered a cup of tea. In *The Changeover*, Laura battles with her own malicious desire to keep Carmody Braque suffering in eternity, but shortly after she mercifully returns him to oblivion the narrative moves from supernatural battlefield to the home, to making sandwiches and looking after Jacko. Harry feels elevated to enchantress status at the end of *The Tricksters* but the final chapters show her retreating into the background of the family drama once more. By placing the heroines firmly back into domesticity and reality as soon as they have become comfortable with their magic, it is clear that, although witchcraft empowers the female, it is not a simple means of escape from the difficulties of growing up within constraints of gendered expectations.

Simon Frith's overview of subcultures suggests that teenagers employ controversial elements of style and behaviour in order to 'cast spells' against their limited status in society. Adolescence is perceived as a period of trying out extreme identities as a way of reclaiming some kind of power. Frith is quick to point out that this posturing is a temporary strategy and that young people are ultimately content to return to mainstream and conventional modes of behaviour, surrendering their radical attempts at empowerment for the safety and comfort of adult life.

Fantastic realism provides a fictional arena for exploring these very dynamics. Fantastic spaces, magical powers and enchanted identities all allow teenage protagonists possibilities for resolving the problems of adolescence and actively seeking agency. Those radical prospects that are generated in the fantastic are, however, bound by realist conventions, especially by expectations of both age and gender. It is significant that, in the majority of the texts discussed in this chapter, fantastic abilities and identities are passed on from generation to generation through familial lines. It is clear that, even in the liberating sphere of the fantastic (where teenagers can safely play out family romances or dramatically transform themselves), there is a tendency for fiction to instruct young people how to act out their genders as normal adolescents and to aspire to the ideals of conventional adulthood. In most cases, men impart power to teenage boys and women impart power to teenage girls, and in each entrustment there is also an inherent warning about responsibility. For the superhero, there is a duty to actively pursue good works, while responsibility for witches lies in the obligation to avoid evil or black magic: to not be tempted into misusing fantastic power. The implication, however tentative, is that teenage boys find their abilities a burden of constructive responsibility and yet female adolescents are potentially dangerous if they are endowed with power. Superheroes may be founded in moral strength and active responsibility, but they are trapped by this role, which proves to be a painful, rather than empowering, burden. In turn, although witchcraft novels allow their heroines a sense of empowerment that might signify celebration in the shifting of gender roles in the late twentieth century, these narratives also indicate a certain fear or anxiety surrounding female power. Either way, adolescence in fantastic realism remains locked into certain ways of being through discourses of age and gender which limit teenagers' agency in the fantastic and, in reality, merely proffer a kind of self-help empowerment that is neither political nor far-reaching. The next chapter turns to spaces where teenagers can apparently escape the realities of social inequality and fixed subjectivities: technological and virtual worlds.

Chapter Four
Writing Fantastic Spaces: Real, Virtual and Textual Teens

As we have seen, frameworks of development, identity and agency have helped shape professional and commonsense understandings of adolescence in the second half of the twentieth century and have also influenced the kinds of stories made available to writers of teenage fiction, presenting a range of narratives where fantasy acts as a space or time for growth into desirable adulthood. Within these bounds, fantastic realism has generated a series of worlds where teenagers can experience a sense of progression or power, but where at the same time progression and power is limited by its temporary nature, its gendered ideology, or its reliance on the idea of 'normality'. As the twentieth century drew to a close, alternative ways of thinking about identity and youth emerged alongside new ontological realities. For the Western teenager in the 1990s and early 2000s, important knowledge about their world includes recognition of environmental dangers and global interconnectedness as well as awareness of international conflicts and threats from war and terrorism. Arguably more important for modern adolescence, however, has been the swift rise of information and computer technology (ICT) in the realms of education, communication, media and entertainment. Heralded as a revolution, digital technology has become an almost invisible integral part of the lives of nearly all teenagers across the Western world.[1] Certainly it is the case that ICT, particularly the Internet, has changed the way that young people act, interact and think about their own identities. Moreover, in a real social environment, which is perceived by many adults to be unsafe for teenagers, online worlds also create new spaces for adolescence to exist and thrive within.

In academic circles, attitudes towards electronic technology and children are generally positive,[2] but the 'commonsense' reactions are more divided. In her article on children and cyberspace, Valerie Walkerdine offers up two discourses that function in general conceptions of childhood and developing technology, and which can be applied even more tellingly to attitudes towards teenagers. The first establishes young people as an irrational mass, vulnerable in the face of manipulative new media; and the alternative presents technological advancement as 'a new frontier, a new space for the production of a new, and perhaps super, rationality, a new body without organs' (235).³ Although thoughtful and balanced criticism on the subject appears in educational, literary and cultural studies, this stark dichotomy is often reproduced in popular media battles staged between advocates of teenage reading on one hand and champions of new forms of high-tech literacy such as gaming skills on the other. A rather extreme, albeit high-profile, example of ultra-conservative opinion on the dangers of computer games can ironically be found at the weblog of Boris Johnson, the former Shadow Minister for Higher Education. Johnson cites figures showing the increase in games consoles and the decline in literacy and reading for pleasure. He vividly evokes the nightmare scenario of mass irrationality, describing teenage gamers as 'blinking lizards, motionless, absorbed, only the twitching of their hands showing they are still conscious', and argues that parents should be switching off consoles around the country, to 'strike a blow for literacy' (Johnson). Online feedback on his comments offers various versions of the opposing argument, questioning the privileged position of literature and pointing out that 'games have extremly [sic] complex storylines, require problem solving skills, forward-thinking, spacial [sic] awareness, advanced risk/reward strategies and some of the most impressive storylines of all entertainment medium'.

In this chapter I focus on young adult novels that have emerged from the technological age and which shift fantastic experiences away from the real world and into electronic or cyber spaces. Many of these narratives can be described most accurately as speculative fantasies rather than fantastic realism. As set out in the Introduction, speculative fantasy merges the questioning mode of science fiction or speculative fiction with elements of supernatural fantasy, impossible even in a futuristic reality. On the whole, then, where computers, virtual reality and gaming occur in the novels I turn to now, the world they exist within may be contemporary or futuristic. More importantly, it is inherently realistic. Moreover, the technology at the centre of these stories is more than just a prop: it either has a fantastic quality—a supernatural element for example—or it provides the structure for a fantastical mode, offering ludic possibilities of hypertext or technological narrative. I am not interested in electronic texts or games as entities in themselves, but I am concerned with how they might be used as a kind of fantastic trope. Although technology is often understood as existing in direct opposition to magic or the supernatural (Kimberley Reynolds 162), it can just as easily act as an alternative aspect of the fantastic, since it allows users to travel in time, change their shape or revel in special powers. Many of the texts I explore in this chapter also explicitly imbue technology with supernatural qualities.

My purpose is not to determine whether technologies represented in teenage novels and the new narratives they offer are 'good for' or 'bad for' the teenager (although the texts in this chapter offer arguments for both sides of the debate), but rather to examine how those novels use the trope of digital technology in ways that intersect with discursive frameworks of space and play. Walkerdine's concepts of cyberspace as a new 'frontier' and as a kind of laboratory for subjectivity will provide useful starting points in asking whether gaming narratives and texts about cyberspace and hypertext can provide alternative spaces and ways of being that are less constrained than other forms of fantastic realism. Do cyberspace, virtual reality, games and hypertexts offer greater chances for adolescents to write or rewrite themselves and their stories? I shall begin with a discussion of cyberspace, its construction of virtual landscapes, and its fostering of community and identity amongst young people.

(Cyber)Space

Spatiality

The term 'cyberspace' has its textual origins in dystopian visions of the future. In his *Neuromancer* (1984), science-fiction writer William Gibson describes cyberspace through the voiceover on a television information show. It is: 'A consensual hallucination experienced daily by billions of legitimate operators [. . .]A graphic representation of data abstracted from the banks of every computer in the human system. Unthinkable complexity. Lines of light ranged in the nonspace of the mind, clusters and constellations of data' (51). Gibson was writing before the worldwide web was created, but it is clear that concepts of virtual reality and electronic data sharing were culturally emergent as geographical entities in the 1980s and 1990s (in films like Ridley Scott's *Blade Runner* [1982] for example). The web is spatial. Michael Benedikt goes so far as to suggest that cyberspace is a kind of realisation of Shangri-La—a shared cultural territory free of space and time—so that, although cyberspace might be made up of the 'permanently ephemeral', it represents a definite topography (30–35). Where the geography of cyberspace differs from other geographies is in its disconnection between bodies and minds. Instead of imagining the material interaction between human culture and physical environment, it is necessary to reconceptualise geography as the way that space is inhabited mentally and virtually. Pure cyberspace makes a distinction between body as 'meat' and mind as 'freed from the constraints that flesh imposes', as Allucquere Rosanne Stone puts it (525), although of course it is impossible to completely disregard all things physical, even in the age of 'the technosocial subject', as I shall explore in my analyses below.

Adolescence—so often defined through biology or social interaction—is less often theorised in terms of its spatiality or geography, although it is possible to trace a set of researchers and theorists working on young people and place within the broader project of childhood studies discussed in the Introduction. Tracey Skelton and Gill Valentine argue that youth has traditionally been excluded from geographical studies, partly because 'public space is produced as an adult space' (7) and their aim is to explore youth culture through examining the spaces that young people carve out for themselves (see also Holloway and Valentine). Space is crucial to the cultural concept of the teenager, even if it is *lack* of space or disapproval about the use of space that is most significant. Dance halls, youth clubs and leisure centres attempted to provide refuge over the course of the last century, as cultural historians of teen culture point out (Danesi; Rollin) but public spaces have never been easily available to young people. In a modern world where risk appears constantly to lurk outside the family home, many adults deem sending teenagers out into the unmonitored wilderness—rural or urban—to be unwise. Moreover, to meet on the streets, in a park or in other public spaces as a group sends out certain messages of threatening behaviour to a society nervous of collectives of young people. Public and private spaces available to adolescents are also policed by adult authorities: in the first case, such authorities are concerned about violent dangers on the streets and forbidden substances in pubs and clubs; in the latter, they control the amount of privacy and autonomy a teenager might have in the domestic sphere, worrying about how much time is spent in bedrooms and what activities might take place there. Moreover, the kinds of identities available to adolescents through the places they inhabit are fraught with difficulties. Chapter Three explored ways that public and private space is gendered, but we might add here that these established understandings of masculine and feminine appropriation of the street and the bedroom are potentially being challenged by changes in the way adolescents use, and have access to, outdoor space. For example, Sara McNamee points out that due to increased fears of external dangers and the attraction of indoor computer-based activities amongst teenage boys, 'girls' use of domestic space as a resistance to boys' domination of the streets [. . .] is now being eroded' (204).

Cyberspace and the worlds made available more generally through computers, ICT and different types of games certainly offer an alternative for adolescents seeking both public and private spaces, but the spatial metaphor surrounding 'cyberspace' demands closer examination. If we return to the terminology used by Walkerdine, we find an interesting reference to descriptions of the Internet as a 'new frontier' and, indeed, this is a common metaphor in optimistic visions of ICT's potential. On a global scale, it seems, voyages into cyberspace are constrained only by access to technology and the expertise to use it, while explorations of new territory on planet Earth and throughout the universe might be nearing saturation point, or at least heading towards ecological and financial stumbling blocks. The concept of new frontiers also appeals to a Western (specifically North American) tradition of independence and expansion, key in historical moments of exploration, colonisation and later in specific military and technological policies such as the USA's Strategic

Defence Initiative. One implication of the term is of a courageous explorer, encountering and bending a wilderness to their own purpose, or leaving behind traditional and restrictive social structures in search of a freer and more equitable community. Of course, the frontier spirit often masks a fundamentally colonialist or appropriative urge amongst the explorers, and the same could arguably be claimed for aspects of ICT; specifically in the global commercial monopoly of certain hardware and software brands. However, the Internet at least provides expansion into space that is not undertaken by the powerful few at the expense of the masses. The promising quality of cyberspace is its potential as an arena for anyone who wants to explore, settle and thrive: even—perhaps especially—the spatially disfranchised adolescent.

Dave Healy argues that cyberspace functions less as a representation of a wilderness that requires taming, and more as a 'middle landscape', in between the security of home and the freedom of the unknown. He draws on geographer Yi-Fu Tuan's distinction between 'place'—where civilisation, safety and social involvement can all be found—and 'space'—which suggests independence and natural existence. The middle landscape symbolises 'a fundamental tension deep within human nature: an urge to withdraw into an undisturbed private world, alongside a desire for connectedness and relatedness' (Healy 59). For Healy, the Internet straddles connectedness and disconnectedness by promoting virtual networks at the same time as perpetuating existing divisions. For example, although chat rooms and discussion groups have the potential for bringing together strangers with nothing more in common than an interest in the topic at hand—much like those brought together from great geographical distances to a single frontier point—the reality of these groups is that they tend to become shaped by existing identifiers, so that online groups more often than not remain segregated by age, race, gender, sexuality or religion.

This middle landscape—the simultaneous freedom to explore and encouragement to remain within recognisable communities—is, of course, what makes cyberspace attractive to teenagers and to those who police them. Making new friendships without having to go out into the dangerous world; forming romantic relationships without the risk of actual sexual experience; playing war games without being in real bodily danger: these elements of place/space seem to allow both security and excitement. In fact, concerns about the safety and wholesomeness of the Internet tend to emerge when the place/space balance tips too far in either direction. Usually that anxiety emerges when too much freedom and too broad a sense of community puts teenagers in contact with 'unsuitable' contacts (predatory adults with sexual or political designs on young minds), but sometimes cyberspace is considered too parochial to be healthy for adolescent development. A recent special report called 'Living Online' in *New Scientist* discusses the implications of a generation that is constantly connected and in continual commune with itself. In part of the report, Sherry Turkle, Professor of the Social Studies of Science and Technology at MIT, describes connected teenagers as being 'tethered'. This tethering allows freedom in some respects, because parents and caregivers trust their wards to venture further into the real world alone when they have technology to hand, such as a mobile phone or email. On the other hand, a tethered teenager is one who 'does not have the experience of being alone' (Else and Turkle 48). I shall return to some of these concerns in discussion of virtual reality gaming narratives below. There are certainly limits to the liberating space of ICT and the online community, which are, perhaps, increasing rather than decreasing as the Internet becomes more sophisticated. The worldwide web is more effectively policed now than it was at its inception, so that users can block particular content (keeping sexually explicit material from teenage users, for example), and web-designers can charge fees for entry into certain sites (in stark contrast to the original ethos of the web as a freely available and shared resource). In those areas where content seems much more openly available and malleable—where communities network together or create webpages and information in the form of social software or wikis—users are even more securely monitored and regulated, since Web 2.0 technology effectively *places* its participants, tagging them and creating a digital map of where they have 'visited' and when.

However far the Internet can be described as a monitored *place*, overrun by adult production and security, there is no doubt that a generation of young people have also made it their own *space*, albeit one with certain limitations. The crux of this spatial realm is its potential for combining classic dichotomies of youth: the problems of inside/outside, private/public, individual/subculture. Certainly, one way of understanding cyberspace's importance as a new frontier is by recognising its uses in forging new kinds of interpersonal connections. In his discussion of virtual communities, Robert Hamman draws on Ray Oldenburg's lament for the 'third place', a zone where people can find space for community outside of work and home, and which, according to Oldenburg, is disappearing in American suburban and ghettoised society (Hamman). When extended to the world of teenagers, this third place usually becomes one outside of *school* and home, a place allowing friendship and interaction that is not defined by preordained familial or educational conditions; and it might be argued that this adolescent third place is similarly under threat in modern geographies. For instance, in his popular examination of the social and economic implications of a 'Net Generation', Don Tapscott points out that in the late nineteenth century a typical American teenager would have had ten square miles of wilderness to play in, while a hundred years later the average play space is an indoor room or two (*Growing Up Digital* 162). Interestingly, Tapscott notes the availability of outdoor spaces and implies that opportunities for physical movement, exploration and communing with untamed nature provide the optimum environment for the personal growth of any young person, disregarding the importance that we might set upon indoor activities such as reading and writing or interacting with parents and peers. More crucially, Tapscott collapses temporal and spatial aspects of historical adolescence, making assumptions about the time that a nineteenth-century adolescent might have had available for play and personal development, which perhaps rely on fictional versions of adolescence such as Huck Finn rather than on real experiences of young people living in rural America a hundred years ago (I noted a similar romanticism in historical versions of adolescence in my discussion of time-slip novels in Chapter Two).

Community and Identity

If a third place is at risk from changes in environment and alleged dangers in the public realm, then teenagers are also at risk in their sense of themselves as social and individual identities. In contrast to the individualism we met in Chapter Two—conceptualised as a necessary and healthy aspect of adolescent development as the teenager separates from parent figures and comes to terms with their own unified self—the 'ontological individualism' and 'culture of separation' discussed by Healy 'renders individuals passive and isolated in the face of larger social needs' (59). Community acts as a check to this destructive tendency. As we have seen, teenage communities have been classified by many social scientists as subcultures: groupings that attempt to function outside of the mainstream and resist it. As such, subcultural theory differs from ideas about community because, although it rests on similar concepts of shared interests or behaviour, it does not have the same implications of cooperation, communication and outward-looking philosophy.

Both Hamman and Healy discuss community in terms of people, place and time. Hamman suggests the following definition:

> (1) a group of people (2) who share social interaction (3) and some common ties between themselves and the other members of the group (4) and who share an area for a least some of the time.

Since teenagers can be classed as a group of people whose primary interactions are, in many ways, social, and who certainly have common ties in the form of their shared status as adolescents, their main problem in creating community occurs in the area of interaction. Clearly virtual or online space provides an ideal solution, although according to cultural critic Howard Rheingold this solution is not unique to teenagers: for Rheingold, virtual community is a potential answer to 'the hunger for community that has followed the disintegration of traditional communities around the world' (4). Studies of teenage users of online chatrooms and gaming environments reveal a rich and active sense of community. A great deal of research has been undertaken since the early 1990s, tracking the effects games have on children and young people in their development, their learning and understanding of the world, and, crucially, their ability to interact with others. While arcade, video and console games absorbed teenagers at first (and these feature in both realist and non-realist texts for children and adolescents in this period), throughout the 1990s and 2000s, attention has turned to virtual reality consoles and online games, including role-playing formats such as graphic games and 'MUDs'. MUDs are online textual role-playing games, known as multi-user dimensions or dungeons because of their origins in the role-playing, dice-based board game, 'Dungeons and Dragons'. MUDs work through language, not graphics, each user carefully describing their appearance and actions, interacting through typed conversations, and often helping to create a shared environment through narrative sketches.[4] Simple commands provide the invisible coding that allows MUDs to evolve and continue through the imaginative writing of their players. Sherry Turkle's extensive work in the field suggests that young people using MUDs experiment with identities and seek out new relationships and interactions: 'they are creating communities that have become privileged contexts for thinking about social, cultural, and ethical dilemmas of living in constructed lives' ('Constructions and Reconstructions of Self in Virtual Reality' 166).[5] Indeed, many commentators have argued that MUDs function primarily as narrative or hypertext rather than as games. Certainly, teenage gamers—who also might also act in the guise of emailer and texter—have been at the forefront of the creation of a new language of communication in cyberspace. Alongside much maligned texting contractions such as 'l8r' (later) and 'b4' (before), emoticons and imaginative acronyms develop a new, often ironic, way of interacting.[6] Computer code and creative cyber-language offers writers of teenage fiction rich material for presenting new forms of adolescent interaction, and young adult literature in the 1990s and 2000s has attempted in part to represent the reality of contemporary teenagers' use of online communication. Marla Harris notes a trend in the 'realistic email/internet novel', where electronic interaction provides the action, often for thrillers or romance narratives. Noga Applebaum also traces the influence of the Internet on fiction for children and teenagers, pointing out, however, that a significant number of realist novels using email, websites and electronic games do little more than 'pay simple lip service to popular culture in the service of increased sales' ('Electronic Texts and Adolescent Agency' 253).

    I shall examine one such realist novel (Michael J. Rosen's *ChaseR*) later in this chapter, but my primary interest is in speculative fantasy and fantastic realism. When technology is employed to develop aspects of fantasy, opportunities for exploring concepts of space, community and identity—as well as the prospects and threats it presents to young people—multiply. The novels under consideration in this chapter describe teenage characters interacting in realistic environments, but all focus on electronic gaming in its most advanced sense. Virtual reality games are no longer 2D and conceptual in these texts: instead, full body suits or headsets wired to the brain result in a complete virtual experience, with immersed sensation (if not always taste or smell) being paramount. To clarify the difference between what we might term 'cyber speculative fantasy' and straightforward cyber fiction, I would point to E.M. Goldman's *The Night Room* (1995). In many ways, Goldman's novel for young adults precisely represents the mixture of teen realism and fantastic elements that this book has been analysing. The story deals with a set of high school students who have been chosen to take part in a new personal development initiative. This 'Argus' programme allows them to participate in a computerised simulation, which projects their individual destinies using data from the detailed questionnaires they have completed. They each travel into a kind of personalised future, through what appears to be a supernatural force, similar to Davy's ability to foresee events in *The Gift*.

While the resulting virtual experiences have aspects of the fantastic about them, Goldman makes it clear that there are in fact no paranormal elements to the programme and that it is purely based on the realistic, albeit futuristic, capacity of technology. Any glitches in the programme can be explained through human error or intervention. For instance, when Mac discovers that his classmate Sandra is dead in the future, some participants suspect supernatural forces. As the story unfolds, however, the volunteers gradually learn that the suspicious death is caused by a very human college dropout who has decided to destroy Argus by writing a heart attack-inducing computer virus. The non-fantastic solution to the mystery is even ironically mentioned by Argus's creator (who is a sad and overambitious scientist rather than a paranormal force). When she is confronted by the teenagers and their theory about the malevolent hacker, she tries to dismiss it but is impressed with the plausibility of their allegation: 'The girl could have claimed that an alien life form was attempting to collect brains through Argus. Instead, she decided on a hacker' (*The Night Room* 212). Goldman is careful to convince the reader that technology has no special power and that any threat or gift comes from purely human agency. Other authors of young adult fiction prefer to represent cyberspace as a supernatural space, however, and it is to these visions that we now turn. In particular, I want to examine the way that a virtual reality environment like 'Argus' can become a site for fantasy.

Virtual Reality

Although virtual reality (VR) is flourishing in the realms of entertainment and education, in a way it has taken a curious route, and not one that theorists, commentators and fiction writers of the 1990s and 2000s envisaged. One of the most successful virtual environments at the time of writing is Linden Lab's 'Second Life', a massive online space in which participants do not primarily play games but rather live an alternative life, complete with jobs, recreation and relationships. Instead of providing an escape from real life ('Real Life' or RL), Linden's product offers more of the same: more work, leisure, politics, economics, commercialism and opportunities for entrepreneurship or crime. A teen version was launched in 2005 which is only accessible to those under the age of eighteen, and which is monitored by Linden administration. 'Teen Second Life' allows adolescents to create their own 'avatars' (representations of online selves), explore the constructed world or 'grid' online, build informal communities, and take part in adult-guided projects. One such project is the Open University's 'Schome Park', a virtual space that is 'not school not home', where users can learn, chat and help build their surroundings.[7] These PC-based experiences, which can of course be 'played' with no discernible change of mode from working or doing homework, construct virtual worlds principally through 2D visuals, with some audio input and output. Other virtual spaces for teenagers include social networks, a relatively new phenomenon which thrives on young people's perceived desire to build cliques of friends, to gossip, and share news or information. These are conceptual spaces. Facebook, for example, relies on metaphors for friendly (or otherwise) interactions, including giving other members 'hugs' or 'slaps'.[8] In terms of actual physical immersion in a virtual reality, options are more limited at present. Games manufacturers have worked with various ideas for handheld or wearable movement-sensitive consoles, where players can project real actions onto a gaming screen. Currently popular is Nintendo's 'Wii', but other fashionable consoles have included Playstation's 'Eye-Toy' and Mattel's 'Playglove'.

Virtual reality in its most interactive and immersive sense has extended a powerful conceptual pull over young adult fiction writers, however. In some cases, virtual reality provides the framework for whole societies. For example, in Conor Kostick's speculative fantasy, *Epic* (2004), a futuristic colony functions almost purely through playing a giant VR game, also called 'Epic'. Families and friends play as teams, working together to win real-life schooling, equipment or provisions. Real economic and civic success is dictated by performance within the game, while material resources are controlled by the game's Central Allocations Board. The young protagonists realise that this online world is a fantasy that cannot be sustained, and work to fight the system from inside, particularly the corrupt members of Central Allocations. The top-down structure of a dominant game like 'Epic' is critiqued in Kostick's vision of future manifestations of online technology, and the narrative looks forward instead to a real world that abides by the Internet's initial idealistic notions of collaboration. At the end of the novel the hero, Erik, completes the *Epicus Ultima* quest and destroys the game world of 'Epic' forever. The librarian in charge of its data notices the difference in the configuration of his reality at once, pointing out that there are '[n]o more character menus, no more arenas. No more game at all. Just the operating level', and that the new quest for all young people is to 'make yourself a useful member of society' (*Epic* 312, 314).[9]

Epic presents an alternative society and explores how young people react in a world overwhelmingly structured by the unreal. More often, young adult speculative fantasy prefers to restrict itself to explicitly adolescent concerns and constructs virtual reality spaces as forms of teenage recreation rather than social engines. Such game worlds might offer protagonists a space for exploration and development between other, real, worlds, but those spaces are also unstable and problematic.

Game Worlds: A Middle Landscape for Adolescents

Many of these virtual-reality game narratives play themselves out almost completely inside the parallel entertainment world, perhaps suggesting that problems of real life can best be solved within this expressly adolescent space, or that VR environments are inherently more exciting or interesting for teenage readers. Vivian Vande Velde's *Heir Apparent* (2002), for example, includes only two chapters set in the real (loosely futuristic) world. In the first, Giannine Bellisario travels to the Rasmussem Gaming Centre to spend her birthday gift voucher on a total immersion game; and in the second she wakes up after her virtual reality adventure. The rest of the action occurs within the game 'Heir Apparent', a pseudo-medieval fantasy quest where the player must act strategically in order to be crowned King and win. When Giannine chooses this game she becomes Janine de St. Jehan, shepherdess and illegitimate daughter of the King. Unfortunately, while she is wired up to the system, the protest group 'Citizens to Protect Our Children' (C-POC) storm the Gaming Centre, damaging the equipment and causing Giannine to become trapped in 'Heir Apparent', risking 'fatal overload' unless she can successfully complete the sequence. Giannine/Janine is made aware of her situation when a representative from Rasmussem Enterprises appears like a literal *deus ex machine* to explain the situation:

> suddenly there was a brilliant shaft of light from the sky. Clouds billowed up out of nowhere, then rolled back; harp music sounded, an angelic choir sang a note of infinitely sad sweetness, and a white-robed figure descended on a golden beam [...] 'Giannine,' he said, 'this is Nigel Rasmussem. Don't panic.' (36–37)

It is representative of Vande Velde's narrative style that the overblown gravity of a typical fantasy scenario is punctured by irony, incongruity and teenage humour heavy on the sarcasm. On closer inspection, the descending figure of 'Nigel Rasmussem' is not particularly God-like, especially as he wears glasses and Reeboks, and we later discover that the Director of Rasmussem Enterprises is actually a sixteen-year-old boy who sent his uncle David to appear to Giannine because he would appear more credible.

There are other moments when the artificiality of the game world is observed: Giannine/Janine's adventures are interspersed with emails from the Rasmussem office describing her critical condition, and the heroine retains her modern teenage attitudes and cynicism even when she is reacting to archaic situations in-game. For instance, the messenger who comes from the King's castle to tell Janine she is heir apparent is rather pompous and acts impatiently towards her peasant foster mother. Janine's reaction is very knowing and contemporary: 'Just because she was a computer-generated figment of my imagination was no reason for him to be rude. "Hey," I told him. "That's my mother you're talking to." If my real mother hung around more, I'd defend her too' (16–17). Vande Velde maintains an ironic connection between the fantasy world and a peripheral real world and this minimises the dramatic tension of events within the virtual reality game: we are always aware that Janine's heroic actions and decision-making find reference points in Giannine's real (and in a way rather ordinary) adolescent concerns. When she realises, after many false starts, that her online father has a part to play in her quest and that she must wait for him to arrive and ask him about a magic ring, she points out that her real-life experience does not support the idea that help can be sought from a father figure: 'In this day of fractured families, what made [Rasmussem] think the average gamer would be willing to hang around just for a parental good-bye?' (70). Clearly, Giannine's real-life concerns about her family situation—in which her father 'rarely calls except for the week before my birthday' (13) and her mother cannot find room for her in her cosy New York apartment—emerge in her online gameplay, and the whole narrative acts in a way to help her reassess the forms of parental support she expects and her own part in making her relationships work. Healy's concept of the middle landscape provides a useful model for the heroine's attitude towards the two different worlds she inhabits. 'Heir Apparent' acts as a space in between the real social relations Giannine faces at home and the virtual adventure she has to tackle as Janine. In a way, she uses the game space to try out new solutions to adolescent problems: to try out a loving father/daughter relationship, for example.

Another set of novels which also maintain an uneasy connection between mundane reality and fantastic virtual reality can be found under the collective title of *The Web 2027* (Spanton 1997/1998). The editor of this collaborative project, Simon Spanton, challenged a number of writers of young adult fiction and/or science fiction to come up with a sustained vision of a future where virtual reality dominates youth culture. Spanton created a guidebook outlining the basic components of 2027's futuristic cyber-society and its technical and subcultural language, and the group of writers decided on a shared villain to menace their narratives.[10] A number of the individual novels in *Web 2027* frame their VR fantasy adventure game with a brief preliminary section setting out the realistic, familial background to their teen protagonists' lives. *Gulliverzone* by Stephen Baxter introduces teenage Sarah (web alias Metaphor), her schoolmate Meg (The Wire) and younger brother George (Byte) with some salient details of everyday life, particularly the family dynamics between Sarah and her father and brother, along with Sarah's issues about her mother's death and her own lack of responsibility. When Sarah/Metaphor and her companions enter the VR world (or 'spin into the Web'), however, these daily realities disappear and the dominant narrative mode becomes self-aware fantasy. The VR narrative remains, by and large, a coherent and contained fantasy adventure based on spaces and characters from Jonathan Swift's *Gulliver's Travels* (1726). The young gamers find themselves befriending and helping the Lilliputians, who turn out to be descendants of a computer virus, and during their adventures they encounter Brobdingnagians, the evil Empress Golbasta, and rat-like creatures called 'struldbrugs'. It is what happens in this constructed virtual environment—and not the deconstructed world of the future, where Samuel Jackson is President of the US and Boris Becker is Chancellor of United Europe—that is the focus for action, even if the ultimate outcome in terms of character development is to help Sarah/Metaphor learn the value of her family and friends outside of the web. In some respects, neither the online space of fantasy adventure, nor the real place of adolescent domestic experience, are produced with any authentic meaning in *Heir Apparent* or *Gulliverzone*. For instance, some of Baxter's cybertechnical references—which, like Vande Velde's adolescent humour, act to preserve ironic knowledge of the material reality of virtual reality—effectively efface narrative tension. The rat-like creatures that dwell in the tunnels of the web are portrayed as tangible and living threats, but have evolved from the much more mundane, conceptual risk of computer viruses. The danger they pose to Metaphor as aggressive vermin is counteracted by her knowledge (and the reader's) that they are purely a part of an artificial electronic world; and their efficacy as computer viruses in Sarah's real world is challenged by the embodiment of their metaphorical name. There is a problem here of being caught between two types of world: the reverse of Healy's rather more ideal middle landscape. If 'Gulliverzone' is neither wholly real home nor wholly virtual adventure but a mixture of both, then in some ways the benefits of home and adventure are cancelled out. The Open University's 'Schome' project produces the same conundrum: 'not school not home' may mean not 'a place to relax' nor 'a place to learn' but a place where neither gets done properly.

Gemini Game (1993) by Michael Scott and the *Legendeer* trilogy by Alan Gibbons are less knowing about the interaction between the real world and an adventure set in the virtual world, and rely less on comic incongruity between fantasy conventions and material technology. Instead, virtual spaces become important as genuine sites for adolescent escape, empowerment or reinvention. In *Gemini Game* the fifteen-year-old O'Connor twins are 'Game Makers', expert programmers of hugely successful and popular VR games. The novel begins with them running from the police because one of their games is causing mass breakdown (or 'burnout') amongst users and has been classified as illegal. A lengthy set-up brings BJ and Liz O'Connor to the realisation that they must enter their own game to rid it of the vicious virus, and further short insert chapters set in the real world follow attempts by policeman Eddie Lyons to capture the twins. The main action, however, occurs within the technological world of the game 'Night's Castle', a world instantly recognisable as a composite of settings, creatures and devices from generic fantasy narratives. We gradually discover that 'Night's Castle' has been tampered with and its code corrupted from within by Ariel, the resentful daughter of a failed Game Maker, Harper. For Ariel and the O'Connor twins, VR games provide the ideal arena for demonstrating their technological and gaming prowess. Unlike Ariel's less competent father, these adolescent player-programmers are more at home in virtual reality than in real life. They all see the VR world as simultaneously a natural landscape and as lines of computer code to be analysed and manipulated. For Ariel, in particular, the interior of a computer game is her natural habitat; she explains 'Don't forget I am part of this world, part of the machine. I am the machine' (124). Interestingly, players from an older generation have a more troubled relationship with the virtual world: both Lyons' and Harper's wives were burnouts, killed by their obsession or inferior gaming skills. Scott's world offers an excellent space for adolescents to stretch their abilities, but it is difficult to tell whether or not they will have to 'grow out of it' when they become less technologically able adults.

Alan Gibbons' novels also rely on pre-existing motifs, story patterns and characters to populate their virtual worlds, which protagonist Phoenix Graves accesses through playing a VR computer game. In the first of the series, *Shadow of the Minotaur* (2000), Phoenix is launched into a world of Greek myths when he plays the prototype of a sinister game his father is helping to design. In the first half of this novel, Phoenix and the reader are uncertain of how real 'The Legendeer' game is, but Phoenix becomes addicted to playing it for reasons linked to real emotions of belonging and identity that he can only just articulate. He thinks 'the game [gives] him a sense of himself, of what he might be' (72) and when he tries to explain to his mother what it means to him he declares 'I belong there. I'm . . . I'm home' (73). Phoenix is half-Greek, new in town, and enjoys reading myths and legends; all qualities which make him an outsider in terms of adolescent society. Gaming is not only a much more acceptable pastime for a teenage boy, it also offers a place—an ostensible middle landscape—that appeals to Phoenix's sense of self as hero. The virtual world in *Shadow of the Minotaur* allows Phoenix to embrace his cultural background within a specific zone where he feels comfortable doing so (unlike reading about Greek myths on the school bus), and it also presents him with the chance to feel like a hero instead of a victim. The electronic space is both part of his fraught domestic and school life—developed by his father and played by some of his fellow students—and also a kind of wilderness where he can escape these very things. Thus, in the first half of *Shadow of the Minotaur* virtual reality seems to offer an ideal adolescent space.

There are, however, hints that this space is less than healthy for Phoenix. He feels an addiction to 'The Legendeer' that parallels representations of drug addiction in a text like Melvin Burgess's *Junk* (1996). When Phoenix's father threatens to send the prototype back to the manufacturer, Phoenix is distraught: 'He hardly cared about the danger. There was something in the game, something hidden and exciting. Playing was all that mattered' (41). He is certainly represented as demonstrating signs of dependence. As we shall see, Gibbons delivers a not-so-subtle critique of the ubiquitous popularity of computer gaming, amongst teenage boys in particular. The fact that a commercially successful product acts as a potential cause of zombie-ism throughout the land returns us to Boris Johnson's concerns about the future of today's youth. Thus, through the second half of *Shadow of the Minotaur* and in the other two novels in the trilogy it transpires that 'The Legendeer' is not any kind of useful middle landscape at all. The positive possibilities of online heroism are negated by the fact that virtual reality is ultimately portrayed as an addictive space controlled by outside forces, as I shall explore below.

Other novels in this sub-genre question the distinction between virtual and real worlds, exploring playful interactions between real life and virtual life and placing importance on the way that adolescent protagonists distinguish between the two. Stephen Bowkett's *Dreamcastle* (1997)—part of *The Web 2027*—and Lesley Howarth's *Ultraviolet* (2001) both force the reader and protagonists to question the validity of VR as an alternative space for being and interacting. The former focuses on Robert Miller (alias Surfer), an expert user of the web. His subjectivity rests on being a 'veteran' player of VR games with an extraordinary reputation, and this involves immersing himself in the world of the web, often to the detriment of other forms of interpersonal relationships and knowledge. When challenged by his father about the amount of time he spends 'cruising in dataspace', Surfer puts forward arguments based on the educational merits of advanced technology, drawing on theories of experiential learning: 'What could beat learning geography by going to any virtual location you desire? Or getting into history by fighting in the Civil War [. . .]?' (*Dreamcastle* 122). However, this sense of the web as a safe place of learning, where the player is shaped by external hierarchies, only represents a small part of Surfer's virtual life. In his own mind there are other roles to perform:

> The Web was the New World of the twenty-first century, a vast territory where pioneers still had a part to play. Careers could be forged, fortunes made, ambitions realised in Webtown. What was wrong with wanting to explore there? Surfer wondered as he slid gratefully into his bed. Where was the harm in dreaming large, then following your dream as far as it would take you? (123)

For Surfer, virtual reality is primarily 'the New World', an unknown frontier space where his curiosity and ambition can be unleashed and rewarded. This is also a space where teenagers are the explorers and entrepreneurs, rather than men like Surfer's father, who does not understand his son's obsession with virtual reality. In particular, Surfer's space is 'Dreamcastle', 'a cross between the labyrinth of the legendary Greek Minotaur, a pyramid temple to the great god Ra, and Dracula's Transylavanian mountaintop mansion' with a thousand levels of gameplay (107).[11] The geography of this game is integral to Surfer's sense of himself. Of course, it is worth noting that Surfer daydreams about being a pioneer from the real and comfortable safety of his bed, and this is an indication of Bowkett's ambivalence towards the true freedoms of a virtual landscape for adolescent gamers.

Ultraviolet portrays a future world where the overheated sun reduces possibilities for real exploration or even for social interaction. Moreover, the adolescent protagonist (and the reader) finds it difficult to negotiate space and place, not always knowing where the central VR game begins and where it ends. There are some facts about reality that seem stable on first reading the novel: Violet, or Vi, lives with her scientist father in a future where the sun's mounting heat has forced the population underground. The real world has become a hostile space and inhabitants are constantly constrained by its environmental, social and economic aspects. Adolescents are no longer unique in being denied a meaningful space of their own, because all humans are now monitored and controlled in their social and private actions. For instance, individuals are tagged and checked for their exposure to solar radiation or 'rads', and their recorded levels dictate access to public services and personal funds. Unlike society in *Dreamcastle*, in this dystopic future teenagers are not the only ones to reject the real world: Vi's invention of a protective suit for walking outside in full sunshine is dismissed by her father, who explains that 'people don't like it. Kind of panics 'em to think they have to wear a suit to go outside. Easier to pretend they don't want to and stay indoors' (*Ultraviolet* 18). While adults retrain themselves to not miss wide open space, Vi and her friends play VR games that provide a very simple experience of landscape and nature lost during the environmental disaster. A programme like 'Lambkin' allows gamers to create their own cyber spring and remind themselves of the sight, sound and feel of rabbits and daffodils (although not the most evocative of senses, smell). Despite the verisimilitude of 'Lambkin', the picturesque virtual world created has gaps and anomalies: tulips growing at the same time as snowdrops, missing summer smells and breezes, and a thrush that none of the players can now recall or recognise as being authentic.

For truly active engagement with social and physical space, it seems Vi has to turn to the kind of games that Surfer finds so liberating in *Dreamcastle*. Vi's favourite game, 'QuestHolme', offers 'the next best thing to excitement' (40) and initially has a similar feel to 'Night's Castle', 'Heir Apparent' or 'Dreamcastle' in its immersive fantasy quest-style adventure. Vi certainly demonstrates some of the symptoms of addiction that are also portrayed in Gibbons' *Legendeer* trilogy, as this passage illustrates:

> The battle for QuestKeys rolls on, until at last Vi droops on her cushions, her infrared glove sensors sending crazy signals to the walls, her sleeping brain empty at last but for dreams, while the Quest locks into a holding pattern, endlessly repeating its Overture over her sleeping body. (163)

Violet is a passive subject in the game: here gaming and dreaming are fused as they are in *Dreamcastle*, but this is hardly the representation of a successful and active pioneer spirit.

What also makes Vi's relationship with online gaming seemingly different to Surfer's is the fact that she sees real freedom and adventure outside in the sun-drenched real world and not on the frontiers of cyberspace. Yet, as we shall see later, Vi's own conception of what is real and what is virtual is not straightforward and is problematised by the confused perception of her surroundings. We as readers are never sure that what she thinks of as real is not, in fact, imagined or virtual. For what appears tangible and attractive in cyberspace is not always totally desirable.

This disparity is made clear in the character of Xenia in *Dreamcastle*. Xenia is the beautiful but sinister player who challenges Surfer. It transpires that she only plays the game in order to find out if the web's virtual spaces offer a valid alternative to her own real mortality. She is determined to live there, in some disembodied sense, forever. Xenia's desire to exist within a virtual world is due to her fear of oblivion, a fear closely related to the fact that, in truth, she is ancient and physically failing. In some ways, virtual reality is an ideal space for the elderly rather than the youthful. Mike Featherstone points to the potential that VR technology holds for older users, suggesting that it allows sensory experience that might have been lost through ageing and disability, offers interaction with others and entertainments that are not the sole province of the young, and provides a way for bodies to be reconstructed and re-experienced. He notes the specific problems that VR might pose for older participants, however: 'there may well be all sorts of pressures to steal a march by upgrading or enhancing the beauty and expressive capacity of the virtual face and body. Likewise there might also be pressures to retain last year's simulation—or even one from the last decade' (Featherstone 613). The urge to retain a youthful and everlasting simulation is at the root of Xenia's engagement with the web, indicating a powerful aversion to anything that is not as it seems shared by many young adult fantastic realist novels. In this teenage-centred narrative, however, the danger of simulation is not primarily to do with Xenia's disintegrating sense of self as she races to recreate herself as unnaturally beautiful. The threat is more closely related to Surfer's development: he is deceived by Xenia's beautiful, youthful online avatar and this leads to a near encounter with death for the adolescent protagonist. Since youth and death should never find themselves in such close contact, this use of virtual reality reveals another aberrant product of false simulation in cyberspace.

The risks and peril which contribute to an exciting adventure story in VR gaming narratives are not eradicated or escaped from by 'spinning in' or 'logging on' to the web; indeed, these cyber entertainments are often not the solution but the origin of danger. In addition, like the supernatural forces we have encountered in previous chapters, VR games create tensions where the protagonist is out of control, manipulated by outside influences or threatened at the level of social identity. It is worth asking, then, who dictates action in VR games: the player or the programme?

The Programme(r): Virtual Danger as Embodied Threat

Early watchwords for the Internet were collaboration and cooperation: there was to be no owner and no leading programmer. The brave new world promised to make sharing its main principal, from Tim Berners-Lee's freely disseminated work on the Internet and hypertext which developed into the worldwide web, to the philosophy of shareware and constant connection. However, in fantastic realism and speculative fantasy few texts emphasise an ideology of unproblematic collaboration in their representations of online experience, and few construct a cyberspace that is free of individuals wishing to dominate or control. Instead, the Internet and virtual reality are often delicately critiqued and most usually portrayed as a sinister—sometimes personified—threat to the adolescent protagonist, promoting isolation or over-reliance, anti-social behaviour and a worrying loss of distinction between reality and fantasy. The outlook for virtual reality and online gaming in this kind of narrative is often bleak, reflecting social and educational concerns more closely than any other area examined so far in this book. Kimberley Reynolds points to possible explanations for this bleakness, suggesting that writers of young adult literature may have particular concerns about the imaginative, moral and physical harm ICT engenders, but also arguing that 'they project their own current (adult) sense of anxiety about using IT onto child readers' (166).

To illustrate general concerns about teenagers and technology we can return to the *New Scientist* special report which worried in passing about the changing face of adolescence. According to Turkle, contemporary forms of communication and self-expression, particularly those rooted in technology, actually threaten the very essence of what it is to be a teenager. Constant connectivity to a technological global space means that young people have no time to be introspective or to think through the meaning of complex feelings: instead there is an endless imperative to check that others feel the same way. Moreover, new forms of high-tech communications erode the possibilities for certain rites of passage, such as a first solo trip out into the city: 'Tethering via a cellphone buffers this moment; tethered children think differently about themselves. They are not quite alone' (Else and Turkle 48). In the same special report, an imaginative story-article narrated by a futuristic teenager takes this line a little further and shows how young people in 2026 are forced to live in 'controlled spaces' under constant surveillance by GPS, ID tags and security videocams. There is no space for real adolescence, because all space is corporately owned software or hardware (Sterling).

Interestingly, the conventions of adventure-style narratives, coupled with a clear objective amongst writers and publishers to portray mixed-gender VR users, means that many of the teen protagonists in speculative cyber-fantasy are part of groups or teams rather than being completely isolated or independent. Phoenix has a female companion, Laura, and Metaphor is joined by her brother and The Wire. In *Gemini Game*, the O'Connor twins are never alone because of their connection as siblings, but furthermore they are constantly monitored as they puzzle their way through 'Night's Castle'. First, they are scrutinised by Ariel, who enters the game with the twins and watches their progress. Her father, Aaron Harper, also observes the players from his location in real life. Although the twins are transported to a seemingly desolate and empty landscape when they enter the game, he continues to watch over them, able to communicate with them and pull them out of 'Night's Castle' if things get too dangerous. The virtual reality game feels like a space of freedom and possibility to the teenage gamers, who experience acute sensations of fear, exhilaration, escape and belonging when they enter its arena, similar to feelings Turkle argues they should encounter in the streets and wildernesses of 'Real Life'. Yet this layer of surveillance acts as added security in much the same way a mobile phone acts as a permanent connection to the safety of family or home.

In other texts, the observer is not powerful but maintains a link between teenage player and adult supervisor. In *Shadow of the Minotaur*, Phoenix's mother, Christina Graves, becomes trapped in time while she sits observing her son fight gods and monsters from Greek myths on the computer screen. She continues to watch over and worry about him, despite the fact he is in a completely different, parallel world and is out of reach of her maternal help. A similar scenario occurs in Gillian Cross's *New World* (1994). This is not strictly speculative fantasy because the controlling force behind the technology is human, but the scenario is similar to that in Gibbons' novel. Young teenagers Miriam and Stuart have been invited to test a new computer game, but as they work their way through the stages an older teenager, Will, unwittingly observes and plays against them (unwittingly, that is, because he does not realise they are 'real' human beings on his screen). Unbeknownst to Will, the game's corporate creator is using it to test the limits of adolescent fear. Will discovers that the best way to beat his adversaries is to subject them to their worst nightmares. For Miriam this involves being tortured by the impression of hundreds of eyes looming towards her. In these examples, inert bodies or pixellated representations on the screen keep gamers in a place which is both public and policed and yet which continues to threaten. It seems that technology simultaneously tethers teenagers and subjects them to external adult control. The teenage characters in these particular novels are never truly alone, even if some—like Phoenix—have a sense that they have a lonely destiny awaiting them.

Dreamcastle's protagonist, Surfer, also quests on 'Dreamcastle' flanked by friends, the hacker Rom and the feisty action girl Kilroy. Despite moments of team-playing and shared experience, however, Surfer's movement through the VR world is not, on the whole, communal and, rather than demonstrating an inevitable 'gazed at' version of online adolescence, this novel is fed by a contrasting concern: that the Internet encourages unhealthy isolation and introspection. With Kilroy's fighting skills and Rom's technological know-how, Surfer's determination to win has solid human support, but at a crucial moment in their attempt at level 506 Surfer abandons his team mates—allowing Rom to fall to his virtual death—in order to pursue a fleeing warlock and his own success. From this point on in the narrative, there are pointed suggestions that Surfer is becoming overly embroiled in the game and from hereon in the only communing achieved is with the virtual world or programme itself. Surfer experiences web sickness ('the voms') more acutely than usual because of his deepening immersion in VR and the subsequent disjuncture between his mind and body.[12] He also begins to lose the ability to recognise Real Life. Walking home from the cyber café, he is nearly run over:

> Surfer was lost in these thoughts as he came to the junction of Woodvale and Fox, and crossed over into the Trent Road.
> A sudden bellowing roar snapped him out of his daydream. His head jerked up and he stared along the road towards town.
> For an instant he glimpsed an electram trundling towards him, headlights flaring—
> But then it was gone and the sky was filled with smoke and flames as the firedrake swept on towards him.
> In terror, Surfer reached for his sword, bracing himself for the firedrake's heat. But there was no sword, and the electram's horn blared as the driver swerved round Surfer, cursing. (146–147)

For an instant, Surfer realises the real danger he faces from the oncoming electram, but at the same time he is cast back into the fantasy world of 'Dreamcastle' and its mythical creatures. The narrative in *Dreamcastle* presents a critique of the player who becomes overpowered or submerged, although Surfer's father's concern that research shows 'spending too long in the Web can be dangerous' (148) is not necessarily authoritative here; after all, parental anxiety does not represent truth in teenage fiction. But Surfer's disintegrating sense of self and community indicates the danger that the virtual world presents. By the end of the novel, the heroic and single-minded adolescent from the opening pages is being haunted by elements of the game that invade his real world, and Kilroy has to enter 'Dreamcastle' to fight for him and safely 'bat' him out of the web. As we have seen in previous chapters, loss of self and of identity within a community is dangerous for an adolescent seeking the ultimate stability of adulthood.

In *Ultraviolet*, Violet suffers a similar decline in social competence and coherent subjectivity. In the early part of the narrative she is aware of her privileged position (her father can afford a 'Shielded garden' in which to grow real fruit and vegetables) but is also eager to rouse people from their general malaise. This is signified early in the narrative when her friends knock over a glass of juice while they play 'QuestHolme' and she cleans it up, thinking 'Stupid idiots are sitting right in it. Oblivious to wet jeans' (11). Her initial activist nature and good intentions lead her into a challenging series of events, in which she escapes the tunnels of her protective community and goes 'outside', simultaneously exposing 'BluShield', the manufacturers of UV-resistant material who are restricting the amount of protection available for their own commercial gain. Yet we have already seen how far Vi's absorption in 'QuestHolme' takes over her. This early indication of Vi's physical and mental submission to virtual reality foreshadows the novel's complex ending, where the reader discovers that most of the action 'outside' has merely been part of a gaming experience. I shall return to the structuring of this narrative twist later, but it is worth noting that, in terms of dangerous introspection, the threat of being totally absorbed by a game or taken over by a programme is transferred from the protagonist to the reader in Howarth's novel. Noga Applebaum argues that this novel incorporates a radical literary style shaped by the structure of VR games themselves, because Howarth 'does not overtly signal the shift between the reality of the game and the reality of her protagonist' (257). For Applebaum, its style makes *Ultraviolet* 'surprising' and playful, which is certainly the case, but there is also an underlying thread of sadness and isolation in the gaming theme and structure. Like the boys who unknowingly spill their drinks on themselves, Vi is unaware that all her determined efforts to change the world around her are actually different levels on a computer game. Her quest is lonely and her political action ineffectual.

It may be salient that in many VR gaming novels technology is not employed primarily as a tool, but as entertainment, yet despite the focus on *play* and *pleasure*, it repeatedly acts as the channel for sinister forces to be confronted. Cultural critic Deborah Lupton argues that computer technology is inherently frightening, partly because of its elusiveness and obliqueness. She points out that fear comes from all things incomprehensible and that a way of overcoming this terror is to portray computers as human in some way. It certainly may help make computers more comprehensible to employ 'user-friendly' icons and endow them with human characteristics, but the concept of a sentient computer is surely equally disturbing for the human who comes into contact with it, and it is not surprising that in some young adult speculative fantasies the threatening power from within the machine is indeed personified.

In *Shadow of the Minotaur* the reader is given early hints that there is persona behind the game that Phoenix's father is working on and testing out with his son. The first half of the novel details the innovative technology involved in this game, including the development of a 'Parallel Reality suit', which acts like a second skin and plunges the player directly into a sensory experience of the game, but the plot is interrupted by short chapters written in an anonymous voice which addresses Phoenix without him realising, promising future dangers and complaining violently when the game is abandoned. We are led to understand that the numbers or code that scroll across the Graves' computer screen produce this voice. Eventually, Phoenix recognises that the game is 'alive':

> *The Legendeer* was more than a matter of graphics and a story line. It always had been. It was a living thing, a thing with power and a life independent of the PC. The machine was a vehicle for the game, the sheath for its chrysalis stage, and that's all. *The Legendeer* was somehow both primitive and all knowing. It was able to reach out. It could twist time and space. *It played the player.* (74)

Across the course of the trilogy, this 'living thing' emerges as 'the Gamesmaster' while Phoenix himself becomes the 'Legendeer'. The Gamesmaster is attempting to infiltrate the real world from his own mythic realm of nightmares, and he/it uses computer games as gateways. Despite the superficial importance of VR *technology*, Gibbons stresses the *organic* nature of the force behind the game, using various metaphors, including the one of an emerging insect employed here. To embody the programme and programmer is to make them real, because they can function at the level of code and of essence, as technology and as creature.

'The Sorceress' performs in a similar way to the Gamesmaster in the collection of stories in *The Web 2027*. This collaborative series has a shared villain who uses cyberspace as a realm for her various sinister plots. Each author in the collective has a slightly different way of conceptualising the Sorceress, but in nearly every case her tangible presence is the main threat involved in 'spinning in' to the Web and in many of the stories the technology merely provides a fantasy setting for her to attack the teen protagonists. In *Gulliverzone*, for example, she appears as the Empress Golbasta, a fearsome creature with 'a giant body, a mound of inert flesh, under thick flowing cloth [. . .] sitting like a spider at the heart of her Lilliput-spanning web' (88). In contrast, in *Dreamcastle* this ugly fleshiness is disguised. As we have already seen, in Bowkett's novel she is represented as the beautiful Xenia, whose evil intentions are revealed visually when she metamorphoses: 'her hair, her face, the very bones of her body, began to ooze and stretch like warm plastic towards [Surfer]' (*Dreamcastle* 181). Cyber villains are sinister because they straddle the boundary between organic and inorganic; body and mind. In this way, the Gamesmaster is not just dependent on the players' physical presence through the game suit, but also feeds on their psychological fears. Cyber villains can also assume aspects of the fantastic, as the Empress Golbasta in *Gulliverzone* does in using 'magic dust' to control the size of her subjects and enemies rather than technological strategies. In some senses, purely technological creatures present less of a threat because they exist on the same plane as the teenagers do when they are hooked into the virtual world of their game. There are wholly virtual creatures that attack and maim in VR games—spiders and rats that represent electronic bugs—but they generally only do damage to the virtual version of the player. Pure cyber villains would also seem less unnatural and might indeed reflect a utopian vision of potential virtual subjectivity. As Mike Featherstone and Roger Burrows point out, '[d]espite the persistence of embodied physiognomic notions of the "true self" in contemporary social life, there is some evidence to suggest that the new technology is opening up the possibility of radically new disembodied subjectivities' (12), and surely someone or something caught between the old form of ensnared identity and an evolved free-floating selfhood is bound to be dangerous and abhorrent. Adolescents attempting to lose some of their embodied lives—the realities of being bullied, or bereaved, or bored —discover that the wires and electrons of cyberspace lead them fantastically to problems even more physical and fleshy. Villains in these novels are not purely conceptual but physically tangible, and as such terrifying, but there is also the dangerous question of how the teenage protagonists manage their body/mind splits within cyberspace, which I shall return to in the next section.

Curiously, the very corporality that threatens protagonists within VR games is also regulated by generic patterns. The Gamesmaster and the Sorceress exhibit such villainous characteristics as found in unimaginative high fantasy, comic books or blockbuster films. In *Shadow of the Minotaur* the voice of the Gamesmaster speaks in fantasy clichés ('There will be no peace for the innocent. You must play this game to the end. To the bitter end' [36]) and the Sorceress's representation as hag or temptress returns us to unhelpful binaries of female power left over from discourses of witchcraft. It is not only the villains who are constrained by the limits of the VR programmes, as we discover in Eric Brown's contribution to *The Web 2027, Untouchable*. Brown recognises the imaginative restrictions of virtual subjectivity and knowingly refers to the tendency for players to 'play safe' with their avatars: when his heroine Ana first enters the web she is told by her companion to change her appearance and that '[t]he program has thousands of options, but it'll be quicker if you just stick to the simple ones' (*Untouchable* 218). In anthropological studies of online worlds, researchers continue to uncover predictable narratives and character types amongst programmers and user identities. Most of the best known MUDs are based on high fantasy premises and most players adopt formulaic personas. Elizabeth Reid cites P. Curtis's complaint that in his research he has lost count of 'the number of "mysterious but unmistakably powerful" figures I have seen wandering LambDaMOO' (179). In her critique of virtual reality from the vantage point of 1995, Cheris Kramarae argues against the utopian vision of virtual subjectivity and suggests that revolutionary rhetoric surrounding new technological advances is not matched by its revolutionary sexual politics of representation. She explains: 'Many of the people writing about VR say that its potential is limited only by the imagination of those working on the programs. That's my worry' (41). It is, then, perhaps unlikely that teenager players will have any agency within such pre-programmed, generic worlds.

Symbolic Universes: The Teenager's Ironic Mythology

In Gibbons' VR gaming trilogy, Phoenix fights against Greek mythological characters (*Shadow of the Minotaur*), vampires (*Vampyr Legion* [2000]) and

Norse gods (*Warriors of the Raven* [2001]), and in each case the archetypal fantasy world that makes up 'The Legendeer' game engulfs the protagonist in an easily recognisable set of events and settings, involving familiar figures and tropes. Mythic figures such as Theseus, Dracul and Odin act as signs, provoking expectations of action and meaning in the reader who can identify the original story. Medusa, for example, is easy to judge so long as the reader can spot the tell-tale features of snaked hair and knows the myth of the Gorgons, and, as I have already argued, other villains are made apparent by their formulaic appearance or actions. Just as characters within the realms of virtual reality are drawn from pre-existing stories and legends, so are the landscapes and settings through which teenage protagonists have to journey, and we might question exactly what it means for these heroes or heroines to be moving within virtual spaces that are not new frontiers in narrative terms.

Jean Baudrillard's understanding of virtual reality as a 'simulacrum', a sign masking the absence of any basic reality, offers one way of thinking about these kinds of gaming geographies. For Baudrillard, simulacra are images of reality which deceive the viewer by hiding the fact that there is no reality beneath; that is, virtual reality distracts from the realisation that reality itself is no longer substantial. Marie-Laure Ryan argues that Baudrillard's model does not work when it comes to computer simulation, however. She suggests that VR does not embody deception because it is an active process, which is designed specifically to explore the possibilities of simulation, and that it is also primarily concerned with possible futures and not with representing existing reality. On the other hand, *fictional* representations of a VR gaming world, which in turn are based on mythical and literary landscapes, add an extra layer of artificiality and further worlds within worlds, so it seems impossible to avoid some consideration of simulacrum. Marc Augé's explanation of spatiality in 'supermodernity' (which Baudrillard sought to critique through his explanation of simulacra) is perhaps more useful, simply due to the terminology he uses. Augé describes supermodernity as the obverse of postmodernity, and characterises it as denoting an *excess* of space; or too much exposure to other places through improved technology and transport:

> This spatial overabundance works like a decoy, but a decoy whose manipulator would be very hard to identify (there is nobody pulling the strings). In very large part, it serves as a substitute for the universes which ethnography has traditionally made its own. We can say of these universes, which are themselves broadly fictional, that they are essentially universes of recognition. The property of symbolic universes is that they constitute a means of recognition, rather than knowledge, for those who have inherited them: closed universes where everything is a sign; collections of codes to which only some hold the key but whose existence everyone accepts. (32–33)

Although not masking a complete absence, Augé's symbolic universes, like Baudrillard's simulacra, are easily recognisable because they are available to everyone, through film, television and fiction, or through holiday brochures and satellite pictures. Knowledge of these places is superficial, however, because it is second-hand rather than directly experienced, and because these places are themselves fictions or 'collections of codes'. 'Gulliverzone', for instance, is an excessive space, full of signification for the knowing reader, but otherwise insubstantial, both because it is a virtual world and because it only superficially stitches together parts of other places (such as Swift's original text and the idea of a themepark). In some ways, moral and educational anxieties about technology are partly played out through the discourse of symbolic universes. When Surfer argues with his father about the efficacy of learning through experience as facilitated by virtual learning environments, Mr Miller could easily retort that virtual experiences—however lifelike—are never the same as real experiences. History and geography might be more accessible through webschooling, but time and space also become compressed and decontextualised. Augé's symbolic universes provide a richer explanation than Baudrillard's simulacrum can. What is valuable about this explanation is that new landscapes can be *recognised*, not purely as decoys or deceptions, but also through the way they enact their spatiality. In other words, a collection of geographical codes performs a certain meaning and can therefore be consistently interpreted by always performing them in the same way.

The symbolic universe in *Vampyr Legion* is constructed from elements of Bram Stoker's *Dracula* (1897) and subsequent rewritings and reinterpretations of the vampire myth and its origins in European folklore. In Gibbons' novel, Phoenix and his companion Laura explore Dracul's lair and discover damp walls, creaking doors and murky galleries.

> The daylight itself seemed lost in the great gloom of the castle. It was like a guttering candle on the brink of extinction.
> 'What a foul place!' said Laura.
> 'Did you expect anything else?' asked Phoenix. They moved forward uncertainly.
> 'Which way?' asked Laura, 'And don't you dare say we're going to split up. I never know why they do that in the movies.' (144–145)

It is a surprisingly self-referential moment, since numerous other similar descriptions of castles, mountains, dungeons and so on, are used without irony throughout the narrative. A similar episode occurs in *Gemini Game*, in which the landscapes are familiar from epic high fantasy and gothic narratives. *Gemini Game*'s fantasy VR world parallels the dangers of the real world—where the twins encounter poverty, inequality and dangerously competitive industry—but presents its threats in a decidedly generic manner:

> The Night's Castle, grim and forbidding, appeared as soon as they cleared the forest, crowning the top of a barren mountain and dominating the entire countryside. Dozens of pointed spires and turrets rose into the sky, which had been designed to remain permanently black with thunderclouds.
> 'It looks a bit scary,' Liz said softly.
> 'Exactly,' BJ agreed with a proud grin. (125)

Phoenix, Laura and Liz all recognise the significance of the landscape they find themselves in and, crucially, they know how to participate in the performance of space and meaning presented to them in these gaming scenarios. In rejecting the urge to split up in order to explore a dangerous space more effectively Laura resists playing what she sees as a predetermined part in the horror genre she has entered, but of course she is in fact enacting an alternative generic role just as plainly. When she questions the conventional response to this type of 'foul' landscape, she mimics the endless knowingness of parodic teenage horror movies like *I Know What You Did Last Summer* (1997) and *Scary Movie* (2003), as well as playful television series aimed at young adults such as *Buffy the Vampire Slayer*. Liz's reading of 'Night's Castle' as 'scary' is also ironic, since she is the game's co-designer and has purposely programmed the landscape to appear ominous and threatening. Interestingly, part of the geographical conundrum of VR landscapes like these is the combined infallibility and instability of their spatiality. While games are fixed in fantasy worlds with predictable meanings, the teenage protagonist has clear signals about where they are and how they should act, but this proficiency in recognising meaning also extends to moments when the games disintegrate or depart from their normal landscapes. In *Gemini Game*, Liz's confident readings of her own constructed universe are challenged when Ariel interferes with the computer programme and 'Night's Castle' collapses from within. A similar breakdown occurs in *Heir Apparent* at the moment that the C-POC group wreck the Rasmussem Gaming Centre and Giannine's VR game is damaged.

Teenagers can interpret the symbolic universes of cyberspace and know how to act within them in order to easily assimilate. They are competent readers of code and know when that code is corrupted. By simulating recognisable spaces, the VR games in *Gemini Game*, *Heir Apparent*, and *Vampyr Legion* provide an ideal backdrop for adolescent performance, and unlike troublesome real places they allow those teenagers to manipulate their surroundings. It is telling that the speculative fantasies authored by Scott and Vande Velde, at least, are more concerned with the way their heroes and heroines perform in-game than in the real world, and even Gibbons loses track of the importance of non-virtual experience by the second in his trilogy. Other writers are more concerned with the intersection between virtual and real space, as we shall now see.

Interfaces

The actual point of interaction between protagonist and computer screen is static, sedentary and isolated. Not surprisingly, few teenage novels dwell for very long on the image of the individual at the PC or console, despite the fact that this scenario offers the truth about much adolescent leisure activity. Anyone who has watched another user play a PC game or surf the Internet will know that little drama can be gleaned from the actual physicality of sitting at the interface. On the other hand, there is meaning to be found in that scenario: as Lupton points out, we have an 'emotional and embodied relationship' with our PCs (477), particularly since a large proportion of Western adults and teenagers spend much of their time working on, playing with, and communicating through computers. After using our PC we 'return to the embodied reality of the empty stomach, stiff neck, aching hands, sore back and gritty eyes caused by many hours in front of a computer terminal' (480). Popular media discourses of adolescence *are* concerned with that reality, often agonising over the collective health of Western youth, which no longer runs around outdoors but lives a sedentary and unhealthy life indoors (little mention ever given to the fact that education systems prioritise such deskbound moments as most productive); but although there is some mention of the physical effects of being in virtual reality too long, fictional representations of teenagers sitting at a computer might seem to miss the point. Lupton goes on to explain that the dominant understanding of our connections with computer technology is disembodied and concerned with the 'self as mind' not as corporal fact: a Cartesian model, in fact. It is the mental connection the individual has with technology that is crucial and not the physical reality of late twentieth-century PCs. In the same way, it is the symbolic journeys teenagers take through their interaction with technology that provides drama, on the whole, and not the static moments where they sit at their desks at home and log on. I would like to begin with those instants of real-life interaction with technology, however, because some texts consciously situate their protagonists in particular spacio-temporal intersections.

Screens and Cyborgs: Adolescent Bodies and Minds

For most texts under consideration, the place where the protagonist uses computer technology is relatively unremarkable. In the virtual reality game narratives I discussed above, the site for playing is either domestic (Vi plays at home in *Ultraviolet*, as do Metaphor and her friends in *Gulliverzone*, and Phoenix in *The Legendeer* trilogy) or commercial (gaming centres feature in *Gemini Game*, *Dreamcastle* and *Heir Apparent*). In Eric Brown's *Untouchable*, however, space, place and the physical relationship with a computer are critical. The location of most of these speculative fantasies is unimportant (beyond being a recognisably Western world), but in Brown's novel we are very purposefully placed in developing New Delhi, where Ana and her brother, Ajay, beg on the streets for their survival. They both have physical disabilities: Ana has only one leg and Ajay is blind. When Ajay is stolen away by a frightening old woman in a Mercedes (another incarnation of the Sorceress), Ana follows them into an unfamiliar district. She loses track of Ajay and is offered help by a boy from the 'affluent suburbs south of central Delhi, where all the Brahmin businessmen and their families lived' (Brown 207). The discrepancy in location indicates the difference between Ana and her new acquaintance, Sanjay, but it is his home entertainment system that signals their real distance:

> Ana entered the lighted room, stopped and stared.
> She had once read a story in a comic book about Aladdin's Cave, a place full of fabulous treasures, winking gold and glinting jewels. Now, she was reminded of Aladdin's Cave. [. . .]
> She paused in front of something like a big television screen set into the wall. A multicoloured pattern was playing across its surface. Next to it was what she knew was a computer system. [. . .]
> She turned in a circle, open-mouthed. She could have sold any one of these objects and bought food to last her months. (210)

Ana and Sanjay inhabit different worlds and represent two aspects of the question of adolescent space. For Ana, living on the street is not a leisure activity or an attempt to define herself through subculture, but rather a practical reality. Like any teenager trying to occupy a public space, though, she is subject to fear: feared *for* because of her vulnerability, and herself terrifying because she is visible and different (young, disabled and an 'untouchable'). Sanjay's space, on the other hand, is private and privileged, secluded from social realities like street poverty and free from adult supervision. Brown's novel is notable for highlighting the limitations in universal conceptions of adolescence, not only in his exploration of class, but also through Ana's physical subjectivity and disability. This is made explicit through Ana's response to Sanjay's room. The basic technology required for online gaming is defamiliarised and made excessive when seen through the eyes of a less privileged teenager.

When Sanjay offers to take her to the web for the first time from the comfort of his room, the process of 'spinning in' is unfamiliar to Ana (and to a certain extent to the reader). The narrative therefore focuses on disjointed bodily sensations:

> Ana hesitated, then picked up the suit. The material was cold, and clung on to her skin. She found the opening in the back, sat on the edge of the couch and worked her good leg into the legging, then slipped the stump of her right leg into the second. The material hung loose where her right leg should have been. She pulled the suit around her body and worked her arms inside. It gripped her limbs, squeezing. (214)

Writing Fantastic Spaces • 173

Like Lupton's acknowledgement of the physicality of sitting at a computer screen, the narrative recognises the user's embodied experience of gaming equipment and their material sense of space and identity in relation to technology. For the teenager and for the individual with a disability, such persistent reminders of the body become troublesome. Without wishing to suggest that age and physical ability are anything like direct parallels in terms of identity, it is surely significant that Ana personifies both adolescence and disability. The fantastic world of the web not only allows Ana to search effectively for her brother (who is being held in the virtual world to be experimented on by the Sorceress), but also provides an ideal space for her to reinvent her body. Her virtual self has two legs and can walk or run freely, and she programmes her avatar to be sixteen years old and well dressed: 'She had breasts, and long legs, and her hair was long and sleek, not the tangled mess it was in real life' (221). Both illusions are held in uneasy tension with the reality of Ana's experience of herself in real life. When she concentrates she can feel the material of the websuit enveloping her, and when she is given positive attention in her new guise she reflects on the way people in non-virtual places treat her according to her real appearance. Her virtual leg is also a constant reminder of how travelling in cyberspace does not involve the profound effort that walking does in real life (where Ana usually leans on her brother and 'shares' his legs) and that physical difference is evened out online.[13] This realisation is mirrored in real teenagers' reported experiences of navigating virtual spaces (Subrahmanyam, Greenfield and Tynes).

As Lupton's description of day-to-day interactions with computers suggests, virtual reality worlds are not the only embodied experiences available to users. The teenage protagonists in Michael J. Rosen's *ChaseR* and Nicola Morgan's *Mondays are Red* have very specific spatial relationships with their computer screens; relationships which relate to mapping external and internal gaps. These texts differ from most of the novels I have discussed so far in this chapter in that they are not examples of speculative fantasy. *ChaseR* has no fantastic elements and deals with contemporary realist issues, but is narrated purely through the medium of email and therefore locates its protagonist unvaryingly at the computer screen. *Mondays are Red* is more recognisably fantastic realist, using computer technology as a conceptual image for the fantastic changes that occur in the protagonist.

The protagonist of Michael J. Rosen's contemporary version of the teenage epistolary novel is Chase Riley, also self-portrayed as ChaseR or through the 'smiley'

q:¬)

a visual representation of a thirteen-year-old boy in a cap. ChaseR has moved with his parents from his city home to a new life in the Ohio countryside, where he faces a set of challenges that include missing his friends and encountering his new rural neighbours' traditional love of hunting. The whole novel is constructed through ChaseR's emails, mainly directed to friends back home and his sister, Mallory. As readers, we do not receive any guidance from a narrator's voice, nor do we get to read any emailed responses from other characters: instead, the text positions the reader alongside ChaseR as he composes at his PC. The distance between him and his old friends is relatively small (only 60 miles in fact) but is amplified by the sense that his only mode of contact is electronic and often one-sided. After all, although email is often mooted as a communication solution which shrinks distances between people, the medium arguably also diminishes individuals' abilities to interact face-to-face or in larger social situations. Moreover, the fact that ChaseR is only 60 miles away from his old community does not really make any difference to his sense of material isolation, and indeed his early emails signal the meagreness of friendships maintained in cyberspace. His closest friend, Jeremy, is a frequent writer, but although ChaseR appreciates the contact he clearly misses physical companionship, appending an early email with the postscript 'You ARE going to get out here sometime. Soon' (21). Most of his acquaintances from home do not even take advantage of the possibilities of email for staying in contact:

> Subject: :=8:| You baboons out there?
> You guys are in serious danger of having your subscription to my e-newsletter canceled [sic] and missing out on all the news from Beaver Creek.
> Write back! Snail mail, even. I've heard from everyone else but you four! Come on. I miss seeing you so, I've got to hear from you. (23)

The novel shows ChaseR using electronic language creatively, demonstrating its potential for different registers (emails to friends and family, more formal emails to strangers, and newsletters for general mailouts, for example) and the possibility of manipulating symbols into new meanings: turning type characters into emoticons such as

Q:¬Grrrrr

and suggestive pictures such as

(o) (o)

(representing a female body), rather than limiting them to conventional forms of linguistic communication. The effect of this multiplicity of playful codes within the text is to suggest a protagonist at ease with the discourse of electronic communication and expert in the expressive possibilities of technology. Indeed, a bolder text might go further and offer up a utopian image of ChaseR contentedly existing within this medium rather than having to give up on most of his old friends and develop a 'real' social life in his new locale. In fact, despite the contemporary atmosphere conferred by the use of email, Rosen's trajectory for his teenage hero is rather conventional. The main plotline in the novel follows ChaseR's outrage at the fact that his new hometown loves hunting deer and finds the pursuit and consumption of wild animals more acceptable than society does in ChaseR's previous urban environment. He outlines his own version of a liberal and environmentalist ideology in emails to his friend Jeremy and to Mallory, and sets out to thwart his neighbour's efforts to shoot the local wildlife (deterring the deer by marking boundaries with his own urine). The campaign naturally takes him away from his online life and brings him into contact with the pleasures of the outdoors. Much of his correspondence details the bugs, birds and creatures he encounters, and the friends he eventually makes within the rural community. By the end of the novel there is the sense that ChaseR has moved away from the interface with his PC towards a more active, healthy and *natural* life. He explains to Jeremy, '[m]y parents HELPED ME decided that if I spend only one hour per day on the computer that could "improve things" ' (139) and, although this policing of online time is ostensibly enforced by parental authority, ChaseR clearly benefits from the shift to pre-technical subjectivity. In the final newsletter to friends back home included in the novel, ChaseR lists the 'Top Ten Reasons to Live in the Country':

> Oh, and maybe my favorite [sic] part of being out here is the sky. The dogs and I go out after dark and lie in the grass, just staring up at the stars. They're the same stars as the ones above Columbus, but without the city glow—and there's no other glow from our own village—I can see them like they never really existed before. (149–150)

Without the glow from the computer screen, ChaseR is free to see the bigger picture, which includes not only stars but also driving lessons and the object of his nocturnal desires, Marylynne, who significantly does not have a computer and who ChaseR represents through comic image of him thinking of her in bed:

lq'¬)\ | /|

Nicola Morgan's *Mondays are Red* does not deal with the literal point of interface between teenager and computer, but offers instead a fantastical connection between adolescent identity and the ubiquitous PC. In the first chapter, Luke wakes up in hospital feeling very strange:

> It was as if a huge transparent computer screen had been put really close to my face. In fact, it was more like being IN a computer and looking out, so that I was seeing first the things on the screen and in my head and then everything outside the computer, the real, other world beyond. (4)

After suffering from a severe bout of meningitis, Luke's phenomenological experience of the world changes dramatically and, although Morgan explores this shift of perspective in various ways—most noticeably through her inventive language, in phrases such as 'A volcano spat me furiously with a roar from its mouth' (1)—the image of a self located within a computer screen presents a particularly interesting metaphor. Unlike ChaseR, Luke is not representative of a normal teenage user of technology. In contrast to the gaming narratives explored in the section above, where electronic worlds act as middle landscapes and spaces in which adolescents are under surveillance, Luke's 'transparent computer screen' offers a way for the teenager to gaze outwards, back at the 'real' world. Luke does not really sit at a PC in the way Lupton discusses, but his sense of self is based on the way that he is embodied through the computer metaphor. His meningitis has brought on symptoms that the author identifies in a postscript note as synaesthesia: he tastes colour, feels sound, and has 'a kaleidoscope in his head' (1). This new way of experiencing the world manifests itself in other fantastic abilities too, most significantly in the gift of flying and the capacity to bring characters and events into being through pure will and the power of description. Early in the story, for example, Luke's friend Tom visits him in hospital and both boys are shocked and embarrassed by Luke's physical weakness and the fact he has to use a wheelchair when before he had been a star runner. Luke discovers he can take advantage of being inside a 'computer screen' by programming the perceptions of people around him:

> if I really concentrated, really looked inside and almost turned my brain inside out, I could grasp the images with my mind, as though I had an invisible mouse to control them with. [...] Slowly, and then more quickly, a picture formed, and my mouth started speaking, almost without my control.
> 'Like my new speed-machine? Check the ice-blue gleaming bodywork, cool alloy wheel trim, techno-bubble fibre-glass dashboard.' (23–24)

Although Luke can see that the wheelchair is still the 'clanky heavy old hospital wheelchair' (24), he simultaneously sees it as a fantastic racing car. More importantly, Tom perceives it as such, and the boys are able to resume their usual relationship based on physical equality. Throughout the novel, Luke uses his power for projects of varying ambition, from fashioning exotic ice-creams to summoning the girl of his dreams. In effect, the metaphorical computer interface allows Luke to create and control aspects of his real existence and brings him closer to being a form of cyborg rather than a mere user of a PC for email or VR equipment for immersion into a pre-programmed world.

David Bell points to the different conceptions of 'cyborgisation', ranging from intimate connections such as electronic implants to less obvious types of human/machine symbiosis, such as car driving and PC use (150). According to Donna Haraway, a cyborg is 'a cybernetic organism, a hybrid of machine and organism, a creature of social reality as well as a creature of fiction' (149). Haraway's interest in cyborgs focuses on their potential for structuring new ways of thinking about identities, particularly gendered ones. Cyborgs have partial identities, confused boundaries and no natural origins, and therefore escape most of the old problems of sexual representation and can instead symbolise an active adoption of new subjectivities. Interestingly, Haraway argues that people with severe disabilities might have 'the most intense experiences of complex hybridisation with other communication devices' (178), becoming whole in ways that make organic holism redundant. Indeed, as we have seen in Brown's *Untouchable*, Ana's experience of becoming whole through merging with technology brings to attention not only her ecstatic realisation that she has the use of two legs once more, but also highlights her sense of empowerment in reinventing herself as a confident sixteen-year-old avatar. In Morgan's novel, the text implies that Luke's metaphorical cyborgisation is a direct result of his severe illness and that his subsequent 'disability' is simultaneously a new kind of 'ability'.[14]

Luke's gendered identity as cyborg is less straightforward, and his subjectivity is perhaps more clearly influenced by his status as adolescent. Haraway's vision of cyborgisation is optimistic and draws on feminist traditions of 'writing the body', albeit employing a new and unsettling formulation of that body. In many respects, Luke's fantastic power in manipulating the world is only partly controlled through the computer screen: its other source of energy comes from inventive and descriptive language. Luke literally evokes real objects and outcomes through synaesthesia-tinged linguistic depictions. Sometimes this works as a form of writing his own body, as when he talks his frail, convalescing self into running and then—fantastically—flying:

> I thought for a moment, looking deep into my head, and the computer screen reshaped before my eyes, full of possibilities. 'It's being light itself, the fastest thing in the universe, weightless. It's knowing you could touch a star, sucking speed from the Milky Way. It's sugared space dust bursting on the back of your tongue.' And as I said it I felt it, melon sherbet singing through my veins. [...] Without thinking, I stood up and walked, walked to the garden gate. I looked back at the house and then turned to the woods. I took off. [...] We raced, Amber and I, and my legs were springs, steely-strong. Both legs. Over the spongy grass we sped, my arms pumping the air, my body weightless. [...] Suddenly I couldn't feel my feet and when I looked down the ground was way way way below me.
>
> I was flying. (34–35)

Here, the technological interface brings Luke closer to his sense of physical being and his body is both 'steely-strong' and 'weightless', indicators of his developing adolescent body and his fantastical fusion with a virtual space through the computer screen. The poetic, synaesthetic phrases he uses to incite his body to move fluidly are wholly sensual and reminiscent of the language used by some feminists to describe the connection between the process of writing imaginatively and awareness of bodily and sexual being.

At other moments, however, Luke's cyborgisation facilitates writing other, sexualised bodies instead. Seraphina, the girl he creates for himself through language is constructed as soft, sweet, and mysterious: 'Her skin is cinnamon in the sun, cake-warm, her hair long as honey. She flows like cream, blows candy-floss bubbles in the air' (53–54). More ominously, Luke sees his sister, Laura, as a series of slimy, slug-like creatures appearing in his computer screen. His negative feelings and these related abject images are based on the fear that school gossip about Laura's sexual activity is true, and this anxiety provokes him into unwittingly creating a real horror story or virtual reality in which Laura is punished. This scenario initially occurs to Luke spontaneously: 'Before I could think further, without warning I was looking through the computer screen. Now Laura looked like the jerky victim in a video game, being pursued by a black metal man, faceless, with a mercury mask' (28). But before long he is manipulating the bodies of Laura and the masked man through storytelling so that his attempt to suppress Laura's adolescent sexuality becomes a real attack on her life. Like a designer of violent computer games, Luke's creativity threatens to fulfil feminist fears about cyber-sexuality rather than satisfy a programme of writing the body (see the concerns expressed by Kramarae, p. 167).

The dangers of an adolescent cyborg at large in a contemporary world are embodied in the figure of Dreeg, a fantastical, shape-shifting creature who resides in Luke's computer screen 'like a little icon' (7) and both coaches and tempts him. Rather like a more sinister version of Bridget's 'threshold guardian', Xiii, in *The Other Ones*, Dreeg also has much in common with the Sorceress from *The Web 2027* or the Gamesmaster in *The Legendeer* trilogy. Like these villains, he is simultaneously attractive and repellent, changing as his relationship with Luke shifts from sweet to sour. He also competes for control of the virtual world that Luke creates, and often takes the role of programmer while his teenage comrade is a mere player. For instance, Luke realises that through Dreeg's powers his fictional man with the metal mask has become real and is pursing Laura. In comprehending the unpleasant side-effects of his new gift he tries to break free of Dreeg, but losing him would also mean losing the ability to run and fly, not to mention losing his own Seraphina. Luke finally recognises that Dreeg is the fantastic personification of the 'ugly part' of his own brain, however, and uses the 'virtual scalpel' from his computer screen 'toolbox' to cut him out. In many respects, this conclusion leaves Luke in the same position as so many fantastic realist protagonists at the end of their narratives: bereft of their fantastic ability, returned to reality and ushered towards a more conventional (offline) adult space. Most disturbingly, we discover that Luke's initial illness was triggered by his disgust at his sister's promiscuity, but his psychological pain is resolved when it is revealed that Laura is actually still a virgin and suddenly regrets dressing and acting provocatively.

The conservatism of Morgan's gender politics is perhaps tempered by Luke's complex identity, which merges elements of computer programmer and of cyborg, of aggressive shaper of the material world and serene manipulator of language. Besides, this is Luke's story, not Laura's, and although her behaviour is policed, his understanding of gender and sexuality is only just beginning to develop and grow. There are some ways in which Morgan's novel actively transcends the ideologies of other young adult fantastic realism or speculative fantasy however. Her use of the computer screen offers something recognisable and contemporary for the teen reader, but it does not fix the adolescent by trapping them within virtual worlds or tethering them to technology. By using the computer as a creative metaphor, *Mondays are Red* suggests that technology is a tool, not a prison or a malevolent force. This means that it is possible for some remnants of Luke's supernatural power to remain at the end of the novel. Although, like most fantastic realist texts, the growth of the teenage character corresponds with a loss of the fantastic (here in the shape of Dreeg and the ability to fly), Morgan's novel allows the continuation of Luke's cyborgisation in the form of his synaesthesia. The computer screen has vanished, but Luke can still manipulate the world around him because he has the power of imagination and language. Through his difference (which like Ana's is made up of adolescence and disability) Luke's mind triumphs over his body.

Young adult literature like Morgan's resolves conflicts between mind and body and allows a space for adolescence that is both fantastic and sustainable. I have pointed to several authors who attempt to create innovative narratives of adolescence using fantastic realism, magic realism and other forms that might more accurately be called 'postmodern'. I would like to revisit one of those texts now, along with two cyber novels, to further consider the role that language, imagination and creativity play in constructing new forms of adolescence. These texts might be understood through the basic technological language of hypertext.

Hypertext: Codes of Adolescence

Like virtual reality, hypertext is a phenomenon that has generated great excitement and discussion in the late twentieth century. As Dan Thu Nguyen and Jon Alexander state, 'the Web's basic design principle is in its underlying architecture of hypertext' (111) and it is this design which turns the use of a personal computer into an interactive experience, on the level of code and language rather than the kinds of bodily virtual immersion discussed above. Hypertext links pages of content to each other and allows the user to move between these pages at will, changing the order and pace of their engagement with the material available. Proponents argue that creative versions of ICT, such as hyperfiction, challenge traditional concepts of authority and textual stability, and more generally that the fluid movement of user through cyberspace via hyperlinks promotes multiple and multi-directional subjectivities. It is therefore not surprising that teenagers are often perceived as having a natural affinity with this conceptual space and language at play in cyberspace: they are cyber-*literate*. Thus, in the same way that teenagers inhabit the spaces of virtual reality, they also successfully navigate textual geographies online. Tapscott uses the term, 'the Net Generation' or 'N-Gen' to describe 'children born with technology' and explains that 'for many kids, using new technology is as natural as breathing' (40), while Peter Hunt points out that this natural expertise shapes young people's relation to the form of electronic and hypertextual fiction: 'we might say that those untrained in certain ways of thinking (conveniently children) do not see narrative in the same way as older readers' ('Futures for Children's Literature' 17). For Tapscott and Hunt hypertext is both natural to and naturally suited to the uninformed person: the child or adolescent. Of course, an alternative reading might argue that non-traditional narrative forms also provide an appropriate figurative landscape for the adolescent who is unformed, capricious and open to constant change. William Sleator's *Rewind* (1999) is one such narrative for slightly younger than teenage readers, described by Applebaum as encompassing 'a rich variety of options' for the reader (258). In this short novel, eleven-year-old Peter is given the chance to rewrite his own destiny after a fatal road accident. He is offered twelve hours to consider how to rerun events leading up to his death, and each time he 'rewinds' and goes back in time he returns to an earlier point in his life. The story is a strange mixture of supernatural and time-travel elements, but key to the narrative is Peter's shifting identity as he learns more about how his actions affect other people's behaviour, and how small changes in the choices he makes on a day-to-day basis cannot change fate unless the more important attitudes behind those choices are also transformed. Crucially, Peter has to accept the new knowledge that he was adopted as a baby and will soon have to accommodate the birth of his parents' natural child, because it was this news that initially led him to argue with his mother and father and run off into the road. The unidentified, supernatural voice that guides Peter when he first dies explains that he has to overcome this unconscious self-destructive urge, and must 'fix things more deeply. Your emotions are as much a solid fact as the car being there' (5). Peter only gradually realises that he cannot simply avoid the time and place of his death but has to mend the relationship he has with his parents, and each time he goes back into the past he tries out different tactics, employing the knowledge he has about the future to manipulate other characters or work out who to trust.

    The structure of Sleator's novel offers the suggestion of choice and multiplicity of endings that mirrors the texture of a computer game, but it is not a true hypertext because neither Peter nor the reader are allowed complete freedom to choose their route through the narrative: rather, Peter is compelled to rewind and replay a series of actions in a particular order so that he can learn from his previous mistakes and finally 'win' at life. In this way, *Rewind* resembles Vande Velde's *Heir Apparent*, as although much of the headway made by both Giannine/Janine and Peter is down to unsystematic combinations of actions reminiscent of the randomness in computer game techniques, there remains a cumulative effect to their gameplay which only works when the narrative episodes are read in a particular order. Many critics of hyperfiction have noted that the inherent freedom, even anarchy, of hypertext is antithetical to the essence of narrative because of this very issue. In an early critique of the medium, Jurgen Fauth suggests that while hypertext might offer 'great opportunities for playful interactions [. . .] it seems to be an artistic dead end as far as narrative is concerned.' He points out that the 'hyperstructure' of hypertext—the unstable mass of choices, links and pathways through textual material—does not result in a different form of narrative at all because ultimately each reader chooses a linear text from amongst the mass of options. John Miller goes even further and argues that readers of hypertext do not even benefit from any playful aspect of the medium:

> a hyperfiction author and critic, argues that a hyperfiction 'invites the reader not to ratify its wholeness, but to deconstruct it ('Reading From the Map' 129). But hyperfictions don't need deconstruction, as the reader assumes they are not constructed in the first place. [. . .] It is hard to play with a text that 'yields,' that doesn't fight back.

Certainly, it seems problematical to argue that the very structure of any traditional printed novel can ever be hypertextual or, as Applebaum suggests, that texts like *Rewind* are really non-linear, because the nature of textual *narrative* is to have a shape or direction. The kinds of electronic texts that avoid such linear structure cannot provide new *narratives* of adolescence, only already deconstructed sets of meaning. Instead of directly comparing the structure of young adult novels and hyperfiction or computer games, it might be more useful to suggest hypertext and games act as a further fantastic trope that authors use to explore the adolescent experience.

Ultraviolet's inventiveness might also be understood through the structures of computer games or hypertext because, as several critics have pointed out, Vi's attempts to break out of her protective indoor society in the main part of the novel are revealed to be nothing more than the complex workings of a new version of 'QuestHolme' ('Edition Eight': *QuestHolme Futures*) (Applebaum; Kimberley Reynolds). Once the reader realises that Vi's story has been a web of real moments in her apartment and unreal gaming moments in her cyborgised imagination, it is impossible to work out where the initial point of reality is located. The final few chapters build an alternative reality, where climate change begins to slow and reverse, society is encouraged to 'log off—go out—tune in', and Vi enjoys idyllic outdoor picnics and barbeques with friends and family. Textual clues suggest that this scenario is also part of QuestHolme, however, and that Vi and her father are now playing together and working out different endings. The novel's final paragraphs shift the site of reality once more, as Vi and her father emerge from the game and discuss its narrative problems. Vi explains, 'We're supposed to care about the story, but it's just a string of events, not much character development, no humour in it or anything' (243), a statement that offers a sly critique on the problems of hypertext. In fact, Vi is left with a printed-out version of her own personalised 'QuestHolme' experience, 'a book of the game', and in a way we are returned to the beginning of the narrative. Like a hypertextual journey through cyberspace, Howarth suggests that Vi's story could have taken many different routes and that her 'fifth different ending' is only the start of the potential for writing and rewriting herself. An early reference to the game's instruction manual foreshadows this idea: '*With a "multiple path" feature as standard, many levels will have two exits, and different exits will lead to different levels. There are over twenty thousand ways to finish the scenario as a result!*' (14).

One of the ways that Vi 'writes' herself in *Ultraviolet* is through a form of direct programming. Her adventures in QuestHolme are influenced by her own actions and surroundings, since the new version of the game allows the player to 'paste in some pretty personalised scenarios with realistic "home" backdrops' (15) and to stimulate visceral experiences by preparing 'feelies', real objects that appear virtually in the game when you touch them. Vi's response to her excessive gaming is to ask 'how could anyone have seen it as a substitute for smelly, glorious, disappointing, thrilling life?' (216), but she is truly a product of her own hypertext and is more real when she is playing—or writing herself—than when she is simply existing. This kind of constructedness is not new but it does reveal interesting ways that adolescence can be created and queried through concepts of programming or coding in literary representations. Aidan Chambers' *Breaktime* is perhaps the most effective example of adolescent self-production through language, and I would like to conclude by examining the way this pre-cyber novel shares hypertextual elements with later fictions of adolescence.

Chambers' *Breaktime* was published in 1978, before the Internet, virtual reality and other electronic technologies were ubiquitous in the lives of teenagers. In fact, the closest the narrative comes to reflecting technological sophistication is when its hero uses a public payphone. In many ways, however, Chambers' novel epitomises aspects of technology; specifically the playful, non-linear structure of hypertext or electronic games. The basic plot seems straightforward: after a fight with his sick father, seventeen-year-old Ditto feels he needs to escape from home so he arranges to go camping with a girlfriend. His time away turns into an adolescent adventure, as he gets drunk, makes friends with some part-time burglars, and loses his virginity with the obliging Helen. In fact, this abundance of events is undercut by a complex framing device and a tricky narrative style. *Breaktime* is not really *about* Ditto's coming of age through drink, violence and sexual experience. Instead, it is about the construction of his identity through language and play; a process that is expressly active and self-aware. The reader encounters the plot through a series of different textual and pictorial devices, including extracts from letters, fragments of dialogue, lists, encyclopaedia entries, images made out of typeface, and cartoon frames, to mention just a few. These are all attempts on Ditto's part to defend 'literature' from his friend Morgan's attacks: namely, that literature is dated, untrue, overly neat and a pretence. Morgan's final accusation is that 'Literature is a sham, no longer useful, effluent, CRAP' (10). Ditto's method of responding to his friend's claims is to present his own life as fiction in a series of vignettes in different narrative styles and from various perspectives.

To compare the structure of these vignettes to the structure of hypertext may at first seem tenuous: after all, there is no mention of non-linear linking in the style of Internet browsing, nor does *Breaktime* play with time and experience in the way that *Ultraviolet* or *Rewind* do. On the other hand, temporal disruption does occur in more specifically *textual* ways, in that the narrative constantly shifts from past to present tense and back again, and Ditto's concurrent experience is interspersed with flashbacks to when he was a child first noticing the schism between himself and his father. Moreover, Chambers plays with conventions of the novel, using what might be termed a more interactive or hypertextual mode of narrative by incorporating visual elements into the text or setting different perspectives against each other in columns on the page. Like an online surfer, the reader has to deal with a range of different mini-narratives and viewpoints, and make their own meaning, rather than being led through a sustained and logical narrative pathway. As a result, Ditto himself is a fluid and multi-subjective character who, although recognisably adolescent in his tendency to be overly smart and self-conscious (in Eriksonian terms, as if constantly aware of a personal imaginary audience), is also able to try out new voices and act as both narrator and protagonist of his story. He provides an honest real-time account of himself masturbating over a photo of Helen she sends to him in a letter:

> but this letter now maybe all the time she was waiting was wanting was after it me me her after it was she me her me her legs breasts skin face legs legs o legs her her her   there there there   there   there (20)

but then the text switches to third-person:

> Ditto rose from his rumpled bed, straightened the cover, examined the scene for clues of his concupiscence [. . .] and sat at his desk, the better to frizzle his eyes on the tormenting photograph while musing on his unexpected letter and the inexperienced nature of his being. (21)

In the first instance Ditto is represented rather touchingly as completely subject to his physical urges and simplistic in his vocabulary, while the latter

Ditto—in control of the narrative—offers a more knowing and self-aware selfhood. A similar effect is achieved in the well-known description of Ditto and Helen having sex, where a left-hand column of text combines an idealised and romantic description of the sexual act interspersed with Ditto's conscious mind reciting times tables and quotations to keep himself from climaxing too quickly, and a right-hand column offers text from *A Young Person's Guide to Life and Love*, by Dr Benjamin Spock. The event culminates with the phrase 'no more words no more thoughts' (125), signifying a moment of pure body over mind. However, since this sexual encounter is most likely a figment of Ditto's literary imagination, it might just as easily be argued that this is a moment of pure virtual experience to match any virtual reality game. Crucially, Chambers manages to combine the Cartesian self and the corporal self through textuality in the same way that cyber narratives attempt to capture the embodied nature of virtual existence. Geoff Moss argues for the metafictional quality of *Breaktime*, arguing that the alternating perspective in this sequence 'shows how much the character of Ditto is constructed by the novelist and the reader rather than by reference to reality [. . .] he is exactly what we make him to be' (49). I would argue that in Ditto's case, however, and to some extent in the case of *Mondays are Red*'s Luke as well, selves are not produced through and directed by external programmes, games or technological media, and nor is the novelist/reader totally autonomous. Rather, Ditto is his own author, the programmer in control of the code that he uses to produce himself.

> Ditto explains his plan of textual defence of literature to Morgan:
> I intend a jaunt [. . .] I also intend recording the events of my jaunt, as they happen (or shortly thereafter). And this record shall be xx [sic] my fiction, the raw material for it anyway. (31)

We might note that this attempt by Ditto to record his outward experience and his inner reactions truthfully and as near to real time as he can corresponds closely to Bakhtin's definition of fantastic realism: that unfeasible access to an individual's world that a writer like Dostoevsky manages to reconstruct. But I would also argue that *Breaktime* reveals that the ideal space for adolescence to exist and self-reflect is not necessarily technological and virtual, but can in fact be textual. The narrative explicitly deals with the issues of spatiality and adolescent identity that have been central to this chapter. For instance, Ditto is distressed by the version of himself represented by his bedroom, a 'neatly precise collection of outgrown junk and second-hand propositions' (21), and is forced to seek freedom and the space to explore his own subjectivity by travelling beyond home and school, into the wilderness (of the Yorkshire Dales). But this idyllic 'third place' could just as easily be the space that Ditto creates through text as the rural spot he picks to pitch his tent, since the reader realises at the end of the novel—along with Morgan—that the whole narrative of escape and adventure may only be Ditto's fictional version of events. As he puts it himself,

'How do you know I didn't sit in my room at home all week making the stuff up?' (138). This is virtual space, where physical and character reinvention is possible in the same way it is for users of virtual reality like Ana or Surfer.

Breaktime, and to some extent *Mondays are Red* seem to offer the Shangri La that many are seeking from cyberspace, and that Walkerdine identifies as 'a new space for the production of a new, and perhaps super, rationality, a new body without organs' (235). In contrast, the majority of young adult speculative fantasies specifically dealing with virtual worlds and the incredible potential of ICT present adolescence in conflict with technology, if not quite the irrational mass that Walkerdine specifies. At risk from external forces through the medium of VR games; threatened by slippage between spaces real and virtual; and shaped by pre-existing codes and geographies: these teens are not wholly at home in the computer. They can, however, successfully exist in magical spaces provided through the virtual language of textuality. This openness to text and language play rather than cyber-spatiality may be partly due to adult writers being used to thinking of themselves as textual creatures. It will be interesting to see how ways of imagining the self in space change as cyber-literate members of the Net Generation begin writing their own versions of adolescence.

Conclusion
New Evolutions: Fears and Pleasures of Young Adult Fantastic Realism

Fictional adolescents, 'word teenagers', appear in many guises: as images of youth that adults desire and fear; as mirrors showing contemporary teenage life 'as it really is' according to dominant discourse; sometimes even as a strange band of witches and metamorphs, time-travellers and the haunted, doppelgangers, superheroes, and virtual or textual gamers. In this book I have demonstrated the value of reading adolescence through a particular generic lens, examining fiction that has previously been ignored or conflated unthinkingly with other forms of fantasy or magical realism. I have argued that structurally and thematically the combination of fantastic and realist modes implicitly constructs adolescence as a liminal state between childhood and adulthood. I have also attempted to indicate the anxieties that are generated when adolescence threatens to appear on its own terms, rather than as a progression towards unified adulthood, a conventional form of agency or an acceptable inhabitant of appropriate spaces.

The discursive frameworks I have employed to structure this book—frameworks of development, identity, space and virtual subjectivity—do more than describe ways of thinking about young people, I would argue. They help to *construct* the very concept of adolescence and provide common sets of meaning from which emerge not only professional and scientific models, but also cultural artefacts such as film, games and literature. Malcolm Bowie has previously stressed these kinds of connections, pointing out that fiction and theory are 'alternative names for the verbal productions of those who indulge in "as if" thinking about the world' (Bowie 5). Others have noted how 'there is now a conjunction between at least the intentions of some literary critics and of some sociologists' (Burns and Burns 9) and that 'literature and sociology are not as far apart as one might think [. . .] sociology too is a kind of art form' (Routh and Woolf 6).[1]

If it is the case that theoretical and fictional representations of adolescence converge, then we might see value in identifying current or imminent discursive frameworks and asking whether similar themes and techniques can be found in emerging fiction for young adults. This is necessarily a tentative methodology, since we might also argue that it is a difficult task to step back from the discourses that surround us in order to see their influence and influences, not to mention their cultural pervasiveness. I would like to use this Conclusion to suggest a test case for just such a methodology and introduce one further discursive framework which may provide fertile ground for debating the construction of adolescence in young adult literature.

Evolutionary Psychology

As we discovered in Chapter One, if individual human development is compared to the trajectory of the whole human race through history, adolescence can be couched in crudely evolutionary terms as 'neo-atavistic'. Initial employment of Darwin's theories in the human sciences suggested that 'primitive' peoples offered us a glimpse of early humanity, while psychologists such as Granville Stanley Hall applied such thinking to personal stages of development. In the kind of 'cultural epoch' theory he propounds, adolescence illustrates the human being in a state of evolution, revealing characteristics of fitness that were not apparent in 'primitive' childhood.

These terms are crude, of course, not only in their propensity to locate certain races and tribes as 'adolescent' in their evolutionary context and therefore make value-judgements about higher and lower peoples, but also due to the common misunderstanding that human evolution can be traced as a direct line from ape to highly cultured civilised man. This philosophy (the 'Great Chain of Being') assumes that humanity is the pinnacle of evolutionary history instead of accepting that all species have their own histories and are no lesser or greater than others. Voices from the discipline of evolutionary psychology are swift to point out that Darwin's ideas should be extricated from the grasp of thinkers who would use them to construct a hierarchy of human and animal traits and therefore label certain peoples as less evolved or innately animalistic in any way. Rather, evolutionary psychology aims to understand human characteristics in terms of the specific ways the species has evolved.

Evolutionary psychology is a relatively new discipline, with the first course textbook on the subject published in 1999[2] and the majority of monographs on the subject still including some kind of defence or apology. Early ventures into this field focused on biological impetuses in human behaviour and argued that particular actions are shaped by natural selection: that is, we act in the way we do because it has an evolved function to ultimately help us survive and reproduce. E.O. Wilson's 1975 study, *Sociobiology: the new synthesis*, defined the theory as 'the systematic study of the biological basis of all social behaviour'

(343) and Richard Dawkins continued the discussion in his *The Selfish Gene* (1976), focusing on the way natural selection occurs through genetics. Sociobiology prepared the way for evolutionary psychology, which focuses more closely on how human thought, brains and evolved biology are interlinked, and Wilson's later book, *Conscilience* aims to explore the potential for linkage between the sciences and humanities and an interlocking theory through which to explain the universe.

Evolutionary psychologists argue that human actions are based on a mixture of 'ultimate' and 'proximate' mechanisms. Proximate mechanisms (such as environmental, personal or cultural histories), which make us react in certain immediate ways to situations we find ourselves in, are overlaid by ultimate mechanisms, which relate to ancient and evolved methods of promoting survival and reproduction. These ultimate predispositions mean that we act in ways that will advance certain functions or qualities, and these become adapted for our survival. Even though evolutionary processes take millions of years, evolutionary psychologists investigate how evolutionary predispositions and overriding reproductive forces can provide explanations for how we think and develop today.

One consequence of thinking about adolescence in evolutionary terms is to deny purely culture-based definitions and to indicate instead that there are universal predispositions amongst humans rooted in the way our species has adapted to fit its environment over the last million years. According to Glenn Weisfeld and Donyell Coleman, then, it is unfortunate that modern study of adolescence has focused on Western societies and commonalities across cultures, since shared characteristics in social and sexual behaviours at puberty across races reveals that adolescence is not culturally specific. Weisfeld and Coleman claim that adolescence cannot be accounted for in socio-cultural terms, suggesting instead that 'we need to seek its explanation in our evolutionary prehistory' (331). This means that arguments defining adolescence as a cultural construction and by-product of industrialisation or highly developed culture are not valid: contrary to social constructivist theory, evolutionary thought presents adolescence as a biological fact.

This is not to say that there are not complex reasons for the stage of humanity we know as adolescence, but according to an evolutionary perspective these reasons are only tangentially cultural and social. Explanations are based instead on the adaptive purpose of adolescence: that is, why it is useful for there to be an extended period of youth before the process of survival through reproduction begins in adulthood, and how this affects the success of the species. Workman and Reader point out that any pre-mature behaviour is in some ways a waste of resources:

> Childhood presents us with something of a paradox. Evolutionary theory teaches us that the only valid strategy in the game of life is to pass on more copies of your genes than your competitors, in which case it might seem

strange that humans (and many other organisms) spend such a large amount of time being unable to reproduce. (139)

The evolutionary explanation for childhood is that it is required as a period of storing up energy, learning strategies and forming the physiological requirements for reproduction. Anthropologist Barry Bogin explains that in many mammals this period is kept short, to minimise danger and non-productivity, but that in humans the adaptive strategy is to 'develop toward adulthood slowly, increase the time for learning, and produce higher-quality adults' (120). In the same way, adolescence is an adaptive strategy and a crucial part of how humans have become human through evolution. In other words, social and cultural theories suggesting that adolescence is the product of an infantilised society or that it has only psychological implications for safe maturation do not take into consideration ultimate biological explanations.

This conceptual battle between the ultimate and the proximate—the underlying species-related influences and the more immediate social, cultural, environmental and personal ones—is characteristic of the fraught ground that evolutionary psychology inhabits, particularly in the case of theorising the behaviour of young people. Proximate explanations feed into common concerns about the *problem* of youth, allowing for solutions to be found in developmental abnormality, psychosis or social ineptness. In contrast, although evolutionary psychologists on the whole accept that proximate motivations can affect adolescent behaviour, they argue that this is because such motivations either confirm ultimate mechanisms or run counter to them. Weisfeld and Coleman argue that Western societies allow young people to become 'outsiders inhabiting a suspicious world of odd dress and musical tastes', which grates against their adapted purpose, whereas traditional societies, which are more in tune with their evolutionary pathways, provide means for adolescents to perform the preparatory functions they are designed for (350). In radical education studies, ultimate evolutionary mechanisms are employed to help defend strategies for teaching through experience rather than through traditional schooling methods. For example, in their work for the '21st Century Learning Initiative', John Abbott and Terry Ryan suggest that changes in the human brain at adolescence are crucial for adaptation in the species. These changes force the adolescent to question authority, challenge earlier ways of learning, fear less and risk more: qualities essential in a hunter-gatherer society. Abbott and Ryan argue that, in subduing these tendencies and attempting to contain them within structured educational institutions, human beings are working against evolutionary psychology and actually creating the kinds of educational and behavioural problems that appear to be rife in schools and on the streets across the Western world.

In making ultimate motivations key, evolutionary psychology sets itself against the Standard Social Sciences Model (SSSM), which assumes that human behaviour is determined by cultural forces. Influential social science theorists such as Emile Durkheim, Margaret Mead and Albert Bandura—and later constructionist thinkers, including Prout, James, Rose and Lesnik-Oberstein, whom we met in the Introduction—can be viewed as fearing biological explanations and therefore finding themselves diametrically opposed to evolutionary psychology's concept of innate and universal species behaviour. At times, this opposition is fiercely hostile, as demonstrated by Robert Wright's defence in *The Moral Animal*:

> The new Darwinian social scientists are fighting a doctrine that has dominated their fields for much of this century: the idea that biology doesn't much matter—that the uniquely malleable human mind, together with the unique force of culture, has severed our behaviour from its evolutionary roots; that there is no inherent human nature driving human events, but that, rather, our essential nature is to be driven. (5)

Wright uses fighting talk, as though evolutionary thought retains the revolutionary tenor it had in the nineteenth century and must be shielded from the reactionaries of the SSSM. Most evolutionary psychologists feel this need to defend what they consider to be a new, controversial and wide-ranging worldview, although not all are as militant as Wright. John Alcock, for instance, points to the fact that cultural determinists disagree amongst themselves on issues of 'precisely which environmental (proximate) influences are responsible for shaping the personality, attitudes, morals, and behavior of individuals' but that they do not realise 'that every behavioral trait depends on evolved physiological systems' (129), even if those systems develop partly through proximate mechanisms.

I cannot judge the scientific validity of evolutionary psychology, but it does seem to be increasingly influential in discussions about human subjectivity and behaviour and therefore cannot be ignored in any study of adolescence. Moreover, as a discursive framework it does offer certain interesting and affirmative understandings of young people: for instance, the whole idea of teenage delinquency can be revisited and instead of seeing such behaviour amongst teenagers as abnormal, problematic or regressive—and therefore as 'correctable' —an evolutionary psychologist is likely to argue that it is simply an evolutionary trait and, as such, is of use to the human race as a whole. In this approach we might see a revolutionary indication that adolescence is important in its own right and should be considered as a crucial state of being—one that requires separate considerations of identity, behaviour and space from either childhood or adulthood.

On the other hand, I am wary of any discourse that returns identity to biology and biological forces, even with a nod to proximate mechanisms such as psychology or culture. Moreover, Wilson's desire to create 'conscilience' can appear like yet another grand narrative, emerging to take the place of Christianity or Marxism in order to provide a unifying theory of everything.

Wright's attitude is terrifying to social scientists, who embrace cultural relativism and nuanced difference:

> Here 'worldview' is meant quite literally. The new Darwinian synthesis is, like quantum physics or molecular biology, a body of scientific theory and fact; but, unlike them, it is also a way of seeing everyday life. Once truly grasped (and it is much easier to grasp than either of them) it can entirely alter one's perception of social reality. (4–5)

That this almost evangelical stance also appears to return identity to an essentialist understanding of biology has to be anathema to constructionists, particularly those with feminist or queer approaches. More generally, ultimate mechanisms suggest a substantial loss of individual agency and control. While the phrase 'survival of the fittest' (Herbert Spencer's metaphor, not Darwin's) implies individual success, it is actually rejected by most evolutionary psychologists because it is imprecise and problematises their basic tenet of fitness and adaptation being innate and unconscious. As Alcock points out, 'neither socio-biology nor evolutionary psychology requires that humans be any more self-consciously desirous of achieving personal genetic success than are red-winged blackbirds' (26).

While the Standard Social Science or constructionist model has its problems, I am convinced of the equal power of culture in forming identity and prefer to reject the idea that culture is subsumed or overpowered by evolutionary forces. Culture may be a more recent impulse, but it has the power of human imagination behind it and must surely supersede evolutionary drives in some arenas. Evolutionary explanations of adolescence are fascinating, but since I am proposing that fiction is as important as theory or science in creating our understanding of, and behaviour towards, young people, I would resist a wholehearted acceptance of the theory. I should, of course, point out that not all evolutionary psychologists subscribe to joyful abandonment of considerable cultural influence. Some merely apply evolutionary methodology to culture itself. Dawkins' work on genes has been highly influential, but he is also important for introducing the concept of 'memes'; that is, units of cultural transmission or imitation. According to Dawkins, genes have replicated themselves from the very origins of life in the primeval soup, but now '[t]he new soup is the soup of human culture' (206). Although the metaphor seems rather to stretch scientific theories, it is interesting because it adopts a certain constructionist premise. Cultural beliefs and ideas replicate themselves and regenerate through history, led by evolutionary urges perhaps, but alternatively by the controlling force of Culture itself.

Can we begin to see any correspondences between evolutionary frameworks for understandings of adolescent behaviour and recent fantastic realism for young adults? Here I am immediately drawn to two older books that may or may not have been directly shaped by Wilson and Dawkins in the early moments of socio-biology: Peter Dickinson's *Eva*, which I have already discussed in Chapter One, and his *A Bone from Dry Sea*, published four years later in 1992. In content and theme alone these novels engage in controversial ideas about the power of evolution working through individual adolescent agency. In *Eva*, the teenage heroine's actions are initially shaped by her own desires to be allowed to exist as both human girl and female chimp, but those very actions lead not only to her own emancipation and fulfilment but also to the potential rebirth of the human race, or at least to the beginning of a new, hybrid species. It is possible to argue that the fantastic possibilities introduced through Eva's metamorphosis are a fictional expression of adolescent evolutionary psychology: her fearless challenging of authority and risk-taking result in a direct evolutionary leap, as she mates with the chimps and begins to educate them in 'human' skills. Dickinson professes that his later novel is directly influenced by debates raging in the world of evolutionary theory, specifically the argument that humans used to be sea-dwelling mammals. In this novel, adolescence is once more represented as the crux for human change, offering curiosity, energy and an almost magical quality that ignites species development.

Other titles offer alternative ways of figuring the evolved teenager through the interaction between fantasy and realism. Annette Curtis Klause's *Blood and Chocolate* (1997) provides an interesting take on adaptive processes, following Vivian as she struggles with her identity as one of the 'loup-garoux'—humans endowed with the supernatural ability to transform into wolf-like creatures. More recently, David Almond explores alternatives for the human story in his *Clay*, which has the teenage protagonists dabbling in creation myths when they make a living being out of clay.

A Constructionist Reading

What remains is the task of drawing together the threads of this argument and explaining further why young adult fantastic realism affords a crucial lens through which to view late twentieth-century and early twenty-first-century adolescence. Teenage fantastic realism belongs very clearly to a certain cultural moment; it is a form that relies on an established teenage market in Western societies and conditions of competency in recognising fantastic and (teen) realist modes. In other words, for the dramatic tension between contemporary realism and impossible or fantastic elements to function—and for the special relationship of fantastic realism to discourses of adolescence to become apparent—literary, social and cultural circumstances must take a certain shape. Peter Hollindale indicates 1970 as a turning point when the study of children's literature took 'a great leap forward' and teenage fiction, by which he means teen *realism*, 'suddenly came into prominence' ('The Adolescent Novel of Ideas' 83–84). Julia Eccleshare offers some explanations as to why teen realism should emerge at this moment:

> Post-war teenagers were a far more vociferous and independent group than their predecessors and their experiences had never been explored in fiction. 'Teenage' became a separate fashionable entity, and so did its fiction. From the mid-1950s on, and increasingly with the social liberation of the 1960s and 1970s, books for 'young adults' were making their mark. [. . .] Writers needed to understand the dilemmas that were posed for this generation by their new freedoms and to offer sensible discussion of choices without too much moral instruction. (388)

Eccleshare brings together a range of reasons for the general appropriateness of realism: a burgeoning and strong-willed teenage community who demanded a literature that would offer them a 'mirror image of their lives'; anxiety over unmediated social liberation for young people; and a desire on the part of both readers and writers for the kind of fiction that would help to understand and shape these changes. There are additional social circumstances for a rise in teen realism. The influence of prominent studies of adolescence in the growing fields of psychology and sociology is likely to have mapped out certain conditions or, in terms taken from sociology of genre, a 'limiting situation' for teen realism. In particular, many theories of adolescence prominent in the 1960s and 1970s prioritise the idea that it is a stage when difficulties must be overcome and tasks solved. Early teenage realism sits easily within this framework of social and individual 'problem', particularly because, as Catherine Sheldrick Ross points out, public and critical reaction to the genre emphasised its taboo content and consequently focused on the problems being treated in each text: 'running away, drug addiction, premarital sex and abortion, suicide, alienation, divorce, the one-parent family, and the like' (175). Moreover, the often uncomfortably didactic qualities of 'the problem novel' and teen realism in general are surely part of a wider pedagogic impulse towards young people, combined with traditional humanist beliefs in the educational power of literature. Empathic moral education provided an ideal intellectual climate for publishing literature that dealt with social issues.

If teenage realism operates ideally within such social conditions then what changes occur to allow the surfacing of fantastic realism, a genre that splices teen realism with fantastic tropes? A simple explanation lies in the increasing market and commercial success of young adult literature as a whole. Michael Cart describes the state of affairs in America during the 1980s, when teenagers had become demanding 'arch-consumers' and bookshop chains and original paperbacks heralded the rapid expansion of young adult publishing (102–106). As young adult literature became established and increasing numbers of publishers created teenage imprints, so the body of work found space and the opportunity to expand and experiment. Thus commentators note the rise of alternative genres to realism in the 1980s and into the 1990s, which provide the adolescent readership with respite from endless well-meaning problem novels, with more challenging material or with different modes that incorporated inventive ironic and intertextual elements.[3] I have tried throughout this book to make it clear that literary trends cannot be extricated from wider discursive fields, and that fiction remains one of a number of ways in which identities are constructed and shaped. As teenage fiction expanded and diversified during the second half of the twentieth century, so too did the field of adolescent studies. Influenced by changes in the social fabric of Western societies, and by post-structural and social constructionist movements, alternative academic and professional approaches to adolescence surfaced to interrogate the representations of young people, introducing increasingly fractured, plural and complex concepts of the teenager.

Fantastic realism represents an alternative genre for young adult literature, which materialised partly because literary, social and cultural indices opened up the opportunity for new ways of conceptualising adolescence and adolescent experience. Rather than being presented through realism—which as a mimetic form was employed in part to describe and classify adolescence as a new cultural category—the teenager could be recodified in interactions between realism and fantastic elements. The general programme for fantastic realism might be defined as representing adolescence with new possibilities and challenges within and beyond the real world. Or, put another way, it provides ways of reading adolescence metaphorically and ideologically as ordinary and yet extraordinary. What might be conceived of as a status constrained by the pressures, limits and practicalities of reality can fictively be represented as realising identity and power in fantastic spheres. In this respect, fantastic realism would seem to offer writers and readers a form that explores pertinent adolescent themes within a constant dynamic between reality and fantasy, as well as providing the potential for radical retellings of adolescence, which test dominant discursive frameworks. At the very least, fantastic realism questions the validity of everyday experience and 'normal' adolescence by incorporating impossible, fantastic elements.

Despite the innovatory form of many teenage fantastic realist novels, the values invoked by them are often conventional or even reactionary, however, and display anxiety about adolescents transgressing what are considered to be their natural boundaries. Chapter One showed how this disquiet is revealed explicitly through tropes of unnatural development, such as animal metamorphosis, as well as implicitly through themes of time-travel that defy dominant developmental frameworks of adolescence. In Chapter Two, close readings suggested that a fetishisation of individualism and personal growth is inscribed through fantasies of difference and disappearance. Discourses privileging individual development and identity formation provide a basis for fantastic realism's resistance of radical or post-structural explorations of subjectivity. Chapter Three explored possibilities for agency and empowerment at adolescence through active identities of witch and superhero, but found that these figures are curbed by their teenage status and by considerations of acceptable gendered behaviour. My final chapter sought new spaces for adolescence in virtual reality and cyberspace, discovering instead that the most liberating geographies for teenage protagonists are textual and narrative.

Why should fantastic realism indicate a region of cultural history that calls forth traditional representations of adolescence when structurally and thematically the genre posits such an exciting realm of parallel reality? Perhaps the answer lies in the fact that that ideological change has some distance to go in what is still an emergent literature. Many of the problems and strictures of teenage realism hold true for the short history of teenage fantastic realism. Structurally, the realist mode remains crucial in teenage fantastic realism and acts to confirm those concepts of adolescence already shaped in part by early teen realism. Adults still generally produce and control the fiction aimed at young adults and a matrix of anxiety/desire continues to be significant in the contemporary discursive field of adolescence. The status of adolescence is also continually shifting and being re-evaluated, and yet ideas of youth and 'growing up' remain bound by older frameworks. More recent theories of identity as performative, subjective or plural appear infrequently in fictional forms, with notable exceptions by authors such as Chambers, Dickinson and McCaughrean. More experimental representations will, no doubt, take time to filter through from radical theoretical work, and it will be interesting to see how discursive frameworks such as evolutionary psychology shape young adult fiction of the future. It is also possible that teenage fiction suffers from its position as 'in opposition' to adult literature. Where identity is considered a valid site for deconstruction in adult literary endeavours, teenage fiction is restricted by its continuing relation to education, edification and appropriateness. It is not considered to be a space suitable for breaking down 'reality'.

If, unlike the literary fantastic, fantastic realism refuses to truly break down reality, then what cultural action does it take? This book has established the genre's overall conservative tendencies, which imply that liberal humanist impulses endure in literature for young people. Adolescence is represented as a minor stage in the process of becoming adult, whole and empowered within appropriate parameters. Nonetheless, there are underlying concerns and anxieties in these texts that also portray adolescence as potentially out of control, abnormal and unacceptably playful or powerful. The tensions have not yet generated narratives that explore the realm of adolescence without recourse to the teleology of development and adulthood, but they do perhaps hint at an embedded appreciation that adulthood itself is neither universal nor unified and may itself be constantly shifting, often unfulfilled, and in a constant *state of becoming*.

* * *

The focal period for this study of fantastic realism is somewhat artificial as there are certainly texts in this genre that pre-date 1967 and it has in no way died out or dramatically transformed since the turn of the new millennium. These forty-odd years have proved to be a useful conceptual epoch for more than their function as practical boundaries. Over this period, for instance, the field of children's literature criticism has emerged and burgeoned to become a widely accepted discipline within literary and cultural studies, and it is only within this fresh critical tradition that a serious consideration of young adult fiction can proceed without having to first clear its way into academic acceptance. It is, moreover, not only intellectual awareness that has widened in the last few decades. The increasingly successful and diverse children's and teenage fiction market has produced in its wake a general curiosity about literature for young people, with both children's and young adult novels winning major literary awards and being made into Hollywood films in the 1990s and 2000s.[4] Perhaps a further reason for the enhanced interest in young adult literature is its inherent potential as 'crossover fiction'. This is described by one commentator as 'books written and marketed with adults as well as children in mind' (Mooney 70) and the most famous examples are J.K. Rowling's Harry Potter novels and Philip Pullman's *His Dark Materials* trilogy. Although neither of these series falls into the precise category of fantastic realism, they do indicate the particular popularity of fantasy genres within children's and young adult crossover novels. With these commercial and generic possibilities opening up in the twenty-first century, teenage fantastic realism is likely to find further ways of developing to challenge the current ideologies and discursive field of adolescence.

Notes

Introduction

1 For early deconstructionist approaches to childhood within sociology, see Chris Jenks' edited volume, *The Sociology of Childhood: essential readings*, which includes essays by Philippe Ariès, Emile Durkheim, Jean Piaget and Erik Erikson, amongst others. See also Stainton-Rogers, 'The Social Construction of Childhood'.
2 The character of Peter Pan has appeared in various stories, plays and latterly in film versions. See Rose's account of this history, passim.
3 Adolescence itself takes on a metaphorical function in other discursive fields and frameworks. Thus, the study of postcolonialism might employ adolescence as a way of discussing the transitory and disempowered nature of newly decolonised nations. See, for example, Mackay.
4 Kimberley Reynolds has attempted a similar project on a smaller scale in her chapter on youth culture and children's literature.
5 See also Weisfeld for a discussion of biological development and its social contexts.
6 See Hall and Coles. Around 2,500 fourteen-year-olds were surveyed for their study of children's reading choices. In a more recent study, however, boys at Key Stage Three and Four did not see themselves as any more reluctant to read than those in Key Stage One. See Maynard, MacKay, Smyth and Reynolds.
7 'The English Programme of Study', National Curriculum Online, 7 Aug. 2007 <http://www.nc.uk.net/nc/contents/En-3-2-POS.html>.
8 John Storey outlines a number of definitions for popular culture, ranging from a quantitative classification according to how many people enjoy it, or defining it as substandard in comparison with 'high culture', to identifying popular culture as a site of struggle between dominant and resistant groups (*An Introductory Guide to Cultural Theory and Popular Culture* 6–17).
9 Possibly the closest that teenage fiction comes to a kind of grassroots

popular culture is through new media and internet texts, where multi-user domains, web-logs, fanzines and fantastic realism fiction can interact directly with young adult novels. This will be discussed in greater detail in Chapter 4. The online 'Francesca Lia Block's Community's Journal' is a good example of a web community where readers can actively engage with texts and construct their own meanings and narratives without input from the author. See Shannon Babcock's discussion of the online journal <http://www.livejournal.com/community/francesca_lia/> in 'Fiction Fandom: Francesca Lia Block and Internet Adolescence'.

10 Peter Hollindale makes this distinction in his *Signs of Childness in Children's Books* (28).

11 For a developmental approach to the study of teenager reading practices see Jack Thompson's 'Teenagers Reading: developmental stages of reading literature'; Hall and Coles.

12 J.K. Rowling's Harry Potter novels are an example of children's literature later published in adult editions.

13 The matter of *Fade*'s fantasy is a contentious one: Cormier argued that the novel was always meant to be realist and that Paul's 'fade' is a manifestation of purely psychological activity. As a reader I disagree with this interpretation (see Waller, '*Fade* and the Lone Teenager').

14 Interestingly, Hollindale employs a classic realist metaphor in his use of the mirror, which is a favourite conceit in discussions of mimesis and realism.

15 For discussions of the problem novel and teen realism, see Sutton; Egoff, 'The Problem Novel'; and Ross. These articles reveal that the limitations of (often American) problem novels such as Gertrude Samuels' *Run, Shelley, Run!* (1974) and Bette Greene's *Philip Hall Likes Me, I Reckon, Maybe* (1976) were a matter of concern in the 1970s and 1980s, but similar novels continue to be popularly published: Jean Ure's *Just Sixteen* (1999) is a clear example of the issue of unwanted pregnancy taking over the narrative.

16 Todorov's use of the term 'uncanny' adds to the significance of Freud's '*unheimlich*'. Freud classes the uncanny as something that once was familiar but which has been repressed and then re-experienced as frightening or uncomfortable (see 'The "Uncanny"').

17 Head is also particularly interested in layers of narrative building up and knocking down the possibility of the fantastic, and the reading strategies teenagers must use to interpret this metanarrative novel.

18 See John King, *Modern Latin American Fiction* and Patricia Hart, *Narrative Magic in the Fiction of Isabel Allende*. Magic realism is typically recognised as originating in Latin America, with Gabriel García Márquez's *One Hundred Years of Solitude* (1970) often cited as the definitive example.

19 Maria Nikolajeva appropriates C.S. Lewis's concept of the other world and discusses secondary worlds in children's fiction in *The Magic Code* (35).

20 Cosslett's article suggests that the time-slip device clusters in books for

children produced in the 1960s and 1970s, whereas my research has found increasing numbers published in the 1990s.
21 Burgess and Welford use a parodic approach to explore this motif, while Dickenson's *Eva* is more strictly science fiction.

Chapter 1

1 Coleman and Hendry's solution is a focal model which presents a variety of different key issues that are faced during adolescence; there is no fixed sequence, no age restrictions and no need for resolution before the individual can progress.
2 Piaget's theories are complex and shift in focus over the various periods of his career. Here only a concise overview is provided. For a complete account see Elkind, 'Egocentricism in Children and Adolescents' and Piaget, *The Growth of Logical Thinking from Childhood to Adolescence*; *Play, Dreams and Imitation in Childhood*; *The Language and Thought of the Child*; *The Psychology of the Child*.
3 For a summary of Erikson's ideas, see also Muuss (42–57).
4 In their survey of young people's reading habits, Christine Hall and Martin Coles note this broad selective tendency amongst readers: 'Children at the age of ten, twelve and fourteen read a wide range of books. They are highly eclectic in their reading habits' (15).
5 This novel actually reveals an intricate engagement with developmental frameworks, as we shall discover later in this chapter.
6 McCallum in fact concentrates on a series of complex multi-stranded narratives (or adolescent novels of ideas), which confuse any obvious teleology, and she argues that many such texts are (in her Bakhtinian terms of reference) dialogic. Unlike this book, her study is not concerned with how discourses of adolescence are reflected.
7 According to McCallum, a documentary approach to the past requires processing primary sources to construct a closed narrative, whilst dialogic methods involve a conversation with the past and inspire critical responses to understood history (170). She suggests that these methods are gendered male and female respectively, but here Tim employs both. I shall explore the possible gendering of fantastic devices in Chapter Three, but here it is the interaction with fantastic history as developmental that is most important.
8 Tess Cosslett explores the ways that the past is produced and reproduced in time-slip books for children, with specific reference to their part in constructing heritage and 'history from below'; that is, new practices of oral, local and family history as opposed to history of the 'great society'. She questions whether these versions of history are regressive or radical. While this is an important and subtle debate concerning this fantastic realist sub-genre, it is not directly relevant to my argument here.

202 • Constructing Adolescence in Fantastic Realism

9. Lassén-Seger acknowledges gender specificity in metamorphosis narratives and notes that boy/animal transformations occur more often whatever the age of the protagonist.
10. 'Row Over Teen Novel,' *BBC News*, 8 August 2001 <http://news.bbc.co.uk/1/hi/entertainment/arts/1480163.stm>.
11. It is possible that the title of Burgess's novel itself makes an oblique reference to Disney's *Lady and the Tramp* (1955), in which the heroine is a real dog called Lady, but an immaculately well-behaved one who would never revel in the idea of being a bitch or going any further than eating meatballs with her rough companion, Tramp. I am grateful to Sharon Ouditt for this potential connection.
12. 'Questions to Melvin Burgess about *Lady: my life as a bitch*', Andersen Press, 20 Jan. 2003 <http://www.andersenpress.co.uk/Biogs/Melvin%20Burgess/Interviewwithmelvin.html>.
13. Further work on this text can be found in Neil Philip's excellent *A Fine Anger: a critical introduction to the work of Alan Garner*.

Chapter 2

1. Ian Watt argues that capitalism and Protestantism produced individualist circumstances vital for the rise of the novel, arguing that 'society must value every individual highly enough to consider him the proper subject of its serious literature' (60).
2. See Waller, 'Is Holden Caulfield Still Real?'
3. In addition, the philosophy of individualism contends that collective properties or classes do not exist, and that only individual entities can be considered. Politics draws upon this idea to refute any suggestion that organisations, nations or other collective abstractions can have any inherent qualities, instead arguing that only individuals should be considered.
4. James, Jenks and Prout discuss the perception that 'children play while adults work' in *Theorizing Childhood* (81–123). For an early survey of children's games and play styles that is still influential see Peter and Iona Opie's *Children's Games in Street and Playground*.
5. I discuss this process with reference to my own childhood experience in '*Fade* and the Lone Teenager'.
6. Erikson (*Identity, Youth and Crisis*) suggests that social play follows on from childhood play, and that adolescents use their status in order to experiment with fantasies of who or what they might be in the future.
7. See Luce Irigaray's *This Sex Which is Not One*, where it is argued that likeness produces multiplicity and completeness in sexual and social experience; also McNaron.
8. McCallum uses this concept to read Lois Duncan's *Stranger with my Face*, which, however, I shall argue is less straightforward than a good/evil schema might suggest.

9 See also 'Ghost Stories: exploiting the convention', where Armstrong modifies her original argument to clarify that the ghost should not merely be explained away as a product of the protagonist's imagination but should be allowed a robust existence.
10 A much cruder example of this tendency to conflate historical and contemporary adolescence can be found in Julian Thompson's *Ghost Story* (1997), in which the ghost that haunts the protagonist signals her difference purely through an 'olde-English' dialect, rather than any specific historical experience or social context.
11 I shall return to Park's *Playing Beatie Bow* to discuss the role of family in Chapter Three.
12 See Fowler (*Stages of Faith*) and Kohlberg for more detailed work on moral and religious practice at adolescence.
13 See Coleman (11–18) for a succinct description of these views.
14 I use the term hysteria in a general sense to mean excessive panic or irrational behaviour, rather than as a medical term. Elaine Showalter complains that many feminist critics write about hysteria with a disregard for medical history (93).
15 See Chapter Three for further discussion of subcultures.
16 I am indebted to Anna Heiða Pálsdóttir's comments on the online discussion list, children-literature-uk for this insight. Anna Heiða Pálsdóttir, 'Ghost Stories', online posting, 7 March 2000 <http://www.jiscmail.ac.uk/cgi-bin/webadmin?A2=ind00&L=CHILDREN-LITERATURE-UK&D=0&I=-3&P=14500>.
17 See Baudry for a discussion of the ideology of the cinematic practices and apparatus which hide the labour of production in the cinema, giving an impression of reality through the supposed scientific objectivity of optical instruments.
18 In my Introduction I refer to Stuart Hall's use of this Derridean strategy when considering the term 'identity', which is no longer valid in an uncomplicated way but has not been superseded by a more useful terminology and must be constantly scrutinised (Hall, 'Who Needs Identity?'; Derrida).

Chapter 3

1 For further discussion of the sociological aspects of adolescence, see Willis; Hebdige; Brake; and Hendry.
2 I am unfortunately uncertain whether Hinton or her publishers were influenced by Becker's earlier sociological work, *The Outsiders*, in their choice of title for her first novel.
3 Gillian Cross's *Chartbreak* (1986) appears to provide a completely 'authentic' voice in the character of Finch, particularly as the novel includes metanarrative features such as newspaper articles and song lyrics that blur the boundaries of fiction and 'fact'.

4. The term is taken from Lévi-Strauss's concept of the re-ordering of magical symbols to communicate new meanings in primitive cultures. It has been applied to subcultural theory, most notably by Dick Hebdige.
5. As already noted in Chapter Two, Janice Radway's *Reading the Romance* provides an interesting and influential examination of how women readers use popular literature as a useful flight into fantasy which allows an empowering privacy and escape from the potentially limiting single roles of mother or wife. Unfortunately, the scope of this book does not allow for a serious examination of reader response to fantasy.
6. For further discussion of gender and agency, see McNay.
7. A spate of television documentaries on adolescence at the turn of the century consciously drew upon scientific discourses to illustrate the inevitability of certain ways of acting at this age stage. Channel Four's documentary *Teen Dreams*, for instance, plays out a drama of male and female adolescent development with computer graphic sections depicting biological changes and impacts. The result is an impression of individuals hopelessly controlled by hormones and chemicals, thereby reducing the possibilities for active agency. Moreover, the programme focused on the difference between boys' sexual urges and girls' emotional development. See also Weisfeld for a more balanced view of the importance of biological influences on behaviour at adolescence.
8. One aspect of Michel Foucault's influential theory of power suggests that power is localised and shifting rather than a set of fixed positions. Accepting this means that it is impossible to declare that power lies either in fantastic or in realistic representations and modes (see Foucault, *The History of Sexuality* 92–102).
9. See Coleman and Hendry (74–77) for a survey of work in this area.
10. In the Welsh *Mabinogion*, Cerridwen brews divine knowledge in the cauldron of the underworld for her son, but when Gwion accidentally tastes the mixture instead Cerridwen angrily pursues him in a number of different animal forms. When he finally changes into an ear of corn, Cerridwen turns herself into a hen and swallows him, only to give birth to him nine months later.
11. See Ruth Starke's article, 'The Absent Mum in Children's Literature', which refers to Australian literature. The online discussion group Child_Lit uncovered similar thoughts about British and American texts (May 2000) <http://www.rci.rutgers.edu/~mjoseph/childlit/about.html>.
12. We might be reminded, here, of Karen Connors and her dream of her future child.
13. These ideas are explored further in the section on witchcraft, below.
14. This is a more adult model—and can be found in more adult style comic books—and will not inform this discussion as fully as earlier superhero archetypes.
15. A series of seventeen Superman cartoon shorts were released for the

cinema by Paramount with Fleischer Studios between 1941 and 1943 (see *Superman Homepage* <http://www.supermanhomepage.com/movies/movies.php?topic=m-fleis>).

16   Foucault uses Jeremy Bentham's Panopticon tower as a principle of discipline through surveillance, enclosing, separating and observing the masses (*Discipline and Punish* 195–228).

17   The characters of Wolf and Granny link this novel to the 'Little Red Riding Hood' theme already identified in Cross's *Wolf*. Fairy tales are popular narrative devices in young adult fiction. Robyn McKinley and Francesca Lia Block, for example, rework the stories into magical realist, often feminist, teenage fiction.

18   See Mel Gibson ('Wonder Women and Invisible Girls'). Gibson has helpfully provided me with a later version of her original paper.

19   Hoffman also refers to Eve, although perhaps Lilith is a more obvious precedent.

20   The idea of covens was probably introduced by the Egyptologist Margaret Murray in *The Witch Cult in Western Europe: a study in anthropology*. Her argument that the witch trials of the Middle Ages persecuted practitioners of a surviving pagan religion has been mostly refuted amongst historians.

21   I discuss this further in ' "Solid All the Way Through": Margaret Mahy's Ordinary Witches'.

22   It should be noted that, although Mahy uses the potent image of a burning girl, many more witches were hanged than burnt in the European Witch Craze of the sixteenth and seventeenth centuries.

23   See Hoffman for discussion of excess in witches and their precursors.

Chapter 4

1   According to one set of statistics, 73 per cent of twelve- to seventeen-year-olds use the Internet (cited in Subrahmanyam, Greenfield and Tynes, 652).

2   See, for example, Margaret Mackey, *Literacies Across Media* and Peter Hunt, 'Futures for Children's Literature'.

3   Walkerdine points to the complexities hidden between these two poles of understanding. She considers the specifics of class-bound and gendered practices of reading and game-playing, which offer different experiences of technology dependent on financial access to computer games, or a preference for platform-style games over 'beat-'em-ups', for example. More interestingly, Walkerdine also hints at the crucial relationship between child/teenage identity and online selves, although she stops short of exploring this idea in depth.

4   Technically, MUDs that allow players to programme changes in the fabric of the game are called TinyMUDs or MOOs, but these subtleties of terminology are not crucial to my discussion.

5   See also, Turkle, *Life on the Screen*.

6   For clarity's sake these are best exemplified in a footnote. Some examples of complex emoticons include a rose: —-<—{@; no comment: :X; and rolling eyes: S-)
7   Schome <http://slurl.com/secondlife/Schome%20Park/50/216/22>.
8   Facebook <www.facebook.com>.
9   M.T. Anderson's *Feed* (2002) is another text that explores the social and political consequences of the cyber-technological age.
10 In some respects it could be argued that this style of creative writing mirrors aspects of computer programming.
11 These settings are stock ones in fantasy VR, as we might deduce from the themes in *The Legendeer* series.
12 Web sickness is a real ailment.
13 It could also be argued that other differences are erased or flattened out through online existence. It is uncertain whether Giannine Bellisario's transformation into Janine de St. Jehan in *Heir Apparent* marks a racial change.
14 Incidentally, the other physical disability that Luke suffers alongside synaesthesia is a damaged leg. This appears to him like 'fog', much as Ana's virtual leg is a ghostly version of her lost one.

Conclusion

1   I have explored elsewhere the tendency in literary criticism, particularly of children's or teenage fiction, to conflate fact and imagination, theory and representation (Waller 'Is Real Holden Caulfield Still Real?'), and part of the purpose of this book has been to examine more closely the traffic between the two fields of science and fiction.
2   David Buss, *Evolutionary Psychology: the new science of the mind*.
3   See, for example, Cart's survey of popular American young adult fiction (*From Romance to Realism*), Hollindale's discussion of the 'adolescent novel of ideas' ('The Adolescent Novel of Ideas') and Charles Sarland's treatment of horror genres ('Attack of the Teenage Horrors').
4   Philip Pullman's *The Amber Spyglass* won the overall Whitbread Book of the Year Award in 2001 and was the first children's or young adult novel to do so. His work has been adapted for theatre and *The Golden Compass* (the film of *Northern Lights*) was released in cinemas in 2007. Louis Sachar's teenage magic realist novel *Holes* (1998) became a hugely successful film in 2003. Interestingly, the 2003 ManBooker and Whitbread winning novels both featured teenage characters (D.C.B. Pierre's *Vernon God Little* and Mark Haddon's *The Curious Incident of the Dog in the Night Time*).

Bibliography

Primary Sources

Almond, David. *Skellig*. London: Hodder Children's Books, 1998.
Almond, David. *Kit's Wilderness*. London: Hodder Children's Books, 1999.
Almond, David. *Secret Heart*. London: Hodder Children's Books, 2001.
Almond, David. *Clay*. London: Hodder Children's Books, 2005.
Anderson, M.T. *Feed*. London: Walker, 2002.
Baxter, Stephen. *Gulliverzone*. 1997. *The Web 2027*. Ed. Simon Spanton. London: Orion, 1999. 1–102.
Blume, Judy. *Forever*. Scarsdale, NY: Bradbury Press, 1975.
Bowkett, Stephen. *Dreamcastle*. 1997. *The Web 2027*. Ed. Simon Spanton. London: Orion, 1999. 103–194.
Bowler, Tim. *River Boy*. Oxford: Oxford University Press, 1997.
Brown, Eric. *Untouchable*. 1997. *The Web 2027*. Ed. Simon Spanton. London: Orion, 1997. 195–286.
Burgess, Melvin. *Burning Issy*. London: Puffin, 1992.
Burgess, Melvin. *Junk*. London: Puffin, 1996.
Burgess, Melvin. *Tiger Tiger*. London: Andersen, 1996.
Burgess, Melvin. *Lady: my life as a bitch*. London: Andersen, 2001.
Burgess, Melvin. *Doing It*. London: Andersen, 2003.
Burningham, John. *Granpa*. London: Cape, 1984.
Butler, Charles. *Calypso Dreaming*. London: HarperCollins, 2002.
Carter, Angela. *Nights at the Circus*. London: Chatto & Windus, 1984.
Chambers, Aidan. *Breaktime*. London: Red Fox, 1978.
Cleary, Beverley. *Fifteen*. New York: Morrow, 1956.
Cooper, Susan. *King of Shadows*. London: Bodley Head, 1999.
Cormier, Robert. *The Chocolate War*. New York: Pantheon, 1974.
Cormier, Robert. *I am the Cheese*. London: Gollancz, 1977.
Cormier, Robert. *The Bumblebee Flies Anyway*. London: Gollancz, 1983.
Cormier, Robert. *Fade*. London: Puffin, 1988.
Cross, Gillian. *The Dark Behind the Curtain*. Oxford: Oxford University Press, 1982.
Cross, Gillian. *Chartbreak*. London: Penguin, 1986.
Cross, Gillian. *Wolf*. 1990. London: Puffin, 1992.
Cross, Gillian. *New World*. 1994. London: Puffin, 1996.
Cross, Gillian. *Pictures in the Dark*. Oxford: Oxford University Press, 1996.
Curley, Marianne. *Old Magic*. London: Bloomsbury, 2000.
Dickinson, Peter. *The Gift*. London: Puffin, 1973.
Dickinson, Peter. *The Healer*. London: Victor Gollancz, 1983.
Dickinson, Peter. *Eva*. London: Victor Gollancz, 1988.
Dickinson, Peter. *A Bone from Dry Sea*. London: Victor Gollancz, 1992.
Dickinson, Peter. *The Lion Tamer's Daughter*. 1997. London: Macmillan, 1999.
Downham, Jenny. *Before I Die*. Oxford: David Fickling, 2007.
Duncan, Lois. *The Eyes of Karen Connors*. 1984. London: Pan, 1986.
Duncan, Lois. *Stranger with my Face*. 1981. London: Puffin, 1995.

Ellis, Sarah. *Out of the Blue.* New York: Margaret K. McElderry Books, 1995.
Farmer, Penelope. *Thicker than Water.* London: Walker, 1989.
Gaiman, Neil. *Coraline.* Oxford: Heinemann New Windmills, 2002.
Garner, Alan. *The Owl Service.* London: Collins, 1967.
Garner, Alan. *Red Shift.* 1973. London: Lions Teen Tracks, 1988.
Gibbons, Alan. *Shadow of the Minotaur*, vol. 1 *The Legendeer.* London: Orion, 2000.
Gibbons, Alan. *Vampyr Legion*, vol. 2 *The Legendeer.* London: Orion, 2000.
Gibbons, Alan. *Warriors of the Raven*, vol. 3 *The Legendeer.* London: Orion, 2001.
Gibson, William. *Neuromancer.* London: Victor Gollancz, 1984.
Goldman, E.M. *The Night Room.* 1995. London: Puffin, 1997.
Greene, Bette. *Philip Hall Likes Me, I Reckon, Maybe.* New York: Dial, 1974.
Gross, Philip. *The Wind Gate.* London: Scholastic Children's Books, 1995.
Haddon, Mark. *The Curious Incident of the Dog in the Night Time.* Oxford: David Fickling, 2003.
Hinton, S.E. *The Outsiders.* 1967. London: Collins, 1995.
Howarth, Leslie. *Ultraviolet.* London: Penguin, 2001.
Isherwood, Christopher. *Goodbye to Berlin.* 1939. London: Vintage, 1998.
Ishiguro, Kazuo. *The Unconsoled.* London: Faber & Faber, 1995.
Johnson, Pete. *We, the Haunted.* London: Mammoth, 1989.
Kaye, Geraldine. *Forests of the Night.* London: Scholastic Children's Books, 1995.
Kindl, Patrice. *Owl in Love.* London: Puffin, 1993.
Klause, Annette Curtis. *Blood and Chocolate.* New York: Delacorte Press, 1997.
Kostick, Conor. *Epic.* Dublin: The O'Brien Press, 2004.
Lasky, Katheryn. *Beyond the Burning Time.* New York: Scholastic, 1994.
Lawrence, Louise. *The Earth Witch.* London: Collins, 1982.
Lawrence, Louise. *The Power of Stars.* 1972. London: Collins, 1990.
Lewis, C.S. *The Lion, the Witch, and the Wardrobe.* London: Geoffrey Bles, 1950.
Lively, Penelope. *The Ghost of Thomas Kempe.* London: Heinemann, 1973.
Lowry, Lois. *The Giver.* 1993. London: Collins Modern Classics, 2003.
McCaughrean, Geraldine. *A Pack of Lies.* Oxford: Oxford University Press, 1988.
Mack, Louise. *Teens.* 1897. London: Andrew Melrose, 1903.
Mahy, Margaret. *The Haunting.* London: Puffin, 1982.
Mahy, Margaret. *The Tricksters.* London: Puffin, 1986.
Mahy, Margaret. *The Changeover.* 1984. London: Puffin, 1995.
Mahy, Margaret. *24 Hours.* London: Collins, 2000.
Morgan, Nicola. *Mondays are Red.* London: Hodder, 2002.
Park, Ruth. *Playing Beatie Bow.* London: Puffin, 1980.
Peyton, K.M. *A Pattern of Roses.* Oxford: Oxford University Press, 1972.
Peyton, K.M. *Unquiet Spirits.* London: Scholastic Children's Books, 1997.
Pierre, D.C.B. *Vernon God Little.* London: Faber & Faber, 2003.
Pilling, Ann. *Black Harvest.* London: Collins, 1983.
Price, Susan. *The Bearwood Witch.* London: Scholastic Children's Books, 2001.
Pullman, Philip. *Northern Lights*, vol. 1 *His Dark Materials.* London: Scholastic Children's Books, 1995.
Pullman, Philip. *The Subtle Knife*, vol. 2 *His Dark Materials.* London: Scholastic Children's Books, 1997.
Pullman, Philip. *The Amber Spyglass*, vol. 3 *His Dark Materials.* London: Scholastic Children's Books, 2000.
Rees, Celia. *Ghost Chamber.* London: Hodder Children's Books, 1997.
Rees, Celia. *Witch Child.* London: Bloomsbury, 2000.
Rosen, Michael J. *ChaseR.* London: Walker Books, 2002.
Sachar, Louis. *Holes.* London: Bloomsbury, 1998.
Salinger, J.D. *The Catcher in the Rye.* London: Penguin, 1951.
Samuels, Gertrude. *Run, Shelley, Run!* New York: Crowell, 1974.
Scott, Michael. *Gemini Game.* Dublin: The O'Brien Press, 1993.
Sedgewick, Marcus. *Witch Hill.* London: Orion Children's Books, 2001.
Sleator, William. *Rewind.* New York: Penguin. 1995.
Spanton, Simon (ed.). *The Web 2027.* London: Orion, 1997.
Thesman, Jean. *The Other Ones.* London: Puffin, 1999.
Thompson, Julian F. *Ghost Story.* London: Bloomsbury, 1997.
Tiernan, Cate. *Wicca: Book of Shadows.* London: Puffin, 2001.
Tolkien, J.R.R. *The Lord of the Rings.* London: George Allen & Unwin, 1954–1955.

Ure, Jean. *Plague 99*. London: Methuen, 1989.
Ure, Jean. *Just Sixteen*. London: Orchard Books, 1999.
Vande Velde, Vivian. *Heir Apparent*. Orlando, FL: Harcourt, 2002.
Welford, Sue. *The Night After Tomorrow*. Oxford: Oxford University Press, 1995.
Westall, Robert. *The Wind Eye*. London: Macmillan, 1976.
Westall, Robert. *The Devil on the Road*. London: Macmillan, 1978.
Westall, Robert. *Yaxley's Cat*. London: Macmillan Children's Books, 1991.
Whyman, Matt. *Superhuman*. London: Hodder Children's Books, 2003.
Zindel, Paul. *The Pigman*. London: Bodley Head, 1968.

Secondary Sources

Abbott, John and Terry Ryan. *The Unfinished Revolution: learning, human behaviour, community and political paradox*. Stafford: Network Education Press, 2000.
Abrams, Mark. *The Teenage Consumer*. London: London Press Exchange, 1959.
Alcock, John. *The Triumph of Sociobiology*. Oxford: Oxford University Press, 2001.
Andrae, Thomas. 'From Menace to Messiah: the history and historicity of Superman.' 1980. *American Media and Mass Culture: left perspectives*. Ed. Donald Lazere. Berkeley, University of California Press, 1987. 124–138.
Applebaum, Noga. 'Electronic Texts and Adolescent Agency: computers and the Internet in contemporary children's fiction.' *Modern Children's Literature: an introduction*. Ed. Kim Reynolds. Basingstoke: Palgrave Macmillan, 2005. 250–262.
Armitt, Lucie. *Theorising the Fantastic*. London: Arnold, 1996.
Armitt, Lucie. *Contemporary Women's Fiction and the Fantastic*. London: Macmillan, 2000.
Armstrong, Judith. 'Ghosts as Rhetorical Devices in Children's Fiction.' *Children's Literature in Education* 9.2 (Summer 1978): 59–66.
Armstrong, Judith. 'Ghost Stories: exploiting the convention.' *Children's Literature in Education* 11.3 (Autumn 1980): 117–123.
Aronson, Marc. *Exploding the Myths: the truth about teens and reading*. Metuchen, NJ and London: Scarecrow, 2001.
Augé, Marc. *Non Places: introduction to an anthropology of supermodernity*. Trans. John Howe. 1992. London: Verso, 1995.
Babbitt, Natalie. 'Between Innocence and Maturity.' *The Horn Book Magazine* (Feb. 1972): 33–37.
Babcock, Shannon. 'Fiction Fandom: Francesca Lia Block and Internet Adolescence.' Lifestyle Narratives Conference (Liverpool John Moores University: Association for the Research in Popular Fictions, 22–23 November 2003).
Bakhtin, Mikhail. *Problems for Dostoevsky's Poetics*. Ed. and trans. Caryl Emerson. 1929. Minneapolis: University of Minnesota Press, 1984.
Bator, Robert, ed. *Signposts to Criticism of Children's Literature*. Chicago: American Library Association, 1983.
Baudrillard, Jean. *Simulacra and Simulations*. Trans. Paul Foss, Paul Patton and Philip Beitchman. *Modern Criticism and Theory: a reader*. Ed. David Lodge and Nigel Wood. 2nd edn. 1983. London: Longman, 1988. 404–412.
Baudry, Jean-Louis. 'Ideological Effects of the Basic Cinematographic Apparatus.' 1970. *Narrative, Apparatus, Ideology*. Ed. Philip Rosen. New York: Columbia University Press, 1986. 286–298.
Beck, Ulrich and Elisabeth Beck-Gernsheim. *Individualization: institutionalized individualism and its social and political consequences*. London: Sage, 2002.
Becker, Howard. *The Outsiders: studies in the sociology of deviance*. Glencoe, IL: Free Press, 1963.
Belbin, David. 'The David Belbin Interview.' *Achuka* 1 Oct. 1999. <http://www.achuka.co.uk/archive/interviews/dbint.php>
Bell, David. *An Introduction to Cybercultures*. London: Routledge, 2001.
Belsey, Catherine. *Critical Practice*. London and New York: Routledge, 1980.
Benedikt, Michael. 'Cyberspace: first steps.' *The Cybercultures Reader*. Ed. David Bell and Barbara M. Kennedy. London: Routledge, 2000. 29–44.
Benjamin, Jessica. *The Bonds of Love: psychoanalysis, feminism, and the problem of domination*. New York: Pantheon Books, 1988.
Bettelheim, Bruno. *The Uses of Enchantment: the meaning and importance of fairy tales*. 1976. London: Thames & Hudson, 1995.
Bignell, Jonathan. 'Writing the Child in Media Theory.' *The Yearbook of English Studies* 32 (2002): 127–139.

Bind, Jean. *Young Teenage Reading Habits: a study of the Bookmaster scheme.* British National Bibliography Research Report 9. London: The British Library, 1982.
Blos, Peter. 'The Second Individuation Process of Adolescence.' *Psychoanalytic Study of the Child* 22 (1967): 132–186.
Bogin, Barry. 'Evolutionary Perspectives on Human Growth.' *Annual Review of Anthropology* 28.1 (1999): 109–153.
Bowie, Malcolm. *Freud, Proust and Lacan: theory as fiction.* Cambridge: Cambridge University Press, 1987.
Brake, Mike. *The Sociology of Youth Culture and Youth Subcultures: sex and drugs and rock'n'roll?* London: Routledge & Kegan Paul, 1980.
Briggs, Julia. *Night Visitors: the rise and fall of the English Ghost Story.* London: Faber, 1977.
Bunting, Madeleine. 'Adolescent Angst.' *The Guardian* 8 April 2002: 15.
Burns, Tom and Elizabeth Burns, ed. *Sociology of Literature and Drama.* Harmondsworth, Middx: Penguin, 1973.
Buse, Peter and Andrew Stott, eds. *Ghosts: deconstruction, psychoanalysis, history.* London: Macmillan, 1999.
Buss, David. *Evolutionary Psychology: the new science of the mind.* London: Allyn& Bacon, 1999.
Bynum, Caroline Walker. *Metamorphosis and Identity.* New York: Zone Books, 2001.
Carlsen, G.R. *Books and the Teenager Reader: a guide for teachers, librarians, and parents.* 2nd rev. edn. New York: Harper & Row, 1980.
Cart, Michael. *From Romance to Realism: 50 years of growth and change in young adult literature.* New York: HarperCollins, 1996.
Cavaliero, Glen. *The Supernatural and English Fiction.* Oxford: Oxford University Press, 1995.
Clarke, Bruce. *Allegories of Writing: the subject of metamorphosis.* Albany: State University of New York Press, 1995.
Clarke, John, Stuart Hall, Tony Jefferson and Brian Roberts. 'Subcultures, Cultures and Class.' *Resistance Through Rituals: youth cultures in post-war Britain.* Ed. Stuart Hall and Tony Jefferson. 1976. London: Routledge, 1993. 9–74.
Clément, Catherine and Hélène Cixous. *The Newly Born Woman.* 1975. Trans. Betsy Wing. London: I.B. Tauris, 1986.
Clute, John and John Grant, eds. *The Encyclopedia of Fantasy.* London: Orbit, 1997.
Cohen, A.K. *Delinquent Boys.* New York: Free Press, 1955.
Cohen, Stanley. *Folk Devils and Moral Panics: the creation of Mods and Rockers.* London: McGibbon & Kee, 1972.
Coleman, John. *Relationships in Adolescence.* London: Routledge & Kegan Paul, 1974.
Coleman, John C. and Leo B. Hendry. *The Nature of Adolescence.* 3rd edn. 1980. London: Routledge, 1999.
Cooke, Rachel. 'It ain't half hot, mum.' *The Observer* 23 Feb. 2003, Review: 1.
Cosslett, Tess. ' "History from Below": time-slip narratives and national identity.' *The Lion and the Unicorn* 26.2 (2002): 243–253.
Culler, Jonathan. 'Literary Competence.' *Reader-Response Criticism: from formalism to post-structuralism.* Ed. Jane Tompkins. London: Johns Hopkins University Press, 1980. 101–117.
Danesi, Marcel. *Cool: signs and meanings of adolescence.* Toronto: University of Toronto Press, 1995.
Dawkins, Richard, *The Selfish Gene.* Oxford: Oxford University Press, 1976.
Deleuze, Gilles and Félix Guattari. *Kafka: toward a minor literature.* Trans. Dana Polan. 1975. Minneapolis: University of Minnesota Press, 1986.
Denzin, Norman K. *The Cinematic Society: the voyeur's gaze.* London: Sage, 1995.
Derrida, Jacques. *Of Grammatology.* Corrected edn. Trans. Gayatri Chakravorty Spivak. 1976. London: Johns Hopkins University Press, 1997.
Doane, Mary Ann. 'Film and the Masquerade: theorising the female spectator.' *Screen* 23.3–4 (1982): 74–87.
Duff, David, ed. *Modern Genre Theory.* London: Pearson Education, 2000.
Eccleshare, Julia. 'Teenage Fiction: realism, romance and contemporary problem novels.' *International Companion Encyclopaedia of Children's Literature.* Ed. Peter Hunt. London: Routledge, 1996. 387–396.
Eco, Umberto. 'The myth of Superman.' *The Role of the Reader: explorations in the semiotics of texts.* Ed. Umberto Eco. Bloomington: Indiana University Press, 1979. 107–124.
Egoff, Sheila. 'The Problem Novel.' *Only Connect.* Ed. Sheila Egoff. Toronto and Oxford: Oxford University Press, 1980. 356–369.
Eisenstadt, S.N. *From Generation to Generation: age groups and social structure.* London: Routledge & Kegan Paul, 1956.

Elkind, David. *Children and Adolescents: interpretive essays on Jean Piaget.* 3rd edn. 1970. New York and Oxford: Oxford University Press, 1981.
Elkind, David. 'Egocentrism in Children and Adolescents.' 1967. *Children and Adolescents: interpretive essays on Jean Piaget.* 3rd edn. Ed. David Elkind. New York: Oxford University Press, 1981. 74–95.
Else, Liz and Sherry Turkle. 'I'll Have to Ask My Friend.' *New Scientist* .2569 (16 Sept. 2006): 48–49.
Erikson, Erik. *Identity and the Life Cycle.* New York: International Universities Press, 1959.
Erikson, Erik. 'Youth: fidelity and diversity.' *The Challenge of Youth.* Ed. Erik Erikson. Garden City, NY: Doubleday/Anchor, 1965.
Erikson, Erik. *Identity, Youth and Crisis.* New York: Norton, 1968.
Evans, Walter. 'Monster Moves: a sexual theory.' *Sexuality in the Movies.* Ed. Thomas R. Atkins. Bloomington: Indiana University Press, 1975.
Fauth, Jurgen. 'Poles in Your Face: the promises and pitfalls of hyperfiction.' *Mississippi Review* Sept. 1995. <http://www.mississippireview.com/1995/06-jurge.html>
Featherstone, Mike. 'Post-Bodies, Aging and Virtual Reality.' *The Cybercultures Reader.* Ed. David Bell and Barbara M. Kennedy. London: Routledge, 2000. 609–618.
Featherstone, Mike and Roger Burrows. 'Cultures of Technological Embodiment: an introduction.' *Cyberspace, Cyberbodies, Cyberpunk: cultures of technological embodiment.* Ed. Mike Featherstone and Roger Burrows. London: SAGE, 1995.
Fish, Stanley. 'Literature in the Reader: affective stylistics.' *Reader-Response Criticism: from formalism to post-structuralism.* Ed. Jane Tompkins. London: Johns Hopkins University Press, 1980. 70–100.
Fiske, John. *Television Culture.* London: Routledge, 1987.
Foucault, Michel. *Discipline and Punish: the birth of the prison.* Trans. Alan Sheridan. 1975. London: Penguin, 1977.
Foucault, Michel. *The History of Sexuality vol. 1: an introduction.* Trans. Robert Hurley. 1976. London: Penguin, 1978.
Foucault, Michel. *Power/Knowledge: selected interviews and other writings, 1972–1977.* Ed. and trans. Colin Gordon. Brighton: Harvester, 1980.
Fowler, Alastair. *Kinds of Literature: an introduction to the theory of genres and modes.* Oxford: Clarendon, 1982.
Fowler, James. *Stages of Faith: the psychology of human development and the quest for meaning.* London: Harper & Row, 1981.
Freud, Sigmund. 'The "Uncanny"'. *The Pelican Freud Library*, vol. 14, Ed. James Strachey. 1885. London: Penguin, 1995. 335–376.
Frith, Simon. *The Sociology of Youth.* Ormskirk, Lancs.: Causeway Books, 1984.
Galbraith, Mary. 'Hear My Cry: a manifesto for an emancipatory childhood studies approach to children's literature.' *The Lion and the Unicorn* 25.2 (2001): 187–205.
Gennep, Arnold van. *The Rites of Passage.* Trans. Monika B. Vizeldom and Gabrielle L. Caffee. London: Routledge & Kegan Paul, 1909.
Gibson, Mel. 'Wonder Women and Invisible Girls: case study of Supergirl and Ms Marvel.' *Future Perfect?* Sheffield: Association of Media, Communication and Cultural Studies Conference Proceedings, 1997.
Gilead, Sarah. 'Magic Abjured: closure in children's fantasy fiction.' *Literature for Children: contemporary criticism.* Ed. Peter Hunt. London and New York: Routledge, 1991. 80–109.
Gilligan, Carol. *In a Different Voice: psychological theory and women's development.* Cambridge, MA: Harvard University Press, 1982.
Gregory, Thomas West. *Adolescence in Literature.* New York: Longman, 1978.
Griffin, Christine. *Representations of Youth: the study of youth and adolescence in Britain and America.* Cambridge: Polity, 1993.
Hall, Christine and Martin Coles. *Children's Reading Choices.* London: Routledge, 1999.
Hall, Granville Stanley. *Adolescence: its psychology and its relation to physiology, anthropology, sociology, sex, crime, religion, and education.* New York: D. Appleton & Co., 1904.
Hall, Stuart. 'Who Needs Identity?' *Questions of Cultural Identity.* Ed. Stuart Hall and Paul du Gay. London: SAGE, 1996. 1–17.
Hall, Stuart and Tony Jefferson, eds. *Resistance through Rituals: youth subcultures in post-war Britain.* 1976. London: Routledge, 1993.
Hamman, Robert. 'Introduction to Virtual Communities Special Edition.' *Research and Cybersociology Magazine* 2. (20 Nov. 1997). <http://www.cybersociology.com/files/2_1_hamman.html>

Haraway, Donna J. *Simians, Cyborgs, and Women: the reinvention of nature.* London: Free Association Books, 1991.
Harris, Marla. 'Contemporary Ghost Stories: cyberspace in fiction for children and young adults.' *Children's Literature in Education* 36.2 (June 2005): 111–128.
Hart, Patricia. *Narrative Magic in the Fiction of Isabel Allende.* London and Toronto: Associated University Presses, 1989.
Harter, Susan. 'Self and Identity Development.' *At the Threshold: the developing adolescent.* Ed. Shirley Feldman and Glen R. Elliott. Cambridge, MA: Harvard University Press, 1990. 352–388.
Havighurst, Robert J. *Human Development and Education.* New York: Longmans, Green & Co., 1953.
Head, Patricia. 'Robert Cormier and the Postmodern Possibilities of Young Adult Fiction.' *Children's Literature Association Quarterly* 21.1 (1996): 28–33.
Healy, Dave. 'Cyberspace and Place: the internet as middle landscape on the electronic frontier.' *Internet Culture.* Ed. David Porter. New York: Routledge, 1996. 55–68.
Hebdige, Dick. *Subculture: the meaning of style.* 1979. London: Routledge, 2003.
Heidmann, Ute and Jean-Michel Adam. 'Text Linguistics and Comparative Literature: towards an interdisciplinary approach to written tales. Angela Carter's translations of Perrault.' *Linguistic Approaches to the Literature Text.* Ed. Donna R. Miller and Monica Turci. London: Equinox Linguistic Books, 2006.
Heldreth, Leonard G. 'The Beast Within: sexuality and metamorphosis in horror films.' *Eros in the Mind's Eye: sexuality and the fantastic in art and film.* Ed. Donald Palumbo. New York, Westport, CT: Greenwood, 1986. 117–125.
Hendry, Leo B. *Growing Up and Going Out.* Aberdeen: Aberdeen University Press, 1983.
Hoffman, Katheryn. 'Flying Through Classicism's Night: the witch in myth and religion.' *Racine et/ou le Classicisme: actes du colloque conjointment organisé par la North American Society for Seventeenth Century French Literature et la Société Racine.* TÅbingen: Gunter Narr Verlag, 2001. 495–470.
Holland, Isabelle. 'What is Adolescent Literature?' *Writers on Writing for Young Adults.* Ed. Patricia E. Feehand and Pamela Petrick Barron. Detroit: Omnigraphics, 1991.
Hollindale, Peter. 'The Adolescent Novel of Ideas.' *Children's Literature in Education* 26.1 (1995): 83–95.
Hollindale, Peter. *Signs of Childness in Children's Books.* South Woodchester: Thimble, 1997.
Holloway, Sarah L. and Gill Valentine, eds. *Children's Geographies: playing, living, learning.* Abingdon: Routledge, 2000.
Hunt, Caroline. 'Young Adult Literature Evades the Theorists.' *Children's Literature Association Quarterly* 21.1 (1996): 4–11.
Hunt, Peter, ed. *Children's Literature: the development of criticism.* London: Routledge, 1990.
Hunt, Peter. 'Winnie-the-Pooh and Domestic Fantasy.' *Stories and Society: children's literature in its social context.* Ed. D. Butts. London: Macmillan, 1992. 112–124.
Hunt, Peter. 'Defining Children's Literature.' *Only Connect.* 3rd edn. Ed. Sheila Egoff, E.T. Stubbs and L.F. Ashley. Toronto: Oxford University Press, 1996. 2–17.
Hunt, Peter. 'Futures for Children's Literature: evolution or radical break?' *Cambridge Journal of Education* 30.1 (2000): 111–119.
Husain, Shahrukh, ed. *The Virago Book of Witches.* London: Virago, 1993.
Hutton, Ronald. *The Triumph of the Moon: a history of modern pagan witchcraft.* Oxford: Oxford University Press, 1999.
Isherwood, Christopher. *Goodbye to Berlin.* London: Hogarth Press, 1939.
Irigaray, Luce. *This Sex Which is Not One.* Trans. Catherine Porter and Carolyn Burke. Ithaca, NY: Cornell University Press, 1985.
Jackson, Rosemary. *Fantasy: the literature of subversion.* London: Routledge, 1981.
James, Allison, and Alan Prout, eds. *Constructing and Reconstructing Childhood: contemporary issues in the sociology of childhood.* 1990. 2nd edn. London: Falmer, 1997.
James, Allison, Chris Jenks and Alan Prout. *Theorizing Childhood.* Cambridge: Polity, 1998.
Jenks, Chris, ed. *The Sociology of Childhood: essential readings.* London: Batsford Academic, 1982.
Jenks, Chris. *Childhood.* London: Routledge, 1996.
Johnson, Boris. 'Computer Games.' *Boris Johnson MP Blog.* 28 Dec. 2006. <http://www.boris-johnson.com/archives/2006/12/computer_games.php>
Kafka, Franz. 'The Metamorphosis'. In *The Metamorphosis and Other Stories.* Trans. Malcolm Pasley. 1915. London: Penguin, 2000.
Kertzer, Adrienne. 'Reclaiming Her Maternal Pre-Text: Little Red Riding Hood's mother and three young adult novels.' *Children's Literature Association Quarterly* 21.1 (1996): 20–27.

Bibliography • 213

Kimmel, M. 'Rethinking "Masculinity": new directions in research'. *Changing Men: new directions in research on men and masculinity.* Ed. M. Kimmel. Newbury Park, CA: SAGE, 1987, 9–24.

King, John. *Modern Latin American Fiction.* London: Faber & Faber, 1987.

Knowles, Murray and Kirsten Malmkjër. *Language and Control in Children's Literature.* London: Routledge, 1996.

Kohlberg, Lawrence. *The Philosophy of Moral Development: moral stages and the idea of justice.* San Francisco and London: Harper & Row, 1981.

Kramarae, Cheris. 'A Backstage Critique of Virtual Reality.' *Cybersociety: computer-mediated communication and community.* Ed. Stephen G. Jones. London: SAGE, 1995. 36–56.

Kramer, Heinrich and James Sprenger. *The Malleus Maleficarum.* Trans. Montague Summers. 1928. New York: Dover, 1971.

Kristeva, Julia. 'Women's Time.' *The Kristeva Reader.* Ed. Toril Moi. 1981. Oxford, Blackwell, 1986. 187–213.

Kroger, Jane. 'Separation-Individuation and Ego Identity Status in New Zealand University Students.' *Journal of Youth & Adolescence* 14 (1985): 133–147.

Kroger, Jane. *Identity in Adolescence: the balance between self and other.* London: Routledge, 1989.

Kroger, Jane and Stephen Haslett. 'Separation-Individuation and Ego Identity Status in Late Adolescents: a two-year longitudinal study.' *Journal of Youth and Adolescence* 17 (1988): 59–81.

Lacan, Jacques. *Écrits: a selection.* Trans. Alan Sheridan. London: Routledge, 1977.

Larner, Christina. *Witchcraft and Religion: the politics of popular belief.* Ed. Alan Macfarlane. Oxford: Blackwell, 1983.

Lassén-Seger, Maria. 'Exploring Otherness: animal metamorphosis of the fictive child.' 15th Biennial Congress of the International Research Society for Children's Literature: change and renewal in children's literature. Warmbaths, South Africa, 20–24 Aug. 2001. 12. Oct. 2002 <www.childlit.org.za/irsclpaplassenseger.html>

Latham, Don. 'Discipline and Its Discontents: a Foucauldian reading of *The Giver.*' *Children's Literature* 32 (2004): 134–151.

Lawrence-Pietroni, Anna. '*The Tricksters, The Changeover,* and the Fluidity of Adolescent Literature.' *Children's Literature Association Quarterly* 21.1 (1996): 34–39.

Lee, Alison. *Realism and Power: postmodern British fiction.* London and New York: Routledge, 1990.

Le Guin, Ursula. 'In Defence of Fantasy.' *The Horn Book Magazine* 49.3 (June 1973): 239.

Lehnert-Rodiek, Gertrud. 'Fantastic Children's Literature and Travel in Time.' *Phaedrus: international annual of children's literature* 13 (1988): 61–72.

Lenz, Millicent and Peter Hunt. *Alternative Worlds in Fantasy Fiction: Ursula Le Guin, Terry Pratchett, Phillip Pullman and others.* London: Continuum, 2001.

Lesnik-Oberstein, Karín. 'Childhood and Textuality: culture, history, literature.' *Children in Culture: approaches to childhood.* Ed. Karín Lesnik-Oberstein. London: Macmillan, 1998. 1–28.

Lupton, Deborah. 'The Embodied Computer/User.' 1995. *The Cybercultures Reader.* Ed. David Bell and Barbara M. Kennedy. London: Routledge, 2000. 477–488.

Lupton, Deborah and Lesley Barclay. *Constructing Fatherhood: discourses and experiences.* London: SAGE, 1997.

McCallum, Robyn. *Ideologies of Identity in Adolescent Fiction: dialogic construction of subjectivity.* New York and London: Garland, 1999.

Mackay, Sophie. 'Liminality: post-colonial narratives of migration for adolescents.' Diss. Roehampton University. 2000.

Mackey, Margaret. *Literacies Across Media: playing the text*, rev. edn. London: Routledge, 2007.

McNamee, Sara. 'Youth, Gender and Video Games: power and control in the home.' *Cool Places: geographies of youth cultures.* Ed. Tracey Skelton and Gill Valentine. London: Routledge, 1998. 195–206.

McNaron, Toni A.H. 'Mirrors and Likeness: a lesbian aesthetic in the making.' *Sexual Practice/Textual Theory: lesbian cultural criticism.* Ed. Susan J. Wolfe and Julie Penelope. Cambridge, MA: Blackwell, 1993. 291–306.

McNay, Lois. *Gender and Agency: reconfiguring the subject in feminist and social theory.* Cambridge: Polity, 2000.

McRobbie, Angela. 'Dance and Social Fantasy.' *Gender and Generation.* Ed. Angela McRobbie and Mica Nava. London: Macmillan, 1984. 130–161.

McRobbie, Angela. 'Settling Accounts with Subculture: a feminist critique.' *Feminism and Youth Culture: from 'Jackie' to 'Just Seventeen.'* Ed. Angela McRobbie. London: Macmillan, 1991. 16–34.

Mahler, Margaret, Fred Pine and Anni Bergman. *The Psychological Birth of the Human Infant: symbiosis and individuation.* London: Hutchinson, 1975.

Manlove, C.N. *Modern Fantasy: five studies.* Cambridge: Cambridge University Press, 1975.
Marcia, James E. 'Development and Validation of Ego Identity Status.' *Journal of Personality and Social Psychology* 3 (1966): 551–558.
Márquez, Gabriel García, *One Hundred Years of Solitude.* 1967. Trans. Gregory Rabassa. New York: Harper & Row, 1970.
Massey, Irving. *The Gaping Pig: literature and metamorphosis.* Berkeley: University of California Press, 1976.
Matthews, Dorothy. 'Writing About Adolescent Literature: current approaches and future directions.' *Young Adult Literature in the Seventies: a selection of readings.* Ed. Jana Varlajs. Metuchen, NJ: Scarecrow, 1978. 32–36.
Matza, David. *Becoming Deviant.* Englewood Cliffs, NJ: Prentice Hall, 1969.
de Mause, Lloyd. *Foundations of Psychohistory.* New York: Creative Roots, 1982.
Maxwell-Stuart, P.G. *Witchcraft: a history.* Stroud, Glos.: Temples Publishing, 2000.
Maynard, Sally, Sophie MacKay, Fiona Smyth and Kimberley Reynolds. *Young People Reading in 2005: the second study of young people's reading habits.* LISU, Loughborough University and the National Centre for Research in Children's Literature, Roehampton University: January 2007.
Miller, John. 'Role Playing Games as Interactive Fiction.' *Reconstruction* 6.1 (Winter 2006): <http://reconstruction.eserver.org/061/miller.shtml>
Mitterauer, Michael. *A History of Youth.* Trans. Graeme Dunphy. Oxford: Blackwell, 1992.
Mooney, Bel. 'Crossover Fiction.' *The Reader* 12 (2004): 70.
Morgan, Nicola. 'YA to You.' *The Author* (Autumn 2003): 124–125.
Moseley, Rachel. 'Glamorous Witchcraft: gender and magic in teen film and television.' *Screen* 43.4 (2002): 403–422.
Moss, Geoff. 'Metafiction, Illustration, and the Poetics of Children's Literature.' *Literature for Children: contemporary criticism.* Ed. Peter Hunt. London: Routledge, 1992.
Mulvey, Laura. 'Visual Pleasure and Narrative Cinema.' 1975. *Contemporary Film Theory.* Ed. Antony Easthope. London: Longman, 1993. 111–124.
Muuss, Rolf E. *Theories of Adolescence.* 6th edn. 1962. London: McGraw Hill, 1996.
National Curriculum Online. 'The English Programme of Study.' <http://www.nc.uk.net/nc/contents/En-3-2-POS.html>
Natov, Roni. *The Poetics of Childhood.* London: Routledge, 2003.
Nguyen, Dan Thu and Jon Alexander. 'The Coming of Cyberspacetime and the End of the Polity.' *Cultures of Internet: virtual spaces, real histories, living bodies.* Ed. Rob Shields. London: Sage, 1996. 99–124.
Nikolajeva, Maria. *The Magic Code: the use of magical patterns in fantasy for children.* Stockholm: Almqvist & Wiksell International, 1988.
Nikolajeva, Maria. 'The Insignificance of Time: *Red Shift.*' *Children's Literature Association Quarterly* 14.3 (1989) 128–131.
Oldenburg, Ray. *The Great Good Place.* New York: Paragon House, 1989.
O'Neil, Dennis. *Knightfall.* London: Bantam, 1994.
Opie, Peter and Iona Opie. *Children's Games in Street and Playground.* Oxford: Clarendon, 1969.
Pecora, Norma. 'Superman/Superboys/Supermen: the comic book hero as socializing agent.' *Men, Masculinity, and the Media.* Ed. Steve Craig. London: Sage, 1992. 61–77.
Philip, Neil. *A Fine Anger: a critical introduction to the work of Alan Garner.* London: Collins, 1981.
Piaget, Jean. *The Growth of Logical Thinking from Childhood to Adolescence.* New York: Basic Books, 1958.
Piaget, Jean. *Play, Dreams and Imitation in Childhood.* London: Routledge & Kegan Paul, 1962.
Piaget, Jean. *The Language and Thought of the Child.* London: Routledge & Kegan Paul, 1969.
Piaget, Jean. *The Psychology of the Child.* New York: Basic Books, 1969.
Purkiss, Diane. *The Witch in History: early modern and twentieth-century representations.* London and New York: Routledge, 1996.
Radway, Janice. *Reading the Romance: women patriarchy, and popular literature.* 1984. London: Verso, 1987.
Reid Elizabeth. 'Virtual Worlds: culture and imagination.' *Cybersociety: computer-mediated communication and community.* Ed. Stephen G. Jones. London: SAGE, 1995. 164–183.
Reynolds, Kimberley. *Radical Children's Literature: future visions and aesthetic transformations in juvenile fiction.* London: Palgrave, 2007.
Reynolds, Richard. *Super Heroes: a modern mythology.* Jackson: University Press of Mississippi, 1992.
Rheingold, Howard. *Virtual Reality.* London: Secker & Warburg, 1991.
Riordan, Ellen. 'Commodified Agents and Empowered Girls: consuming and producing feminism.' *Journal of Communication Inquiry* 25.3 (July 2001): 279–297.

Rollin, Lucy. *Twentieth-century Teen Culture by the Decades: a reference guide.* Westport, CT: Greenwodd Press, 1999.

Rose, Jacqueline. *The Case of Peter Pan: or the impossibility of children's fiction.* London: Macmillan, 1984.

Routh, Jane and Janet Woolf, eds. *The Sociology of Literature: theoretical approaches.* Keele: University of Keele, 1977.

Rustin, Margaret and Michael Rustin. *Narratives of Love and Loss: studies in modern children's fiction.* London: Verso, 1987.

Ryan, Marie-Laure. *Narrative as Virtual Reality: immersion and interactivity in literature and electronic media.* Baltimore, MD: Johns Hopkins University Press, 2001.

Sabin, Roger. *Adult Comics: an introduction.* London: Routledge, 1993.

Saïd, Edward, *Orientalism.* London: Penguin, 1978.

Sambell, Kay. 'The Use of Fictional Time in Novels for Young Readers.' Diss. University of York, 1996.

Sanders, Andrew. *A Deed Without a Name: the witch in society and history.* Oxford: Berg, 1995.

Sarland, Charles. 'Attack of the Teenage Horrors: theme and meaning in popular series fiction.' *Signal* 73 (Jan. 1994): 49–61.

Segal, Lynne. *Slow Motion: changing masculinities changing men.* London: Virago, 1990.

Sheldrick Ross, Catherine. 'Young Adult Realism: conventions, narrators, and readers', *The Library Quarterly* 55.2 (1985): 174–191.

Showalter, Elaine. *Hysteries: hysterical epidemics and modern culture.* London: Picador, 1997.

Skelton, Tracey and Gill Valentine, eds. *Cool Places: geographies of youth cultures.* London: Routledge, 1998.

Smith, Karen Patricia. *The Fabulous Realm: a literary-historical approach to British fantasy 1780–1990.* Metuchen, NJ: Scarecrow, 1993.

Smith, Louisa. 'Real Gardens with Imaginary Toads: domestic fantasy.' *International Companion Encyclopaedia of Children's Literature.* Ed. Peter Hunt. London: Routledge, 1996. 295–302.

Spufford, Francis. *The Child that Books Built.* London: Faber & Faber, 2002.

Stainton-Rogers, Rex. 'The Social Construction of Childhood.' *Child Abuse and Neglect.* Eds Wendy Stainton-Rogers, D. Harvey and E. Ash. London: Batsford and Open University, 1989.

Stainton-Rogers, Rex and Wendy Stainton-Rogers. 'Word Children.' *Children in Culture: approaches to childhood.* Ed. Karín Lesnik-Oberstein. London: Macmillan, 1998. 178–203.

Starke, Ruth. 'The Absent Mum in Children's Literature: where have all the mothers gone?' 4 Nov. 2003. <http://family.go.com/Features...8_05/melb/melb58deadmum/melb58deadmum.htm>

Stephens, John. *Language and Ideology in Children's Literature.* London: Longman, 1992.

Sterling, Bruce. 'I Saw the Best Minds of My Generation Destroyed by Google.' *New Scientist* .2569 (16 Sept. 2006): 52–53.

Stone, Allucquere Rosanne. 'Will the Real Body Please Stand Up? Boundary stories about virtual cultures.' *The Cybercultures Reader.* Ed. David Bell and Barbara M. Kennedy. London: Routledge, 2000. 504–528.

Storey, John. *An Introductory Guide to Cultural Theory and Popular Culture.* London: Harvester Wheatsheaf, 1993.

Subrahmanyam, Kaveri, Patricia M. Greenfield and Brendesha Tynes. 'Constructing Sexuality and Identity in an Online Teen Chat Room.' *Applied Developmental Psychology* 25 (2004): 651–666.

Sullivan, C.W. III, ed. *Young Adult Science Fiction.* Westport, CT: Greenwood, 1999.

Summerfield, Geoffrey. 'Oh the Impossibility of Books-for-adolescents.' *Teenage Reading.* Ed. Peter Kennerley. London: Ward Lock Educational, 1979. 3–8.

Sutton, Roger. 'The Critical Myth: realistic YA novels', *School Library Journal* 29.3 (Nov. 1982): 33–35.

Tapscott, Don. *Growing Up Digital: the rise of the Net Generation.* New York: McGraw Hill, 1998.

'Teen Dreams.' *Body Story* (Wall to Wall Productions for Channel Four, April 2001).

Thompson, Jack. 'Teenagers Reading: developmental stages of reading literature.' *International Companion Encyclopaedia of Children's Literature.* Ed. Peter Hunt. London: Routledge, 1996. 584–593.

Thomson, Stephen. 'The Real Adolescent: performance and negativity in Melvyn Burgess's *Junk*.' *The Lion and the Unicorn* 23.1 (1999): 22–29.

Todorov, Tsvetan. *The Fantastic: a structural approach to a literary genre.* Cleveland: Case Western Reserve University Press, 1973.

Tolkein, J.R.R. *Tree and Leaf.* London: Allen & Unwin, 1964.

Townsend, John Rowe. *A Sense of Story: essays on contemporary writers for children.* London: Longman, 1971.

Trites, Roberta Seelinger. *Disturbing the Universe: power and repression in adolescent literature.* Iowa City: University of Iowa Press, 2000.
Tuan, Yi-Fu. *Space and Place: the perspective of experience.* London: Edward Arnold, 1977.
Tucker, Nicholas and Julia Eccleshare. *The Rough Guide to Books for Teenagers.* London: Penguin, 2003.
Turkle, Sherry. 'Constructions and Reconstructions of Self in Virtual Reality: playing in the MUDs.' *Mind Culture and Activity* 1.3 (Summer 1994): 158–167.
Turkle, Sherry. *Life on the Screen: identity in the age of the internet.* London: Phoenix, 1997.
Turner, Victor. *The Ritual Process: structure and anti-structure.* London: Routledge & Kegan Paul, 1969.
Van Druten, John. *I am a Camera.* New York: Random House, 1952.
Walkerdine, Valerie. 'Children in Cyberspace: a new frontier?' *Children in Culture.* Ed. Karín Lesnik-Oberstein. London: Macmillan, 1998. 231–247.
Wall, Barbara. *The Narrator's Voice: the dilemma of children's fiction.* London: Macmillan, 1991.
Waller, Alison. 'Is Holden Caulfield Still Real? The body of theory and practice in young adult literature.' *New Voices in Children's Literature Criticism.* Ed. Sebastien Chapleau. Lichfield, Staffs.: Pied Piper Publishing, 2004. 97–104.
Waller, Alison. '*Fade* and the Lone Teenager: young adult fantastic realism shaping modern individualism.' *Children's Fantasy Fiction: debates for the 21st Century.* Ed. Nickianne Moody and Clare Horrocks. Liverpool: Association for Research in Popular Fictions, 2005. 127–144.
Waller, Alison. ' "Solid All the Way Through": Margaret Mahy's Ordinary Witches.' *The Fiction of Margaret Mahy.* Ed. Sarah Winters and Elizabeth Hale. Wellington, NZ: Victoria University Press. 21–43.
Watt, Ian. *The Rise of the Novel: studies in Defoe, Richardson and Fielding.* 1957. London: The Hogarth Press, 1987.
Weedon, Chris. *Feminism and Poststructuralism.* Oxford: Blackwell, 1992.
Weisfeld, Glenn E. *Evolutionary Principles of Human Adolescence.* New York: Basic Books, 1999.
Weisfeld, Glenn E. and Donyell K. Coleman. 'Further Observations on Adolescence.' *Evolutionary Perspectives on Human Development.* Ed. Robert L. Burgess and Kevin MacDonald. London: Sage, 2005. 331–357.
Whelehan, Imelda. 'Feminism and Trash: destabilising "the reader" '. *Gendering the Reader.* Ed. Sara Mills. Harvester: Wheatsheaf, 1994. 217–235.
Widdowson, John. 'The Witch as a Frightening and Threatening Figure.' *The Witch Figure: folklore essays.* Ed. Venetia Newal. London: Routledge & Kegan Paul, 1973. 200–220.
Wilkie-Stibbs, Christine. *The Feminine Subject in Children's Literature.* London: Routledge, 2002.
Willeman, Paul. 'Voyeurism, the Look, and Dwoskin.' *Narrative, Apparatus, Ideology: a film theory reader.* Ed. Philip Rosen. New York: Columbia University Press, 1986. 210–218.
Williams, Raymond. *Keywords.* London: Fontana/Croom Helm, 1976.
Willis, Paul. *Profane Culture.* London: Routledge & Kegan Paul, 1978.
Wilson, Edward O. *Sociobiology: the new synthesis.* Cambridge, MA: Harvard University Press, 1975.
Wilson, Edward O. *Consilience.* London: Abacus, 1999.
Workman, Lance and Will Reader. *Evolutionary Psychology: an introduction.* Cambridge: Cambridge University Press, 2004.
Wright, Robert. *The Moral Animal: why we are the way we are.* London: Abacus, 1994.

Index

addiction 158–60
adolescence: definitions of 5–6, 8–9; and fiction 26, 33, 50–1, 87–90, 91; frameworks of 1, 30–2, 57–60, 92–6, 147, 189–97, 199n3; as introspective 55–6, 62–3; as social agents 98, 204n7
adolescent literature *see* young adult literature
adolescent novel of ideas *see* novel of ideas
agency *see* power
Almond, David: *Clay* 193; *Kit's Wilderness* 33, 40, 89; *Secret Heart* 45–8
alternateen 49
Anderson, M.T.: *Feed* 206n9
Armitt, Lucie 10–11, 73, 89, 99–100
Armstrong, Judith 66–9, 73, 203n9
Augé, Marc 168–9

Bakhtin, Mikhail 18
Baudrillard, Jean 168–9
Baxter, Stephen: *Gulliverzone* 156–7, 166, 169
belief 73–4
Blos, Peter 58–60
Blume, Judy: *Forever* 16
bodies *see* embodiment
Bowkett, Stephen: *Dreamcastle* 159, 161, 163–4, 166
boys *see* masculinity
Brake, Mike 93, 95–6
bricolage 6, 95, 126, 134, 137, 204n4
Brown, Eric: *Untouchable* 167, 171–3, 177
Buffy the Vampire Slayer 131
Burgess, Melvin: *Lady: my life as a bitch* 50–2, 87, 202n11; *Tiger Tiger* 46–7

camera *see* photography
Carter, Angela: *Nights at the Circus* 87
Centre for Contemporary Cultural Studies (CCCS) 92–3
Chambers, Aidan: *Breaktime* 89, 182–5
Chicago school 92
childhood 2–5, 189–90
Coleman, John 30, 201n1
community 151
computer 171–80, 182; code 152, 179, 182–4; embodied 165–7; *see also* technology
constructionism 3–4, 189–92
Cooper, Susan: *King of Shadows* 22, 36–9
Cormier, Robert: *Fade* xii, 17, 19–20, 79–80, 81–2, 85–6, 114–24, 200n13
coven *see* witchcraft, initiation into
Cross, Gillian: *Chartbreak* 203–4n3; *Pictures in the Dark* 15, 45–6, 47–9, 80–1, 83, 109–10
'culture epoch' 35–6, 43, 188
Curley, Marianne: *Old Magic* 128, 130–1, 138, 140
cyberspace 147–50,
cyborgisation 176–9

delinquency *see* deviancy
developmentalism 30–1, 33–5
deviancy 31–2, 34, 60, 92–5, 130, 190–1
Dickinson, Peter: *A Bone from Dry Sea* 193; *Eva* 52–3, 193; *The Gift* 114–15, 117, 120–1, 122–3; *The Lion Tamer's Daughter* 13, 64–8
discourse 6–7, 187
domestic fantasy 21
doppelganger 25, 64–68
Dostoevsky, Fyodor 18

double *see* doppelganger
Downham, Jenny: *Before I Die* 18–19
dream 85
Duncan, Lois: *The Eyes of Karen Connors* 83–5, 86; *Stranger with my Face* 65–8, 203n8

egocentrism 58, 62, 88
Elkind, David 58, 62–3
Ellis, Sarah: *Out of the Blue* 13
email 174–5
embodiment 166–7, 171–3, 176–7, 184; *see also* computer, embodied
empowerment *see* power
enchantment *see* witchcraft
erasure *see* invisibility
Erikson, Erik 31, 58, 73, 202n6
escape 99–100
evolutionary psychology 188–93

fade *see* invisibility
fantastic, the 19–21, 61–3, 99–100
fantastic realism 1–2, 192–7; definitions of 17–18; sister genres of 21–2; types of 22–5
fantasy *see* fantastic, the
Farmer, Penelope: *Thicker than Water* 104–5
father 107–12, 122; figure 38–9
femininity: and madness 76–8; and power; 97, 137–8; and subcultures 95–6; and witchcraft 126–8, 135
flight *see* escape
formal operational stage 31, 58
Foucault, Michel 7, 119, 204n8, 205n16
Frith, Simon 92–3, 95–6, 142
futuristic teen novel 33

Gaiman, Neil: *Coraline* 85
gaming 154–8, 160–1, 163–7, 182
Garner, Alan: *The Owl Service* 17, 76–7; *Red Shift* 34, 53–4
genre theory 10–12
geography *see* space
ghost *see* haunting
Gibbons, Alan: 'The Legendeer' series; *Shadow of the Minotaur* 158–9, 163, 165–6, 167–8; *Vampyr Legion* 168–9, 171; *Warrior's of the Raven* 168
Gibson, William: *Neuromancer* 147
girls *see* femininity
Goldman, E.M.: *The Night Room* 152–3

Hall, Granville Stanley 8, 36, 75, 188
Hall, Stuart 3, 92–3, 203n18
Haraway, Donna 176–7
haunting 22–3, 66–7, 73–4, 79, 203n9n10
Hendry, Leo B. 30, 201n1
high fantasy 21, 62
Hinton, S.E.: *The Outsiders* 18, 94, 203n2
history 36, 38–9, 41–4, 53–4, 71, 201n7; 'from below' 39, 70, 201n8
Hollindale, Peter 11–12, 18–19, 193, 200n14
horror 49–51
Howarth, Leslie: *Ultraviolet* 160–1, 164–5, 181–2
Hunt, Peter 16–17, 21, 98, 180
hypertext 179–84
hysteria *see* madness

ICT *see* technology
identity 2–3, 56, 59–60; achievement 31, 37, 55, 57–8, 72–3, 84; and fantasy 63; and perception 80, 82; 'under erasure' 3, 79, 83, 86, 203n18
'imaginary audience' 58
individualism 55–7, 64, 72–3, 85, 89, 202n1n3; institutionalised 60–1; second 59–60; separation- 39, 58–9, 101, 106–7, 151
infantilism 1, 61
internet 145, 150, 161; *see also* technology
invisibility 19, 24, 114, 116–17, 120; as erasure 79, 82–3, 85–6
Isherwood, Christopher: *Goodbye to Berlin* 80
Ishiguro, Kazuo: *The Unconsoled* 85

Jackson, Rosemary 18, 20, 56–7, 67, 72, 82–3, 86, 100

kinderschreck 139
Kindl, Patrice: *Owl in Love* 87–8
Klause, Annette Curtis: *Blood and Chocolate* 193
knowledge: as power 121
Kohlberg, Lawrence 122–3
Kostick, Conor: *Epic* 154
Kristeva, Julia 35; *see also* 'woman's time'

labelling theory 87, 92, 130
Lasky, Kathryn: *Beyond the Burning Time* 134
'law of the father' *see* Symbolic

Lawrence, Louise: *The Earth Witch* 102–4, 140; *The Power of Stars* 77–8
lens *see* photography
Lesnik-Oberstein, Karín 5
Lewis, C.S.: *The Lion, the Witch, and the Wardrobe* 101
liminality 32–3, 96
Lively, Penelope: *The Ghost of Thomas Kempe* 67
Lowry, Lois: *The Giver* 114–15, 117–18, 120, 124–5
Lupton, Deborah 165, 171, 173

McCallum, Robyn 35–6, 52, 56, 64, 66–7, 86, 201n6n7
McCaughrean, Geraldine: *A Pack of Lies* 89
McRobbie, Angela 78, 95–6, 141, 204n10
madness 72, 75–8, 203n14
magic *see* witchcraft
magic gift 24
magic realism 21–2, 89, 200n18
Mahy, Margaret: *The Changeover* xii, 22, 105, 106, 108–9, 128, 136, 138–9, 141–2; *The Haunting* 131–3, 140–1; *The Tricksters* 132–3, 135–6, 140, 142
Marcia, James 31, 37
masculinity 107–8, 113–14, 116–17, 120
Matthews, Dorothy 13
menstruation 50
metamorphosis 24, 44–52, 87–8, 202n9; as escape 47–8
'middle landscape' 149, 155–9
mirror stage 64, 66
Morgan, Nicola: *Mondays are Red* 173, 175–9
mother 84, 101–7
MUD, 152, 167, 205n4
myth 127–8, 133–5, 139, 167–9

nanny state *see* infantilism
National Curriculum 10, 199n7
'new frontier' 146–50, 159
Nikolajeva, Maria 29, 53, 200n19
novel of ideas 11, 52, 56

Panopticon 124, 205n16
Park, Ruth: *Playing Beatie Bow* 71–2, 105–7
parody 49–52
past *see* history
PC *see* computer

Piaget, Jean 31–2, 36, 201n2
perception 79–84
'personal fable' 58, 65
Peyton, K.M.: *A Pattern of Roses* 37–8, 39; *Unquiet Spirits* 22, 69–71, 74–5, 78–9
photography 79–83, 203n17
Pilling, Ann: *Black Harvest* 40, 76
power 97–100, 112, 142; of allure 136–7, 204n8; of the father 107; relations between adolescent and adult 103–4; as responsibility/burden 123–5, 141
Price, Susan: *The Bearwood Witch* 139
problem novel 16, 17, 19, 93–4, 194, 200n15
programmer 166
puberty 8, 30, 44, 49, 50, 98, 189, 204n7; *see also* adolescence
Pullman, Philip: *The Golden Compass* 206n4; 'His Dark Materials' series 15, 62, 129–30

realism 80; young adult 17–19, 193–4, 299n15; *see also* problem novel
recapitulation theory *see* 'culture epoch'
Rees, Celia: *Witch Child* 128
representation 2–5, 26
resistance 97, 110, 130–1, 133
rite of passage 32, 44–6
Rose, Jacqueline 4–5, 29, 199n2
Rosen, Michael J.: *ChaseR* 173–5

Salinger, J.D.: *The Catcher in the Rye* 16
Scott, Michael: *Gemini Game* 157–8, 162–3, 169–70
Second Life 153
Sedgewick, Marcus: *Witch Hill* 40, 139
Semiotic 48, 81
sexuality 60, 65, 103; excessive 134–9; and male gaze 120
shape-shifting *see* metamorphosis
simulacra 161, 168–9
Sleator, William: *Rewind* 180–1
sociobiology *see* evolutionary psychology
solipsism *see* egocentrism
sorcery *see* witchcraft
space 147–8, 150–3, 155–61, 168–71, 172–5, 184
speculative fantasy 25, 146, 152–3
Spiderman 121, 123; *see also* superheroes
Standard Social Science Model (SSSM) *see* constructionism

'storm and stress' 75
subcultures 78, 92–6, 98–9, 101, 126, 141–2, 151
subjectivity *see* identity
Summerfield, Geoffrey 55–6, 62
superheroes 24, 112–18, 120–6
Superman 113, 115–17 122–3, 205n15; *see also* superheroes
surveillance 162–3; *see also* perception
Symbolic 48, 107, 109–10
'symbolic universe' 167–70

technology 25, 145–7, 150, 165, 179, 205n3; as threat 162–7
teenage fiction *see* young adult literature
teenager 9; *see also* adolescence
Thesman, Jean: *The Other Ones* 129
'third place' 150, 184
Thompson, Julian: *Ghost Story* 203n10
Tiernan, Cate: *Wicca* 134, 140–1
time *see* history
time-slip *see* time-travel
time travel 22–3, 36, 39–40, 71–2, 201n20n8
Todorov, Tsvetan 19–20, 72, 200n16
Tolkien, J.R.R.: *The Lord of the Rings* 62
transformation *see* metamorphosis
transition 6, 30, 49
twin *see* doppelganger

uncanny 19, 24, 200n16

Ure, Jean: *Just Sixteen* 200n15; *Plague 99* 34

Vande Velde, Vivian: *Heir Apparent* 155–6, 170, 181, 206n13
virtual reality 153–5, 158–70, 173; *see also* cyberspace
vision *see* perception
voyeurism 120, 124

Walkerdine, Valerie 145–8, 185, 205n3
Westall, Robert: *The Devil on the Road* 41–4, 53, 75, 103; *Yaxley's Cat* 76
Whyman, Matt: *Superhuman* 125–6
Wicca 127–8; *see also* witchcraft
Wilkie-Stibbs, Christine 81, 106, 110–11
Wilson, Edward 188–9, 191–2
witchcraft 23, 102–3, 126–43, 205n22; as 'black magic' 127, 139–41; initiation into 128–9, 205n20
'woman's time' 35, 43–4, 47, 81, 89
'word children' 2
'word teenager' 2, 187
World Wide Web *see* internet

young adult 9; *see also* adolescence
Young Adult Library Services Association (YALSA) 9
young adult literature 12, 25, 55–6, 62; definitions of 13–17; material conditions of 9–10, 33, 98–9, 195
youth *see* adolescence

Related titles from Routledge

Crossover Fiction
Global and Historical Perspectives
Sandra L. Beckett

Crossover books transcend the conventionally recognized age barriers within the fiction market. Although crossover literature has recently acquired a prominent status thanks to the extraordinary cross-generational success of J. K. Rowling's Harry Potter, authors and readers have been crossing the boundaries between adult and children's fiction in both directions ever since those boundaries were drawn. In fact, there is a very long tradition of literature shared by audiences of all ages.

In *Crossover Fiction*, Sandra L. Beckett explores the global trend of crossover literature and explains how it is transforming literary canons, concepts of readership, the status of authors, the publishing industry, and bookselling practices. This pioneering study will have significant relevance across disciplines, as scholars in literary studies, media and cultural studies, visual arts, education, psychology, and sociology examine the increasingly blurred borderlines between adults and young people in contemporary society, notably with regard to their consumption of popular culture. Well-written and exhaustively researched, Beckett's newest book will no doubt be the definitive volume on the crossover genre for years to come.

ISBN: 978-0-415-98033-3 (hbk)

For ordering and further information please visit:
www.routledge.com

Related titles from Routledge

The Collected Sicilian Folk and Fairy Tales of Giuseppe Pitrè
Guiseppe Pitrè

Edited by Jack Zipes and Joseph Russo

Giuseppe Pitrè, a nineteenth-century Sicilian physician, gathered an enormous wealth of folk and fairy tales as he traveled and treated the poor throughout Palermo. He also received tales from friends and scholars throughout the island of Sicily. A dedicated folklorist, whose significance ranks alongside the Brothers Grimm, he published a 25-volume collection of Sicilian folk tales, legends, songs, and customs between 1871 and 1914. Though first published in their original Sicilian dialect, these tales have never before been translated, collected, and published in English until now.

This historic two-volume set collects 300 and 100 variants of his most entertaining and most important folk and fairy tales, along with lively, vivid illustrations by Carmelo Lettere. In stark contrast to the more literary ambitions of the Grimms' tales, Pitrè's possess a charming, earthy quality that reflect the customs, beliefs, and superstitions of the common people more clearly than any other European folklore collection of the nineteenth century.

Edited, translated, and with a critical introduction by world-renowned folk and fairy tale experts Jack Zipes and Joseph Russo, this collection will firmly establish Pitrè's importance as a folklorist.

Vol. 1 ISBN: 978-0-415-98030-2 (hbk)
Vol. 2 ISBN: 978-0-415-98031-9 (hbk)
2-Vol Set ISBN: 978-0-415-98032-6 (hbk)

For ordering and further information please visit:
www.routledge.com

Related titles from Routledge

Critical Approaches to Food in Children's Literature
Edited by Kara K. Keeling and Scott T. Pollard

Food in Children's Literature is the first scholarly volume on the topic, connecting children's literature to the burgeoning discipline of food studies. Spanning genres (picture books, chapter books, popular media, and children's cookbooks) and regions (the United States, Britain, and Latin America), the essays utilize a variety of approaches, including archival research, cultural studies, formalism, gender studies, post-colonialism, post-structuralism, race studies, structuralism, and theology.

ISBN: 978-0-415-96366-4 (hbk)

For ordering and further information please visit:
www.routledge.com

Related titles from Routledge

Shakespeare in Children's Literature
Gender and Cultural Capital
Erica Hateley

Shakespeare in Children's Literature considers the genre of Shakespeare-for-children, considering both adaptations of his plays and children's novels in which he appears as a character. Drawing on feminist theory and sociology, Hateley demonstrates how Shakespeare for children utilizes the ongoing cultural capital of "Shakespeare," and the pedagogical aspects of children's literature, to perpetuate anachronistic forms of identity and authority.

ISBN: 978-0-415-96492-0 (hbk)

For ordering and further information please visit:
www.routledge.com

Printed in the USA/Agawam, MA
February 14, 2012